W9-DHJ-889

The Reference Shelf®

U.S. National Debate Topic: 2017-2018

Education Reform

The Reference Shelf
Volume 89 • Number 3
H.W. Wilson
A Division of EBSCO Information Services, Inc.

Published by
GREY HOUSE PUBLISHING
Amenia, New York
2017

The Reference Shelf

The books in this series contain reprints of articles, excerpts from books, addresses on current issues, and studies of social trends in the United States and other countries. There are six separately bound numbers in each volume, all of which are usually published in the same calendar year. Numbers one through five are each devoted to a single subject, providing background information and discussion from various points of view and concluding with an index and comprehensive bibliography that lists books, pamphlets, and articles on the subject. The final number of each volume is a collection of recent speeches. Books in the series may be purchased individually or on subscription.

Publisher's Cataloging-In-Publication Data
(Prepared by The Donohue Group, Inc.)

Names: H.W. Wilson Company.
Title: U.S. national debate topic, 2017-2018. Education reform / [compiled by] H. W. Wilson, a division of EBSCO Information Services.
Other Titles: US national debate topic, 2017-2018. Education reform | United States national debate topic, 2017-2018. Education reform | Education reform | Reference shelf ; v. 89, no. 3.
Description: Amenia, New York : Grey House Publishing, 2017. | Includes bibliographical references and index.
Identifiers: ISBN 978-1-68217-453-1 (v. 89, no. 3) | ISBN 978-1-68217-450-0 (volume set)
Subjects: LCSH: Educational change--United States--History--21st century. | Education--United States--Finance--History--21st century. | Educational technology--United States--History--21st century.
Classification: LCC LA217.2 .U8 2017 | DDC 370.973--dc23

Contents

3

In the Classroom—Skills, Knowledge, Climate

4

Equity and the Achievement Gap

5

Education Technology

Preface

The Education Debate

After a controversial election, there was some degree of initial uncertainty about how newly elected President Trump would approach education, given that education was not a priority of his campaign and that Trump marketed himself as a "radical" conservative willing to break with traditional Republican politics. Despite questions, Trump's cabinet appointments and budget proposals indicated that his administration will follow a traditional conservative approach on many key issues, including education. In general, conservatives invest in corporations and the wealthy and reduce investment in government-run or funded programs, like welfare, Social Security, and education. Trump's initial proposals fall into line with this general policy position. For instance, Trump has proposed reducing corporate tax rates by more than half and he proposed repealing an estate tax that charged taxes on estates of more than $5.49 million.[1] Trump's initial budget blueprint, though not yet finalized, featured a $9.2 billion (or 13 percent) reduction in federal funding for public education.[2] In a further signifier of his educational approach, Trump appointed billionaire heiress Betsy DeVos, an outspoken critic of government spending on social welfare and the public school system, to serve as Secretary of Education.[3]

Social services are paid for through taxation and taxation is based on income. The wealthy therefore pay higher taxes and many see themselves as taking little out of the system, though this is not typically true. For some, this situation seems fundamentally unfair and many wealthy conservatives believe that the government has little right to claim revenues that they or their ancestors earned. In addition, conservatives are more likely to view government programs as poorly managed, corrupt, or inefficient and conservatives are more likely to believe that private investment and free-market competition are superior to investing in social safety nets. In essence, conservative administrations invest in the wealthy and in corporations, trusting that this investment will increase wealth at the upper levels of society and that this increased wealth will lead to greater productivity and more opportunities for advancement at every level. Whether or not this approach benefits most Americans or will be effective in improving education, is a matter of widespread debate.

Compromising Education with Politics

Beyond the specifics of reform legislation or education financing, the effectiveness of any nation's education system is also dependent on the attitudes of the population. Finland has what many experts consider to be one of the best education systems in the world and Finnish students consistently score higher on tests than students in the United States. In comparison to the US education system, Finnish education is more personalized and less focused on quantitative achievement in key subjects. This is possible only because the Finnish population has embraced the idea that a well-rounded education is the best approach, while the United States has increasingly gravitated towards focusing on what is seen as the most "profitable" material, subjects that most directly lead to jobs and earning. Finnish teachers report feeling embraced and supported by their society, while there is a sense that US legislators increasingly want to invest only in the best schools and the best students.[4] The gulf between the United States and Finland is not as much a matter of spending or of better government management, as it is a matter of cultural philosophy and priorities.

Political ideology, which has become more and more stratified in the United States, is also increasingly affecting the way that individuals approach education. In a 2011 review of the Texas State school system, researchers from the Thomas Fordham Institute gave Texas a "D" grade because the state government revised the state's social studies curriculum in such a way that teachers were required to downplay the existence of slavery and segregation and to promote the positive effects of Christianity and free enterprise in US history. While it might be argued that this radical reading of history is an appropriate viewpoint to present to students, the state government's revision mandated that teachers in the state were *only* able to present this highly skewed interpretation. The scholars who study history, social studies, politics, and other facets of human culture can be progressive, conservative, or occupy points between these positions, but the information presented in school curricula must result from a consensus, weighing the research on an issue and presenting, where applicable, various perspectives. When curriculum becomes a tool for inculcating political ideology, the legitimacy of education is compromised and students become the victims of manipulation rather than the recipients of knowledge.[5]

The Culture of Competition

Another factor that compromises educational quality is the distribution of resources, both among schools and among populations in the United States. The United States has an extreme and growing disparity between economic classes that has always existed but has also become more pronounced over time. Sociologists have coined the term "achievement gap," to describe the difference in educational achievement between students from different groups. On the whole, children from wealthy families, as a result of greater resources contributing to better educational preparedness and the availability of assistance when encountering challenges, fare far better in the educational system than students from low-income families. It is also well demonstrated that there is a persistent achievement gap between white and minority students that is distinct but related to the class achievement gap. A 2016 study from Northwestern University found that the stress of racial prejudice alone reduces educational achievement in marginalized groups.[6] Subtle factors like the indirect effects of racism are compounded by institutionalized racism operating at every level of American society that mitigates opportunities for Black and Hispanic students and perpetuates a cycle of disadvantage.[7]

The achievement gap in education contributes to a class, racial, and gender wage gap in the workplace. This wage gap creates a disparity in resources that makes it less likely that children of low-income or minority families will themselves succeed in higher education and thus, the educational divide continues and the wage gap persists and deepens.[8] Though there have been a variety of proposals to address these complex issues, the fundamental challenge is cultural. The unfortunate drawback to living in a nation that embraces free-market competition, with all its potential for commercial growth and innovation, is that those with advantages not only have access to more opportunities, but also utilize and shape the system to further their own advantages at the expense of potential competitors. In this way, big corporations prevent independent businesses and smaller corporations from becoming competitors. This free-market mind-set is not only a factor in business, but affects many other aspects of American culture.

For instance, a suburban public school may have far higher revenues than an inner city public school *because* many suburbs attract wealthier residents who work in the nearby city, but do not wish to live there for a variety of reasons. Despite the fact that living in suburbs is only attractive *because* of the nearby city and its resources, residents of the suburbs often resist contributing tax revenues to the city. As many inner city schools languish due to insufficient resources and funding, even wealthy residents who remain in the city may choose to send their children to private school rather than investing time, donations, effort, or energy in supporting the local school district. This pattern plays out across the United States, with students who have no other options consigned to underfunded, insufficient schools, while those with the resources congregate in better-funded suburban schools or opt out of the system altogether by choosing private or religious schools. Therefore, despite the fact that suburban residents and wealthy urban residents live where they do because of the city and its resources, the competitive mind-set encourages individuals to invest first in themselves and in those facets of society that provide direct advantages.

Having embraced this competitive mind-set in many aspects of society, there are many who argue that education too would be better if it operated on a more competitive model. In every competition there must, by definition, be winners and losers and so, in a competitive educational environment some schools would be seen as winners, and will therefore be deserving of further investment in both human and monetary resources, while other schools would become losers. Some feel that these underperforming schools, those that cannot compete, should essentially be allowed to lose and that this will ultimately benefit society more than sinking further funding into failing systems. Companies that fail to compete lose investors and may go out of business, but this opens up the system for new competitors. However, if education is a competition and, therefore, some schools will lose, the question is, should some students be allowed to lose as well?

Technology Will Save the Day

Digital technology, the Web and the Internet, and mobile digital devices, have revolutionized many facets of American culture, from music and movies to literature and dating. Some have hoped that technology might offer novel solutions for the problems facing the education system as well. Since the 1990s, educational pioneers have experimented with a variety of types of online and virtual education in hopes of reaching out to alternative students and, in general, making formal education more available, attainable, and egalitarian. As of 2017, the online education revolution has not become the great democratizing force that the most fervent supporters had hoped, but this means only that there is still room for new innovations that might bring about a more productive blend of technological education in the future.

One of the most promising approaches to blending education and technology is the emerging personalized education movement. This approach seeks to utilize technology and real-world participatory activities as a way to make education more engrossing, relevant, and interesting to students. Studies of nations in which education is more personalized, like Finland, demonstrate that such a strategy can have very real advantages for students. Technological advancements like learning computers and gamification are creating the possibility of new ways of challenging and evaluating students and of personalizing curricula to make it possible for a single teacher to effectively teach students at vastly different skill levels. Advancements like these could potentially lead away from what some educators and experts feel has been an overly rigid and unproductive focus on standardized testing and core subjects.

In a complex education system influenced by political dissonance, unequal distribution of resources, and widespread disagreement about how to improve the system, the future of education is largely uncertain. The Trump administration's focus is likely to be on privatization, with a reduction of federal funding for public schools. As 91 percent of American students attend public schools, it is unknown whether this experiment will improve educational options or will simply reduce resources for most students and schools. Americans across ideological lines have always agreed that the welfare of the nation's children must be protected and, for many, this will remain a passionate focus even as enduring challenges remain relevant and new difficulties appear on the horizon.

Micah L. Issitt

Works Used

Anderson, Melinda. "How the Stress of Racism Affects Learning." *The Atlantic*. The Atlantic Monthly Group. Oct 11 2016. Web. 30 Apr 2017.

Bendix, Aria. "Trump's Education Budget Revealed." *The Atlantic*. The Atlantic Monthly Group. Mar 16 2017. Web. 30 Apr 2017.

Bukhari, Jeff. "If Trump Repeals the Estate Tax, the Federal Government Will Hardly Notice." *Fortune*. Fortune Inc. Apr 27 2017. Web. 10 May 2017.

Camera, Lauren. "Achievement Gap between White and Black Students Still Gaping." U.S. News. U.S. News and World Report. Jan 13 2016. Web. 30 Apr 2017.

Doyle, William. "Why Finland Has the Best Schools." *LA Times*. Tronc Media. Mar 18 2016. Web. 10 May 2017.

Harding, Luke. "Leak Reveals Rex Tillerson Was Director of Bahamas-Based US-Russian Oil Firm." *The Guardian*. Guardian News and Media. Dec 18 2016. Web. 30 Apr 2017.

Lehmann, Evan. "Conservatives Lose Faith in Science over Last 40 Years." *Scientific American*. Nature America, Inc. Mar 30 2012. Web. 30 Apr 2017.

Patten, Eileen. "Racial, Gender Wage Gaps Persist in U.S. Despite Some Progress." *Pew Research*. Pew Research Center. Jul 1 2016. Web. 3 May 2017.

Stern, Sheldon M. and Jeremy A. Stern. "The State of State U.S. History Standards 2011." *EdExcellence*. Thomas B. Fordham Institute. Feb 2011. Web. 30 Apr 2017.

Stratford, Michael. "A Look at Betsy DeVos' Charitable Giving." *Politico*. Politico LLC. Dec 5 2016. Web. 30 Apr 2017.

Strauss, Valerie. "Why the Movement to Privatize Public Education Is a Very Bad Idea." *The Washington Post*. Nash Holdings. Jul 14 2016. Web. 30 Apr 2017.

Notes

1. Bukhari, "If Trump Repeals the Estate Tax, the Federal Government Will Hardly Notice."
2. Bendix, "Trump's Education Budget Revealed."
3. Stratford, "A Look at Betsy DeVos' Charitable Giving."
4. Doyle, "Why Finland Has the Best Schools."
5. Stern and Stern, "The State of State U.S. History Standards 2011."
6. Anderson, "How the Stress of Racism Affects Learning."
7. Camera, "Achievement Gap between White and Black Students Still Gaping."
8. Patten, "Racial, Gender Wage Gaps Persist in U.S. Despite Some Progress."

1
The State of American Education

Credit: Andrew Harrer/Bloomberg via Getty Images

U.S. President Donald Trump holds up a pen to give away after signing H.J. Res. 57, which overturns a rule on school accountability standards that are part of the Every Student Succeeds Act, during a bill signing ceremony in the Roosevelt Room of the White House in Washington, D.C., U.S., on Monday, March 27, 2017. Trump signed four bills, H.J. Res 37, H.J. Res 44, H.J. Res. 57 and H.J. Res. 58, that nullify measures put in place during former President Obama's administration.

Educational States

In 2016, more than 91 percent of American students attended one of the nation's public schools. Any discussion about the state of education must therefore focus, predominantly, on public education. The public school system emerged in the mid-nineteenth century and, though widely maligned for political reasons, has been one of the most important factors in the effort to combat racial, gender, and class inequality. Public schools are funded by state and federal tax revenues and managed by public servants who are entrusted with ensuring that the school system functions without discrimination and to further public interest. This means that the public school system faces the extreme challenge of educating the most diverse student body in the nation, with a wide spectrum of students from different backgrounds and with vast differences in ability.

For those parents and students with the means or who live in certain areas, there are two basic options outside of the standard public school system: private school or charter school. Private schools are funded by donations and private investment, but also receive federal support in the form of tax breaks. Though only about 9 percent of students attend private schools, 25 percent of the nation's schools are private and the value of the private education industry was estimated in 2016 at over $57billion. Most (over 80 percent) of the nation's private schools offer a religious-themed education.[1] The third option, charter schools, is a hybrid of the public/private school models. Charters are public, in that students attend for free and the schools receive tax revenues, but are private in that they are run by private individuals, corporations, or organizations. As a result, charter schools, like private schools, are more selective in admission and can be operated on either a nonprofit or for-profit model.

In 2017, the landscape of education is changing. Newly elected President Donald Trump and his choice for Secretary of Education Betsy DeVos are both graduates of elite private schools and are critics of the nation's public school system. The new trend in education, known by the marketing term "school choice," is essentially a privatization movement that seeks to transfer tax funds away from public schools to private schools. The movement is based on the idea that allowing schools to compete for revenues will create a more dynamic, free-market system, that will improve educational quality. The privatization movement has been fueled by the perception of a failing public school system and by studies indicating that US students lag behind students of many other developed nations in key subjects.

The Perceived Crisis in Education

Defending his choice of Betsy DeVos for Secretary of Education, President Donald Trump described the US education system as being in a state of "crisis."[2] However, the state of education is largely a matter of perception and political motive. Trump and allies see a crisis because this perspective fits well with the Trump administration's overarching thesis that the United States is worse now than it was in the past and that this is the fault of corrupt Democratic bureaucracy, which includes the bureaucracy of the public schools. Experts in the field, including educators, researchers, and legislators with direct experience, do not generally agree that US education, as a whole, is facing a crisis. Rather, experts see US public education as a mitigated success compromised by numerous complex factors, many of which are woven into the fabric of American culture and not only affect education, but also healthcare, the job market, and many other aspects of life for a majority of Americans.

Public opinion polls demonstrate that there is little consensus about the state of education and that opinions have become increasingly partisan. For instance, a 2016 Gallup Poll found that 53 percent of Democrats but only 32 percent of Republicans approved of the nation's K-12 education system. Gallup Polls from 2014, by contrast, found similar levels of support across partisan lines. The partisan gulf reflects the increasing polarization between conservatives and progressives on major issues. The 2016 Gallup Poll also indicated that only about 43 percent of all Americans were satisfied with the state of education, which is the lowest level of faith in public education measured since 2000.

The fact that a majority of Americans feel at least partially dissatisfied with public education seems to indicate that the crisis seen by Trump and supporters is a verifiable fact and yet this perception is largely illusory. Gallup Poll studies show that 76 percent of parents report being satisfied with their own child's education and with the schools that their children attend, despite the fact that less than 40 percent reported being satisfied with public education as a whole.[3] In another poll by Education Next, 55 percent of parents rated schools in their community as achieving either an "A" or "B" rating, though only 25 percent gave an A or B rating to public schools in general. In fact, the Education Next poll found that opinions of local schools have improved over the past decade (from 43 percent to 55 percent giving an A or B grade), while the perception of the system as a whole has declined.[4]

If a majority of Americans are satisfied with their own educational experiences, why then do so many Americans believe that there is an education crisis? In part, this can be explained by a psychological phenomenon known as the "mere-exposure" effect, in which individuals are more likely to be supportive when they are familiar with the thing in question.[5] There has also been a multibillion-dollar campaign to discourage faith in public schools and to promote privatization, the idea that schools could be more effectively, efficiently, and affordably run by private entities than governmental bureaucracy. Finally, because education is one of the most important aspects of any society, the fear that US education is failing creates a sense of perennial paranoia and motivates the belief that education is always in a state of crisis.

However, experts in the field widely agree that there are regions, districts, and individual schools that are very much in a state of crisis. The distribution of funding is tied to local tax revenues and schools in poor districts therefore suffer from a lack of resources. The effects of these disadvantages are also generational and insidious. Parents who are themselves undereducated and underemployed are concentrated in poor districts where the schools are underserved, producing new generations who are similarly undereducated and more likely to be underemployed.[6] It is this phenomenon, the educational manifestation of America's severe and deepening class inequality, that creates the nation's legitimate education crisis.

The International Perspective

When evaluating the US education system, one common measure is to compare US students to their counterparts in other nations. For instance, the 2015 Program for International Student Assessment (PISA), found that US students achieve average rankings in science, mathematics, and literacy when compared to all nations studied, but rank significantly behind students in many other economically advanced nations. In mathematics, US students ranked 38th out of 71 nations measured, while they ranked 24th in science. Many educators and legislators expressed concern over the results of the 2015 PISA study in part because the vast increase in technological jobs means that math and science are increasingly important for students hoping to participate in the global economy.[7] A similar study focusing on math and science skills at lower grade levels, the Trends in International Mathematics and Science Study (TIMSS), found similar results, with US students lagging behind peers in many developed nations.[8]

The United States spends more money per student than most other countries in which students score higher in math, science, and literacy, indicating that spending alone does not correlate with increased performance. Program for International Student Assessment studies also indicate that socioeconomic class plays a larger role in the United States than in many other nations, in terms of the effects of class on educational achievement. Analyses of 2012 PISA results showed that about 13 percent of low-income students in Korea, Hong Kong, Vietnam, Singapore, and China were "resilient," which means that students performed better on tests than predicted by their socioeconomic status. By contrast, only 7 percent of US students were shown to be resilient to the effects of economic class.[9]

Reform advocates, politicians, and educational entrepreneurs have seized on PISA results to criticize public education. However, experts in the field caution against such conclusions and note that deep cultural differences are likely one of the most important factors preventing US students from matching or surpassing students in many other nations.[10] Parental involvement and cultural attitudes about the value of education are important in determining how students, teachers, and parents approach, utilize, and participate in the system. For US students to beat out students in other advanced nations, it may therefore require deep changes in cultural philosophy that place increased emphasis, regardless of class and political affiliation, on the value of education and the need for parental and community participation.

International comparisons can also provide a reminder of the benefits US citizenship. Around the world, nearly one-in-five adults, or 19 percent of the adult population, have no formal schooling. This includes more than 40 percent of adults in the Middle East and North Africa where even basic education is not guaranteed. By contrast, 98 percent of Europeans and 99 percent of adults in North America attain at least some level of formal schooling. The problem is more severe across gender lines, with nearly 23 percent of women globally receiving no formal schooling.[11] In comparison to the world population, therefore, US students, even those in the most disadvantaged school districts, enjoy advantages that are far from universal.

Micah L. Issitt

Works Used

Desilver, Drew. "U.S. Students' Academic Achievement Still Lags That of Their Peers in Many Other Countries." *Pew Research*. Pew Research Center. Feb 15 2017. Web. 25 Apr. 2017.

Heim, Joe. "On the World Stage, U.S. Students Fall Behind." *The Washington Post*. Nash Holdings. Dec 6 2016. Web. 25 Apr 2017.

Jennings, Jack. "Proportion of U.S. Students in Private Schools Is 10 Percent and Declining." *Huffpost*. Huffington Post. Mar 28 2013. Web. 25 Apr 2017.

Kamenetz, Anya. "Americans Like Their Schools Just Fine—But Not Yours." *NPR*. National Public Radio. Aug 23 2016. Web. 30 Apr 2017.

Lynch, Matthew. "Poverty and School Funding: Why Low-Income Students Often Suffer." *Huffington Post*. Oct 15 2015.

Masci, David. "About One-Fifth of Adults Globally Have No Formal Schooling." *Pew Research*. Pew Research Center. Jan 11 2017. Web. 25 Apr 2017.

"Results from the 2016 Education Next Poll." *Education Next*. Program on Education Policy and Governance. Harvard Kennedy School. 2016. Web. 25 Apr 2017.

Ryan, Julia. "American Schools vs. the World: Expensive, Unequal, Bad at Math." *The Atlantic*. The Atlantic Monthly Group. Dec 3 2013. Web. 25 Apr 2017.

Saad, Lydia. "U.S. Education Ratings Show Record Political Polarization." Gallup. Gallup Org. Aug 17 2016. Web. 24 Apr 2017.

Strauss, Valerie. "How Public Opinion about New PISA Test Scores Is Being Manipulated." *The Washington Post*. Nash Holdings. Dec 1 2013. Web. 25 Apr 2017.

"Trump: Secretary DeVos Right Choice to Address Education 'Crisis.'" *VOA News*. Voice of America. Feb 14 2017. Web. 30 Apr 2017.

Notes

1. Jennings, "Proportion of U.S. Students in Private Schools Is 10 Percent and Declining."
2. "Trump: Secretary DeVos Right Choice to Address Education 'Crisis'", *VOA News*.
3. Saad, "U.S. Education Ratings Show Record Political Polarization."
4. "Results from the 2016 Education Next Poll," *Education Next*.
5. Kamenetz, "Americans Like Their Schools Just Fine—But Not Yours."
6. Lynch, "Poverty and School Funding: Why Low-Income Students Often Suffer."

7. Heim, "On the World Stage, U.S. Students Fall Behind."
8. Desilver, "U.S. Students' Academic Achievement Still Lags That of Their Peers in Many Other Countries."
9. Ryan, "American Schools vs. the World: Expensive, Unequal, Bad at Math."
10. Strauss, "How Public Opinion about New PISA Test Scores Is Being Manipulated."
11. Masci, "About One-Fifth of Adults Globally Have No Formal Schooling."

Ask Better School Reform Questions

By Frederick M. Hess and Paige Willey
U.S News and World Report, April 11, 2017

There's always a "next big thing" in school reform. The pursuit of better schools yields an endless drumbeat, as reformers feel the urge to do *something*. Amid all the new agendas, big ideas and heated debates, it can sometimes be hard to stop long enough to take a hard look at what's worked and what hasn't.

After all, even those who don't pay much attention to the ins and outs of schooling can probably name more than a few high-profile education reforms off the top of their head: Charter schools. Common Core. No Child Left Behind. Merit pay. Class size reduction.

Close observers of schooling can easily name scores more: Site-based management. Eighth-grade algebra. Close reading. Dual immersion programs. Magnet schools. School improvement grants.

You get the idea. But how do we know which of these reforms actually work? More to the point, what does it even mean when we say a reform "works"?

Plenty of researchers and reformers find it convenient to treat the answer as a simple yes-no question that's typically phrased as, "Did reading and math scores go up?" Well, OK. But there are at least three big problems with that way of thinking about things.

First, nearly all reforms show a hugely mixed track record. It's no exaggeration to say that every reform sometimes shows benefits and sometimes does not. Reforms are more likely to work when they're pursued enthusiastically, purposefully, carefully, and seriously—and to disappoint when they're not. The upshot is that it's tough to point to a single reform that reliably and automatically "works."

Second, it's hard to find anyone who truly thinks that we should measure school improvement solely in terms of reading and math scores. And many reforms aren't designed to spark short-term bumps in test scores, making movement in reading and math scores a very limited measure of success. That's obviously true when it comes to revamping career and technical education or arts education. But it's also true of efforts to improve things like governance, curriculum or hiring—changes intended less to move reading scores next spring than to improve teaching and learning over time.

Third, reforms tend to have a lot of moving parts. Consider No Child Left Behind. With its mandates governing testing, accountability, school improvement, teacher qualifications and more, it's hard to know what we're talking about when we state flatly that such a reform did or didn't "work." The same is equally true when it comes to policies like charter schooling or school turnarounds, where the "reform" is actually a basket of different models and approaches. Simply declaring one of these pushes to be a success or a failure tends to obscure more than it reveals.

Given all that, it's worth rethinking what it means to say that a reform is or isn't working. Doing so may help us develop new insights into which reforms are likely to deliver, curtail the temptation to ditch promising measures before they ripen, and make it easier to agree on when it's time to pull the plug. There are four sets of questions that can be especially useful when trying to make sense of all this.

1. The observable impact on students and families. What do the tests show? What's happening to other academic outcomes, such as graduation rates, college readiness or absenteeism? What's the impact on parental involvement, student engagement or school climate?

2. The impact on institutions and arrangements. Has the reform changed assumptions for schools, systems and families? Has the reform led to permanent changes in funding, governance or system mechanics? Has the reform entered the "grammar" of schooling, like NCLB's reading and math tests?

3. The amount of sustained—and sustainable—support for the reform. Is there a committed base of support for the reform, as is the case when it comes to the Individuals with Disabilities Education Act or charter schooling? Is there support among a diverse set of stakeholders such as business leaders and civil rights advocates, or rural and urban officials? Does the reform threaten popular programs or the concerns of influential figures?

4. The costs of the reform. What is the dollar cost of the reform, and where is that money coming from? What does the reform require in terms of time, energy and focus? What's not getting done because of this reform; that is, what's the opportunity cost of putting this reform into place?

Schooling is hugely complex and intensely personal. This means that how reforms are done often matters more than whether they're done. Reforms with too few passionate supporters often fall apart, while those with too narrow a base of support can run into political headwinds. Philanthropy and federal policy can play a critical role, but can also serve as a crutch. They risk undermining the coalition-building needed to make reform sustainable.

Reforms are more likely to work when they're pursued enthusiastically, purposefully, carefully, and seriously—and to disappoint when they're not.

This schema doesn't offer any pat answers. But it just might offer a fuller and more useful way to talk about how reforms are working, in the hope that we can spend less time talking past one another and more focused on what it takes to make good ideas deliver for students.

Print Citations

CMS: Hess, Frederick M., and Paige Willey. "Ask Better School Reform Questions." In *The Reference Shelf: Education Reform,* edited by Betsy Maury, 9–11. Ipswich, MA: H.W. Wilson, 2017.

MLA: Hess, Frederick M., and Paige Willey. "Ask Better School Reform Questions." *The Reference Shelf: Education Reform.* Ed. Betsy Maury. Ipswich: H.W. Wilson, 2017. 9–11. Print.

APA: Hess, F. M., & P. Willey. (2017). Ask better school reform questions. In Betsy Maury (Ed.), *The reference shelf: Education reform* (pp. 9–11). Ipswich, MA: H.W. Wilson. (Original work published 2017)

A Look at the Education Crisis: Tests, Standards, and the Future of American Education

By Ulrich Boser, Perpetual Baffour, and Steph Vela
The Center for American Progress, January 26, 2016

In many ways standards-based school reform is at a crossroads. On one side, the movement has made tremendous strides. The Common Core State Standards Initiative, known simply as Common Core, is now strongly established in more than 40 states. Many teachers believe that the new, higher academic standards have helped them improve instruction. And, most importantly, a solid body of data demonstrates that the standards-based reform movement has shown success in raising student outcomes.

In some areas, outcome indicators are on the rise. Over the past two decades, for instance, the number of students of color performing at grade level in reading and math has more than doubled in elementary and middle school. Meanwhile, high school graduation rates are the highest they have ever been: 81 percent of the class of 2013 received their diploma within four years.

But clearly much work remains. Achievement gaps in many subject areas remain large. For example, only 21 percent of low-income fourth-grade students achieved proficiency on the 2015 National Assessment of Educational Progress (NAEP) reading test compared to 52 percent of nonpoor students. And if students of color graduated at the same rate as their white peers, they would receive nearly two hundred thousand more diplomas each year.

In a way, the question for education advocates boils down to: What's next? For a few vocal observers, the answer to this question is—surprisingly—anything but standards-based reform. In other words, these observers believe that the standards-based reform effort—and its associated assessments and accountability efforts—have been a total failure. In a policy memo released last year, Kevin Welner and William Mathis of the National Education Policy Center argued that "we as a nation have devoted enormous amounts of time and money to the focused goal of increasing test scores, and we have almost nothing to show for it."

Some, such as blogger Anthony Cody, argue that policymakers should not really even focus on raising standards or improving tests or reforming accountability systems. Instead, Cody believes that policy leaders should aim to create a "healthy

From *The Center for American Progress* January 26, 2016

ecosystem" for students. From this perspective, resources would be better invested in improving prenatal care and child nutrition than in reforming public schools.

One of the most vocal proponents of this view is education historian Diane Ravitch. Although Ravitch was once a leading advocate of national standards, the former U.S. assistant secretary of education has shifted her position dramatically in recent years. In interviews, Ravitch is adamant that "the current sense of crisis about our nation's public schools is exaggerated." She criticizes the Common Core as "blind faith in the standardization of tests and curriculum." Or, as Ravitch argues, "We have a national policy that is a theory based on an assumption grounded in hope."

The argument over the scope and nature of the education problem in the United States is particularly important to the political debate over the Common Core. In some parts of the country, there has been a backlash against the standards. For instance, almost 60,000 students in Washington state opted out of Common Core tests. In some affluent Washington municipalities more than 90 percent of high schoolers opted out of the math tests.

Other states, such as Oklahoma, have simply backed out of the standards. And for some political leaders, such as former Louisiana Gov. Bobby Jindal (R), the new standards are a classic example of government overreach. While others, including former Texas Gov. Rick Perry (R), see them as part of a grand conspiracy.

Part of the reason for the backlash against Common Core is the belief that schools are actually doing pretty well—particularly in affluent areas. In fact, many parents give high grades to the schools in their communities, regardless of the school's location or background. According to a 2014 PDK/Gallup poll, around 50 percent of parents gave their child's school an A or B grade.

This sort of optimism about the state of public schools has led some parents to crusade against the new standards, arguing that the Common Core is simply too difficult. "To me we are setting our kids up to fail," one parent told CNN. "The reading passages are three levels above the child's current grade level."

To look more deeply at the state of our education system—and the state of standards-based reform—the authors of this report analyzed the latest data from two national assessments: NAEP and the Trial Urban District Assessment, or TUDA.

The NAEP assessment, long known as the "Nation's Report Card," was administered for the first time in 1969. NAEP exams in math and reading are given every two years to a random sample of schools and students in each state and almost two dozen urban districts.

While NAEP assesses student progress at the national and state level, TUDA is used to report the performance of large urban districts. The TUDA test was first administered in 2002 and served as a way to "focus attention on urban education" by providing district-level NAEP exams. In 2002, there were only six participating urban districts; that number has since increased to 21 districts.

Using data from TUDA and NAEP, this report estimates the absolute number of students at or above proficient for each disaggregated group. We started with the overall percentages of students scoring proficient or above or scoring advanced or above on each NAEP exam in 2015. We then compared these data with estimates of the total school-age population for each group. To our knowledge, this is the first time that such an analysis has been done.

And, most importantly, a solid body of data demonstrates that the standards-based reform movement has shown success in raising student outcomes.

Consider, for example, Cleveland, Ohio, where 6 percent of African American students who took the NAEP eighth-grade math test scored at the proficient level or above. However, only a subset of the district's students actually took the NAEP. We estimated that, if all the African American students in the district had actually taken the test, 6 percent of the approximately 1,340 such students—or approximately 80 total—would have scored proficient or above. For this report, the authors rounded these totals to the nearest ten for the city-specific data because the results were approximations of the exact figure. For the state-level data, we rounded to the nearest hundred, thousand, or tens of thousands.

We looked at proficiency rates for several groups of students, including students of color and students with disabilities. We used these rates to estimate the total number of students in each group that were performing at the proficient or advanced level.

Our research revealed several key findings:

Some States and Districts Are Making Clear Gains

In Massachusetts, the percentage of fourth-graders scoring proficient or above in math jumped from 41 percent in 2003 to 54 percent in 2013. In other words, about 7,000 more fourth-graders in Massachusetts are reaching proficiency now than they were 10 years ago. In other states, such as Florida, the same rate rose from 31 percent to 42 percent, meaning around 22,000 more fourth-graders are scoring at grade level in math than they were 10 years ago.

Many districts have also made clear gains. Since 2002, thousands more students of color in the nation's cities have scored proficient or above on the reading and math NAEP exams. In Boston, for instance, nearly 1,000 more Hispanic fourth- and eighth-graders are now proficient in math. Similarly, the District of Columbia has also seen about 1,000 more fourth-graders scoring proficient or above in math and reading. In Charlotte, at least 2,000 more fourth graders can now do math at grade level.

The State and Local Policy Environment Matters

Many of the cities and states that have embraced standards-based reform have seen clear gains. The District of Columbia, for instance, has been a national leader in the reform movement, and high school graduation rates and other student outcomes have been jumped upwards in the city. Or take Charlotte, North Carolina. The district has long been strong on using accountability systems and data-driven decision-making to bolster achievement and narrow achievement gaps.

Perhaps the best example is Massachusetts, where there is a clear link between the state's standard-based reform efforts and a large jump in student outcomes. Over the past decade, low-income students in the Bay State have seen a 12-point increase in scores on the fourth- and eighth-grade NAEP exams. Today, low-income students in Massachusetts are among the nation's highest performing.

While a rigorous analysis of the policy context in each city is far beyond the scope of this report, some reform-oriented areas have shown clear results.

In Many Locations, Students of Color and Students Living in Poverty Still Have Extraordinarily Low Achievement

According to our analysis, an estimated 120 black students in fourth grade score proficient or above on the NAEP mathematics assessment in Detroit. This is not a misprint: A reliable, high-quality exam shows that just a little more than 100 African American fourth-graders are performing grade-level work in math in the city.

Students in other cities have similarly low results. In Atlanta, a depressing total of around 60 Hispanic fourth-graders score proficient or above on the reading NAEP exam. The numbers are even worse in Cleveland, where based on our estimates, only some 30 Latino eighth-graders would be considered proficient in math.

While this report calculated absolute numbers to highlight the dramatic extent of the education problem, the percentage outcomes for each of these cities is just as shocking. In fourth-grade reading, only 13 percent of Hispanic students in Cleveland reached proficiency. In fourth-grade math, only 11 percent of African American students in Atlanta reached proficiency. In Fresno, California, only 7 percent of low-income eighth-graders can read at grade level.

When It Comes to Students Performing at the Advanced Level, Outcomes Are Also Rock Bottom

In the entire United States, only about 123,000 eighth-graders—or 3 percent—scored at the advanced level in reading on the NAEP exams. Again, this is not a misprint: Just around 120,000 eighth graders are doing excellent work in middle school English language arts in the whole country.

In some states, the issue is also dire when it comes to high-level work, and only a few hundred students have reached the advanced level in some grades. Around 410 eighth-graders in Mississippi, for instance, are reading at the advanced level; in New Mexico, there are approximately 230 eighth-graders achieving at that level. In West Virginia, only about 610 eighth-graders are considered advanced in math.

While there has been substantial progress over the past decade—particularly in cities and states that have embraced standards-based reform—the nation still faces a pressing education crisis, particularly when it comes to students of color and students from low-income backgrounds. The sooner that the American public takes action, the better prepared the nation will be for the future.

Print Citations

CMS: Boser, Ulrich, Perpetual Baffour, and Steph Vela. "A Look at the Education Crisis: Tests, Standards, and the Future of American Education." In *The Reference Shelf: Education Reform*, edited by Betsy Maury, 12–16. Ipswich, MA: H.W. Wilson, 2017.

MLA: Boser, Ulrich, Perpetual Baffour, and Steph Vela. "A Look at the Education Crisis: Tests, Standards, and the Future of American Education." *The Reference Shelf: Education Reform*. Ed. Betsy Maury. Ipswich: H.W. Wilson, 2017. 12–16. Print.

APA: Boser, U., P. Baffour, & S. Vela. (2017). A look at the education crisis: Tests, standards, and the future of American education. In Betsy Maury (Ed.), *The reference shelf: Education reform* (pp. 12–16). Ipswich, MA: H.W. Wilson. (Original work published 2016)

Why the Charter School Debate Has Moved Beyond "Better" or "Worse"

By Joshua Cowen
The Conversation, April 20, 2016

The charter school debate is getting even more heated. Recently, charter opponents launched a campaign from the steps of the Massachusetts State House to warn that charter schools were "sapping resources from the traditional schools that serve most minority students, and creating a two-track system." Similar opposition has been voiced by critics across the country as well.

So when it comes to educating kids, are charter schools good or bad?

Differing Views

Minnesota authorized the first charter schools in 1991. Charter schools are public schools that are independent and more autonomous than traditional schools and typically based around a particular educational mission or philosophy.

Charters' governance structure—who can operate a charter and what kind of oversight they face—varies by state. For example, while charter schools in some states are managed by nonprofit organizations, in other states they are run for a fee by for-profit companies.

Regardless, over the years, an increasing number of students have been enrolling in charter schools. At present there are more than three million students enrolled in 6,700 charter schools across 42 states. Nationally, charter school enrollment has more than tripled since 2000.

The response to charter prevalence is varied: proponents say these schools provide a vital opportunity for children to attend high-quality alternatives to traditional public schools. Especially when those traditional schools are struggling or underperforming.

Opponents, like those in Boston, say charter schools are threats to the very idea of public schooling—they weaken neighborhood schools by reducing enrollment, capturing their funding and prioritizing high-ability students instead of those most in need of educational improvements.

What's the Evidence?

As a researcher who studies school choice, I know that many of these arguments are reflected in evidence. But, the truth is, when you look nationwide, the effects of charter schooling on student test scores are mixed—charters in some states do better than traditional public schools, worse or about the same in others.

Research has been less ambiguous when it comes to educational attainment. We know that kids from Boston charter schools, for example, are more likely to pass the state's high school exit exam "with especially large effects on the likelihood of qualifying for a state-sponsored college scholarship." Charters also "induce a clear shift from two-year to four-year colleges."

What's more, a new study published in the *Journal of Policy Analysis and Management* (the top peer-reviewed policy journal in the country) has shown that students from charter schools not only persist longer in college than those from traditional public schools, but also earn more in income later.

But critics charge that charters achieve these kinds of effects by pushing out kids with learning disabilities or problematic behavior—or avoid such children altogether.

There are also concerns that charter advantages are rooted in new patterns of racial/ethnic segregation because white and minority families may choose schools with more children of the same race or ethnicity.

Then there is the understudied issue of teachers in charter schools. Most of these teachers are not unionized, which remains a source of major tension between charter and traditional public school advocates.

We know, for example, that charter teachers tend to exit schools at higher rates than other public teachers, which, all else being equal, could be detrimental to student outcomes.

But we also know that charter administrators may prioritize teacher effectiveness and other attributes in making staffing and compensation decisions. This differs from traditional schools, where teachers' pay and job retention are not usually linked to their classroom performance.

What Do Parents Think?

Public opinion about charter schools varies along with this evidence.

A recent national poll indicated that 51 percent of all Americans support the idea of charter schooling. Only 27 percent actively opposed charters, which means almost as many Americans either don't like or don't have an opinion about these schools as those who do and support them.

What Might Explain Some of These Differences?

A massive new survey of parents in urban areas across the country provides some insight.

Respondents in these urban areas were far more supportive of school choice generally and charter schools in particular than the national average: no less than 83 percent (in Tulsa) and as much as 91-92 percent (in Atlanta, Boston, Memphis,

New Orleans and New York City) agreed that parents should have more school choices.

No less than 58 percent (in New York City) and as much as 74 percent (in Atlanta, Boston, Los Angeles and New Orleans) believed that overall, charter schools improve education.

Whether charter schools are better for kids than traditional public schools appears to depend on which charter schools we are talking about, and in which states.

In that survey, there was a direct correlation between respondents' perceptions of surrounding public school quality and support for charter schools: the worse parents believed their traditional schooling options to be, the more they favored charter schools.

Charters Are Here to Stay

So, where do we go from here?

Scholars like me tend to conclude our studies by saying "we need more evidence." And on charter schools, that's true: we need to know more. But on the big questions of public policy—and education certainly is one of these—research tends to go only so far.

Rigorous evidence can tell us about differences between charter and traditional schools. But it cannot solve a more fundamental and subjective disagreement about whether public education should or should not continue to exist largely as it has for the last century.

This is especially true whenever we add the caveat— "it depends."

Whether charter schools are better for kids than traditional public schools appears to depend on which charter schools we are talking about, and in which states.

So too does the question of whether charters exist to help all kids or to provide a specialized education to a few. And whether parents see charters as a positive force in their communities appears to depend on their sense that traditional schools will provide what they need for their children.

In my view, one thing seems certain: charter schools are here to stay. Already, there are more of them every year.

So, it's time to move the debate away from "are charters good or bad for kids" and to a more careful consideration of the strengths and weaknesses of the charter approach in many different places.

Charter proponents can and should recognize that not all charter schools are superior to the traditional public model. Charter critics should note that traditional public schools have failed many families—especially poor families and families of color—and there are reasons many have turned to alternative education providers.

More evidence is needed, to be sure, but these basic realities are likely to remain.

Print Citations

CMS: Cowen, Joshua. "Why the Charter School Debate Has Moved Beyond 'Better' or 'Worse.'" In *The Reference Shelf: Education Reform*, edited by Betsy Maury, 17–20. Ipswich, MA: H.W. Wilson, 2017.

MLA: Cowen, Joshua. "Why the Charter School Debate Has Moved Beyond 'Better' or 'Worse.'" *The Reference Shelf: Education Reform*. Ed. Betsy Maury. Ipswich: H.W. Wilson, 2017. 17–20. Print.

APA: Cowen, J. (2017). Why the charter school debate has moved beyond "better" or "worse." In Betsy Maury (Ed.), *The reference shelf: Education reform* (pp. 17–20). Ipswich, MA: H.W. Wilson. (Original work published 2016)

America's Not-So-Broken Education System: Do U.S. Schools Really Need to Be Disrupted?

By Jack Schneider
The Atlantic, June 22, 2016

Everything in American education is broken. Or so say the policy elites, from the online learning pioneer Sal Khan to the journalist-turned-reformer Campbell Brown. As leaders of the XQ project succinctly put it, we need to "scrap the blueprint and revolutionize this dangerously broken system."

This, they explain, is the sad truth. The educational system simply stopped working. It aged, declined, and broke. And now the nation has a mess on its hands. But there's good news, too. As Michelle Rhee's group, StudentsFirst, declares: Americans can "work together to fix this broken system." All it takes is the courage to rip it apart.

This is how the argument goes, again and again. The system used to work, but now it doesn't. And though nobody inside schools seems to care, innovators outside the establishment have developed some simple solutions. The system can be rebuilt, reformers argue. But first it must be torn down.

American education has some obvious shortcomings. Even defenders of the schools can make long lists of things they'd like to change. But the root of the problem is not incompetent design, as is so frequently alleged. Nor is it stasis. Rather, it is the twofold challenge of complexity and scale. American schools are charged with the task of creating better human beings. And they are expected to do so in a relatively consistent way for all of young people. It is perhaps the nation's most ambitious collective project; as such, it advances slowly.

For evidence of this, one need look only to the past. If the educational system had broken at some point, a look backward would reveal an end to progress—a point at which the system stopped working. Yet that isn't at all the picture that emerges. Instead, one can see that across many generations, the schools have slowly and steadily improved.

Consider the teachers in classrooms. For most of American history, teachers received no training at all, and hiring was a chaotic process in which the only constant was patronage. To quote Ted Sizer on the subject, the typical result was one "in which some mayor's half-drunk illiterate uncle was hired to teach twelfth-grade

---

English." There were other problems, too. As late as the 20th century, for instance, would-be educators generally had little if any student-teaching experience prior to entering classrooms, and they received no preparation for teaching particular content areas. Even as recently as mid-century, prospective teachers had no background in adolescent cognition and received no training in how to work with students from diverse backgrounds. All of that has changed. Does that mean that today's system of teacher education is without flaw? Hardly. There's lots of work yet to be done. But there is also no question that the average teacher in the U.S. today is better prepared than the average teacher from any past period.

The same is true of the school curriculum. Sure, it's somewhat arbitrary and, at least for some students, insufficiently challenging. But Americans are regularly told that the modern curriculum is a relic of the past and that it has grown increasingly out of date. That simply isn't true. Prior to the 20th century, high schools focused heavily on Latin and Greek, required coursework in subjects like zoology and mechanical drawing, and rarely offered any math beyond algebra. In 1900, the average school year was 100 days long—40 percent shorter than the current school year—and classes were commonly twice as large as contemporary ones. And well into the 20th century, girls and students of color were regularly offered a separate curriculum, emphasizing domestic or industrial training. Do students still read books? Yes. Do they sit in desks? Typically. Do teachers still stand at the front of the class? For the most part. But beyond that, there are more differences than similarities. Again, this doesn't mean that present practices are ideal—but it does mean that Americans should think twice before dissolving into panic over what is being taught in modern classrooms.

One can see that across many generations, the schools have slowly and steadily improved.

Finally, consider the outcomes produced by the educational system. Critics are right that achievement scores aren't overwhelmingly impressive and that troubling gaps persist across racial, ethnic, and income groups. Yet scores are up over the past 40 years, and the greatest gains over that period have been made by black and Hispanic students. They're right that the U.S. finishes well behind exam-oriented countries like Taiwan and Korea on international tests. But scores are roughly on par with countries like Norway, which was named by the United Nations the best place in the world to live; and students from low-poverty states like Massachusetts outscore most of their global peers. Critics are right that 40 percent of college students still don't graduate. But almost half of all American high-school students now head off to college each year—an all-time high. And whatever the doom-and-gloom about schools failing to address workforce needs, it's worth remembering that the U.S has the strongest economy in the world—by an enormous margin.

Are the schools perfect? No. But they are slowly improving. And they are certainly better today than at any point in the past. So why the invented story about an unchanging and obsolete system? Why the hysterical claims that everything has broken?

Perhaps some policy elites really believe the fake history—about a dramatic rise and tragic fall. The claim that the high school "was designed for early 20th-century workforce needs," for instance, has been repeated so frequently that it has a kind of truth status. Never the fact that the American high school was created in 1635 to provide classical training to the sons of ministers and merchants; and never mind the fact that today's high schools operate quite differently than those of the past. Facts, it seems, aren't as durable as myth.

Yet there is also another possible explanation worth considering: that policy elites are working to generate political will for their pet projects. Money and influence may go a long way in setting policy agendas. But in a decentralized and relatively democratic system, it still takes significant momentum to initiate any significant change—particularly the kinds of change that certain reformers are after when they suggest starting "from scratch." To generate that kind of energy—the energy to rip something down and rebuild it—the public needs to be convinced that it has a looming catastrophe on its hands.

This is not to suggest that educational reform is crafted by conspirators working to manufacture crisis. Policy elites are not knowingly falsifying evidence or collectively coming to secret agreement about how to terrify the public. Instead, as research has shown, self-identified school reformers inhabit a small and relatively closed network. As the policy analyst Rick Hess recently put it, "orthodoxy reigns" in reform circles, with shared values and concerns emerging "through partnerships, projects, consulting arrangements, and foundation initiatives." The ostensible brokenness of public education, it seems, is not merely a talking point; it is also an article of faith.

Whatever the intentions of policy leaders, this "broken system" narrative has had some serious unintended consequences. And perhaps the most obvious of those has been an increased tolerance for half-baked plans. Generally speaking, the public has a relatively high bar for replacing something that works, particularly if there is a risk of failure, and especially when their children are concerned. Historically, this has been the case in education. A half century ago, for instance, the Phi Delta Kappa/Gallup poll asked public-school parents what the schools were doing right. The response: Almost everything. The standard curriculum, the quality of teachers, and school facilities came in first, second, and third on the list. Not surprisingly, when parents were asked in another PDK/Gallup poll if the schools were "interested enough in trying new ways and methods," 42 percent responded that the schools were striking the right balance. Twenty-one percent felt that the schools were "too ready to try new ideas," and 20 percent felt that the schools were "not interested enough."

When it comes to replacing something broken, however, the bar for intervention is much lower. Doing something, even if it fails to live up to expectations, is invariably better than doing nothing. Only by doing nothing, Americans are told, can they fail. Thus, despite the fact that there is often little evidence in support of utopian schemes like "personalized online learning," which would use software to create a custom curriculum for each student, or "value-added measures" of teachers, which would determine educator effectiveness by running student test scores through an algorithm, many people are willing to suspend disbelief. Why? Because they have been convinced that the alternative—a status quo in precipitous decline—is worse. But what if the schools aren't in a downward spiral? What if, instead, things are slowly but steadily improving? In that light, disruption—a buzzword if ever there was one—doesn't sound like such a great idea.

A second consequence of the "broken system" narrative is that it denigrates schools and communities. Teachers, for instance, have seemingly never been more disillusioned. Roughly half of teachers report feeling under great stress several days a week, job satisfaction is at a 25-year low, and almost a third of teachers say they are likely to leave the profession within the next five years. Parents, too, have never had less confidence in the system. According to the most recent Phi Delta Kappa/Gallup poll, roughly 80 percent of Americans give grades of "C," "D," or "F" to the nation's schools—a far larger total than the 56 percent who issued those grades three decades ago. This, despite the fact that 70 percent of public school parents give their children's current schools an "A" or a "B" rating. In other words, despite people's positive direct experiences, the barrage of negative messaging has done serious damage to the public school brand.

The claim that the high school "was designed for early 20th-century workforce needs" has been repeated so frequently that it has a kind of truth status.

Consequently, many anxious parents are now competing with alarming ferocity for what they believe to be a shrinking number of "good" schools. As research indicates, they have exacerbated residential segregation in the process, intensifying racial and economic inequality.

Perhaps the most serious consequence of the "broken system" narrative is that it draws attention away from real problems that the nation has never fully addressed. The public-education system is undeniably flawed. Yet many of the deepest flaws have been deliberately cultivated. Funding inequity and racial segregation, for instance, aren't byproducts of a system that broke. They are direct consequences of an intentional concentration of privilege. Placing the blame solely on teacher training, or the curriculum, or on the design of the high school—alleging "brokenness"—perpetuates the fiction that all schools can be made great without addressing issues of race, class, and power. This is wishful thinking at its most pernicious.

This is not to suggest that there is no space for criticism, or for outrage. Students, families, and activists have both the right and the responsibility to advocate for themselves and their communities. They know what they need, and their needs have merit. Policymakers have a great deal to learn from them.

Still, it is important not to confuse inequity with ineptitude. History may reveal broken promises around racial and economic justice. But it does not support the story of a broken education system. Instead, the long view reveals a far less dramatic truth—that most aspects of public education have gotten better, generation by generation.

The evolution of America's school system has been slow. But providing a first-rate public education to every child in the country is a monumental task. Today, 50 million U.S. students attend roughly 100,000 schools, and are educated by over 3 million teachers. The scale alone is overwhelming. And the aim of schooling is equally ambitious. Educators are not just designing gadgets or building websites. At this phenomenal scale, they are trying to make people—a fantastically difficult task for which there is no quick fix, no simple solution, no "hack."

Can policy leaders and stakeholders accelerate the pace of development? Probably. Can the schools do more to realize national ideals around equity and inclusion? Without question. But none of these aims will be achieved by ripping the system apart. That's a ruinous fiction. The struggle to create great schools for all young people demands swift justice and steady effort, not melodrama and magical thinking.

Print Citations

CMS: Schneider, Jack. "America's Not-So-Broken Education System: Do U.S. Schools Really Need to Be Disrupted?" In *The Reference Shelf: Education Reform*, edited by Betsy Maury, 21–25. Ipswich, MA: H.W. Wilson, 2017.

MLA: Schneider, Jack. "America's Not-So-Broken Education System: Do U.S. Schools Really Need to Be Disrupted?" *The Reference Shelf: Education Reform*. Ed. Betsy Maury. Ipswich: H.W. Wilson, 2017. 21–25. Print.

APA: Schneider, J. (2017). America's not-so-broken education system: Do U.S. schools really need to be disrupted?" In Betsy Maury (Ed.), *The reference shelf: Education reform* (pp. 21–25). Ipswich, MA: H.W. Wilson. (Original work published 2016)

What the World Can Learn from the Latest PISA Test Results

The Economist, December 10, 2016

Football fans must wait four years between World Cups. Education nerds get their fill of global competition every three. The sixth Programme for International Student Assessment (PISA), a test of the science, maths and reading skills of 15-year-olds from across the world, was published by the OECD club of mainly rich countries on December 6th. Its results have telling lessons for policymakers worldwide.

Some 540,000 pupils in 72 countries or regions—each of whom had finished at least six years of school—sat similar tests last year. The OECD then crunched the results into a standardised scale. In the OECD the average result for each subject is about 490 points. Scoring 30 points above that is roughly akin to completing an extra year of schooling.

Singapore, the consistently high-achiever in PISA, does even better: it is now the top-performing country in each subject area. The average pupil's maths score of 564 suggests Singaporean teens are roughly three years ahead of their American peers, with a tally of 470.

Other East Asian countries also score highly across most domains, as they have done since PISA was launched 15 years ago. Japan and South Korea have above-average results in science and maths, as do cities such as Hong Kong and Macau, both autonomous territories of China, and Taipei, the capital of Taiwan.

Elsewhere, Canada and Finland have reading scores as high as Hong Kong's. Then there is Estonia: its science results are indistinguishable from Japan's and its maths scores are akin to South Korea's. It is now equal with Finland as the top performer in Europe. In turn Finland, which topped the first PISA, is still an above-average performer, but its scores have fallen since at least 2006.

Opponents of PISA argue that trying to make sense of all this is like trying to hear oneself over the noise of an obstreperous classroom. They note that education is about more than doing well in tests. And besides, some critics add, there is little useful to learn from the results, since it is parents alone that encourage swots. John Jerrim of University College London suggests that the only way some countries could catch up with the East Asian powerhouses is through more "tiger mothers" and "widespread cultural change".

PISA has flaws. It is one of many standardised tests, and tests are not all there is to learning. But it matters. It is the most influential research report in education for good reason. It offers informed guidance on what policymakers should do to fix their school systems. Just as importantly, it tells them what not to do.

Reforming education is slow and hard, but eminently possible.

It points out that among poorer countries the amount of public spending per pupil is associated with higher test scores. But in richer states that spend more than about $50,000 per pupil in total between 6 and 15 this link falls away. The pupils of Poland and Denmark have, in effect, the same average results in the science tests even though Denmark spends about 50% more per pupil.

Another potential waste of money, if only from the perspective of PISA results, may be sending children to private school. Across the OECD pupils in public schools score lower in science than students in private schools do. But this is not the case once you account for the economic and social background of pupils.

And while poverty is strongly associated with low scores, it is not destiny. In the OECD poor pupils are nearly three times more likely than their rich peers to have less than the basic level of proficiency in science. Those pupils with foreign-born parents tend to do even worse. Nevertheless, 29% of poor pupils score among the top quarter of children across the OECD. In Singapore, Japan and Estonia nearly half of the poorest pupils do.

Money Isn't Everything

That hints at another finding: achievement and greater equality are not mutually exclusive. In Canada, Denmark, Estonia, Hong Kong and Macau pupils have high average scores, with only a weak link between results and children's backgrounds.

One reason for Estonia's gain is demographic loss. Over the past 20 years the population of young people has declined faster than the number of teachers. There is now one teacher for every 12 pupils, down from closer to 20 two decades ago. Although in general reducing class sizes is not the most cost-effective response, Estonian pupils have benefited from the demographic shift, which has made it easier to give pupils, especially laggards, extra help.

But Estonia has also taken a deliberately inclusive approach, argues Mart Laidmets, a senior official at its ministry of education. It tries to avoid at all costs having pupils repeat years of school. Holding pupils back can help. But too often it is used as an excuse not to teach difficult kids. It may also reflect bias or discrimination. In countries such as Russia, Slovakia and the Czech Republic, poor boys are especially prone to being kept back a year, despite decent academic achievements.

Estonia, like Finland and Canada, also tries to keep selection by ability to a minimum. It delays "tracking" children into academic or vocational routes until they are 15 or 16 years old. Mr Laidmets argues that it helps pupils find jobs later in life, since better maths and literacy make it easier for them to adapt to changes in the labour market and to earn new skills.

By contrast, where pupils are diverted from an academic track at an early age, whether towards a vocational school or a less rigorous class in the same school, the gap between rich and poor children tends to be wider. In the Netherlands pupils at vocational schools have results equivalent to about three years less of schooling than their peers at general schools. "The more academically selective you are the more socially selective you become", says Andreas Schleicher, the head of education at the OECD.

All of which suggests what countries should not do. But are there any sure-fire tips from the best performers? Or is their success just down to pushy parents and tuition after school?

Culture matters but so, too, does policy, says Lucy Crehan, author of *Cleverlands*, a new book on PISA-besting countries. She points out that most of these states delay formal schooling until children are six or seven. Instead they use early-years education to prepare children for school through play-based learning and by focusing on social skills. Then they keep pupils in academic courses until the age of 16. Even Singapore, which does divert some pupils to a vocational track at the age of 13, ensures that pupils in those schools keep up high standards in reading and maths.

Top performers also focus their time and effort on what goes on in the classroom, rather than the structure of the school system. For while test scores and pupils' economic background are linked across the OECD, so too are specific things that the best schools and teachers do.

The top performers treat teachers as professionals and teachers act that way as well. They have time to prepare lessons and learn from their peers. They tend to direct classroom instruction rather than be led by their pupils. Their advancement is determined by results, not by teachers' unions. There are high expectations of nearly every student and high standards, too.

A Keener Argentina

The teenagers who took the PISA tests in 2015 were influenced by many years' worth of policies. And focusing on the consistently high performers means that lessons from those that have made recent improvements are neglected.

The city of Buenos Aires had the largest jump in overall scores from three years ago. On average its pupils scored 475 in science (up 51 points), 475 in reading (46 points) and 456 points (38 points) in maths.

For Esteban Bullrich, the minister in charge of education from 2010 to 2015, the initial aim was to make sure that pupils were being taught. Teachers were spending 12-15 days per year on strike, or about 7% of the time they should be in class, according to his calculations. To try to reduce those absences he first made his mobile-phone number public and began fielding calls directly from angry teachers. He extended the school day.

The top performers treat teachers as professionals and teachers act that way as well.

Then he offered teachers something of a deal: higher salaries in exchange for taking their job more seriously. The grip of unions in deciding on promotions was loosened. And he made teacher training more rigorous and practical.

Another impressive mover, albeit more of a tortoise than a hare, is Portugal. Since 2006 it has steadily improved its scores across each subject by about a year of schooling, overtaking the United States as it went from a middling to an above-average performer.

There are three reasons for Portugal's steady progress, says Nuno Crato, the country's former education minister. First, it began to care about results, introducing new standardised tests. Second, a new curriculum with higher standards was introduced from 2011. Third, it has reduced the amount of streaming by ability, keeping its use "temporary and partial". Struggling pupils may get extra tuition but teachers will try to keep them in the same classes as their peers.

For Portugal to become an educational powerhouse, argues Mr Crato, it also needs "better-prepared teachers". This is hard when some teaching unions oppose their members having to pass exams before they are allowed into classrooms. What better education does not necessarily need is bigger budgets, he says. Portugal's improvements have come despite severe cuts to public spending. "Money matters but it is not decisive," adds Mr Crato.

Progress can also be spotted even among countries whose overall scores have remained flat. The economic background of the average American pupil matters much less to their overall test scores than in earlier editions of PISA. Mr Schleicher puts this down to reforms such as President George W. Bush's No Child Left Behind Act, which made local governments more accountable for the results of poorer pupils.

The PISA results are not all happy tales of plucky reform. Australia is one of several countries whose results have dipped. Its average score in maths has fallen from 524 to 494 since 2003, equivalent to a year of schooling. Australia is one of the few rich countries where pupils do not have to take maths in their leaving exams. (Malcolm Turnbull, the prime minister, is trying to make states change this.) It is also a result of a declining quality of teaching, suggests John Hattie of the University of Melbourne. Successful applicants to teacher-training courses have lower results in their school exams than in the 1980s and 1990s.

Nevertheless, while some countries rise and others fall, many are just like England. Its results have barely budged since 2006. (Scotland's have plummeted.) The average result for OECD countries has similarly hardly changed since the tests began. This may reflect well on the test-setters: it would be worrying if the results swung wildly from edition to edition.

Yet it still reflects poorly on many policymakers. Mr Bullrich says PISA is like an X-ray of a country's education policy. It is not a full picture of your health but it can help you spot where things are sickly. Sadly, too many countries are dodging essential therapy.

Print Citations

CMS: "What the World Can Learn from the Latest PISA Test Results." In *The Reference Shelf: Education Reform*, edited by Betsy Maury, 26–30. Ipswich, MA: H.W. Wilson, 2017.

MLA: "What the World Can Learn from the Latest PISA Test Results." *The Reference Shelf: Education Reform*. Ed. Betsy Maury. Ipswich: H.W. Wilson, 2017. 26–30. Print.

APA: The Economist. (2017). What the world can learn from the latests PISA test results. In Betsy Maury (Ed.), *The reference shelf: Education reform* (pp. 26–30). Ipswich, MA: H.W. Wilson. (Original work published 2016)

Where School Choice Gets an A or B

By Mark Silva
U.S. News and World Report, March 29, 2017

When it comes to school choice—allowing parents the option of which schools their children attend—major school districts in some of the states ranking lowest in Pre-K-12 education are operating some of the top-rated alternative offerings.

The grades for school districts offering parental choice—either for public schools, or private schools supported by publicly financed tuition vouchers—come from an annual review conducted by the Brookings Institution.

In the 2016 "Education Choice and Competition Index" released today, one of Denver's school districts holds its place at the front of the pack for large school districts, with a Grade A rating. And by the numbers, it's only marginally ahead of the Recovery School District of New Orleans, also graded A.

In the Best States ranking of all 50 states at *U.S. News and World Report*, Colorado and Louisiana stand below average in the metrics used to evaluate education from Pre-K through high school: Colorado No. 30, Louisiana 44.

At the same time, the top-10 large school districts graded for school choice in the Brookings report include three in states rated among the top-10 for Pre-K-12 education at Best States: The Newark public schools are ranked No. 4 in the ECCI grading, while New Jersey is ranked No. 2 for Pre-K-12 in the Best States measure. And Boston's public schools are ranked No. 5 in the ECCI grades, while Massachusetts is ranked No. 3 for Pre-K-12 in the Best States review.

"The ECCI is not designed to answer causal questions about what system or education delivery mechanism works best," writes Grover Whitehurst, author of the Brookings report. Rather, he notes, the index "describes what is happening on the ground and ranks large districts on the degree and quality of the environment they provide for parents who want to choose the schools their children attend."

Denver County's School District 1, with 270 schools, "has a strong choice system characterized by a centralized assignment process requiring a single application from parents for both charter and regular public schools," he writes. "It has a good mix and utilization by parents of alternatives to traditional public schools."

The report from Brookings' Center for Children and Families examining school choice in the nation's 100 largest districts acknowledges the debate between school choice advocates and defenders of traditional public schooling. It also concludes that school choice is offering valid alternatives to poor neighborhood schools.

"There would be no reason for the ECCI if the traditional school district model of delivery of public education was the monolith that it represented until recently," the author writes. "In the traditional district model that completely dominated public education through the end of the 20th century, publicly-funded education for each state was provided entirely by school districts governed by elected school boards. Each district had an exclusive franchise to provide education services within its geographical boundaries."

"There is no question that alternatives to the traditional school district model are destructive of the traditional school district model," he writes. "Whether they are harmful, neutral, or helpful to students, families, and the nation is, in the end, an empirical question.... There is no question empirically that opportunities for parents to choose among traditional public schools for their children, to choose a charter school, and to receive a financial subsidy to attend a private school have grown leaps and bounds in the last 15-20 years. The traditional school district model is no longer the monopoly it used to be."

The report from Brookings' Center for Children and Families examining school choice in the nation's 100 largest districts acknowledges the debate between school choice advocates and defenders of traditional public schooling.

The Recovery district in New Orleans, with 92 schools, "has a high availability of choice, with all of its public schools being charters (which are universally schools of choice)," the report finds. "It also has a good supply of affordable private schools, and vouchers for private school attendance available from the state."

New to the top-10 list at Brookings this year: Columbus, Ohio, and Chicago. And once again, sixth-ranked Columbus in the ECCI rankings is found in a state that ranks No. 31 for pre-K-12 in the Best States rankings—while seventh-ranked for choice Chicago sits in a state ranked No. 10 for Pre-K-12 at Best States.

The Brookings top 10 is rounded out by other states ranking below average for pre-K-12: New York City's public schools, with 2,547 schools, rank No. 3 in the ECCI report, with a Grade A-minus. New York State ranks No. 23 for pre-K-12 at Best States. Houston, with 488 schools, ranks No. 8 in the Brookings report—while Texas ranks No 41 for pre-K-12 at Best States. The Pinellas County schools in Florida rank No. 10 at Brookings, Florida No. 46 among Best States for pre-K-12. The ninth ranking in the school choice report goes to Washington, D.C. (The federal district is not included in the *U.S. News* measurement of states.)

"We do not know how to create or sustain uniformly great neighborhood schools," Whitehurst concludes. "There is no existing proof that we do, and strong empirical evidence that the performance of schools varies substantially everywhere there are large numbers of schools to compare. An education reform agenda based on the assumption that the solution to the nation's education challenges is to provide a great neighborhood school for every child is fanciful."

Print Citations

CMS: Silva, Mark. "Where School Choice Gets an A or B." In *The Reference Shelf: Education Reform*, edited by Betsy Maury, 31–33. Ipswich, MA: H.W. Wilson, 2017.

MLA: Silva, Mark. "Where School Choice Gets an A or B." *The Reference Shelf: Education Reform*. Ed. Betsy Maury. Ipswich: H.W. Wilson, 2017. 31–33. Print.

APA: Silva, M. (2017). Where school choice gets an A or B. In Betsy Maury (Ed.), *The reference shelf: Education reform* (pp. 31–33). Ipswich, MA: H.W. Wilson. (Original work published 2017)

2
Reform 2017

Credit: Olivier Douliery/Pool via Bloomberg

U.S. President Donald Trump, second right, and Betsy DeVos, U.S. secretary of education, right, participate in a parent-teacher conference listening session inside the Roosevelt Room of the White House in Washington, D.C., on Tuesday, Feb. 14, 2017.

Commercializing Knowledge: Reform in 2017

Driven by the well documented struggle faced by the nation's disadvantaged schools and by fear that US students are falling behind the international curve of achievement, education reform is a perennially popular topic. The reform path explored depends largely on the political ideology that is dominant in the legislature. In 2017 President Donald Trump appointed Betsy DeVos—billionaire heiress and a private and religious school advocate—to serve as Secretary of Education. Despite bipartisan political opposition and little public support (34.5 percent according to Saint Leo University Polling Institute),[1] DeVos was confirmed, becoming the most controversial education secretary in recent history. Both Trump and DeVos are private school graduates who also chose private schools for their children, and, under this leadership, education reform is likely to focus on providing benefits to private schools at the expense of public education.

Free Market Versus Public Trust

A public trust is an institution or system that is operated and managed by elected or appointed public servants and is managed in the interest of the public. Government-managed programs, like public schools or the Social Security system, are typically complex, which is a result of having to adhere to guidelines meant to ensure fairness and prevent discrimination. Conservative Americans tend to be skeptical of government-run programs and often view them as bloated, corrupt, and inefficient. Conservatives are also more likely to believe that free-market competition, in which organizations or corporations compete for revenues and customers, is superior to government ownership or management.

Private schools essentially function like corporations, competing for students and revenue. Private schools, because they do not receive government funding, enjoy more freedom to tailor their admissions and curriculum to serve certain types of students. Some private schools cater to the wealthy elite, while others cater to children with developmental disabilities or other challenges. Supporters of private schooling typically see private schools as a way to avoid the perceived problems of public education, such as large class sizes, a lack of direct student/teacher interaction, and diverse student bodies that some feel compromise high-achieving students by placing them in classes with low-performing students. In 2017, one of the biggest trends in education reform is privatization, or the idea that federal funding should be invested in alternatives to public school, like private and charter schools. The basic tenet is that a competitive educational marketplace will improve the quality of education by forcing schools to compete for students and revenues tied to student enrollment. This competitive environment, in theory, will raise the quality of education on the whole.

Columbia University education specialist Samuel Abrams, in his book *Education and the Commercial Mindset*, argues that privatization only works well when applied to markets dealing with simple services, like retail electronics. This is because consumers can easily compare and judge the quality of simple products and services and can legally seek recourse against companies that violate their contracts by selling inferior or flawed products. By contrast, education is a complex service and it is not possible for parents and legislators to accurately judge the quality of each school's educational product. This is because the quality of education at each school, or within each class, is dependent on highly complex factors like socio-economic environment, parental involvement, and access to resources. As of 2017, there is no reliable system to accurate measure a school's quality and so education cannot be effectively sold in a traditional free-market model.[2]

It is also arguable that free-market competition does not encourage companies to develop the best product, because the best product is not always the most profitable and because it is not always necessary to produce the *best* product to beat competitors. In the free market, companies are encouraged to innovate just enough to beat their competitors and to reserve further innovation for when it is needed. Companies in the free market focus on their most profitable products, even when alternative products might be better for consumers. This reality of free-market economics might help illustrate why standardized testing has failed to raise the quality of schools. The focus on testing encourages teachers and schools to focus on information covered in tests and discourages offering educational options like art, music, and dance, and of experimenting with new programs. The increasingly narrow focus on testing therefore discourages a more well-rounded education that is arguably better for students in favor of a more profitable system that focuses on teaching subjects that are tied to better ratings and thus higher revenues.

Charters and Vouchers

Charter schools, the education trend of the 2000s, are essentially public schools that are run by private individuals, groups, or corporations rather than by public servants. The "charters" of the system are contracts between the schools and the government that elucidate the school's purpose and promise accountability in return for federal and state funding. In addition to government revenues, charters can also utilize donations and private investment. The charter movement gained momentum in the 1990s, with hundreds of charters opening across the country. As charters do not have to adhere to what some see as overly rigid state guidelines, they enjoy greater freedom to target certain groups, such as low-income students or students seeking vocational training.

A 2006 study of charter schools conducted by the National Center for Education Statistics, showed that charter schools, on average, do not offer a higher-quality education than comparable public schools.[3] Further, studies indicate that charters rarely face penalties when they fail to meet state standards because there is no effective system in place to hold them accountable.[4] As charters are not as constrained by state laws designed to prohibit discrimination, studies also indicate that many charters avoid enrolling problems or special needs students in an effort to avoid compromising performance and are also more likely to expel or suspend students in an effort to maintain the perception of quality to potential enrollees and investors. In some cases, because charters can target marginalized populations in areas with underfunded public schools, the programs have been successful at helping certain students. As this occurs, however, the public schools surrounding charter startups, suffer from further disadvantages and the students who remain in public schools are therefore further marginalized by the growth of the charter program.

Critics argue that charters take money from public schools, but proponents counter that this is not the case because the "funds follow the child." When a student leaves public school for a charter option, funding for the student is transferred from the public school to the charter school. Therefore, though the public school loses one student's worth of funding, the school also has one less student to pay for, and thus, supporters argue that there is no net loss. This interpretation is incorrect, because, as schools lose students, they cannot adjust investment in staff, facilities, and services to match their loss in revenue. If a public school, for instance, loses 5 percent of its students to charter schools, the school cannot reduce its facility size by 5 percent, or reduce its staff by 5 percent, without compromising remaining students. A 2014 review of the financial impact of charter schools in Nashville, Tennessee, showed that the growth of charters did result in a net loss of funding and resources for the city's public schools.[5]

In addition, critics argue that opening education to private investment is not in the interest of student welfare as it encourages investors to invest in education for profit rather than out of legitimate concern for students. In Florida, for instance, charter schools grew into a $400-million-a-year business, receiving more than $6,000 per student enrolled, and operating largely without public oversight. It was discovered that the Life Skills Center of Miami-Dade County, for instance, had been paying 97 percent of its revenue to a for-profit investment management company.[6] In a testament to the waning appeal of charters, in November of 2016 Massachusetts voters rejected a bill that would have removed a cap on the number of charter schools in the state. This occurred despite the fact that Massachusetts has what many consider to be the best charter schools in the nation *and* despite a 30-million-dollar campaign to promote charters in the state.[7]

Vouchers, sometimes called "opportunity scholarships," are an emerging alternative to public and charter schools in which state revenues, that would otherwise be used to fund public schools and/or charters, are given directly to parents who can use the funds on any educational option, including private or religious schools. The idea for vouchers emerged in the 1990s through a pilot program in Milwaukee, Wisconsin. Since then, fourteen states have adopted some form of voucher program. Secretary DeVos hopes that a national voucher program would enable underprivileged students to attend private schools. Proposals emerging from the

Trump Administration, under DeVos, indicate that the administration plans to focus vouchers first on low-income and minority families.

Whether or not the voucher program becomes more widespread, there will be many students who are unable to qualify for vouchers or who, even if they do, will be unable to transfer due to a lack of availability or because the amount of assistance provided through vouchers will still be insufficient, in the vast majority of cases, to fund private school tuition. Studies indicate that, even with a voucher program, public schools will remain the only option for most students. Critics therefore argue that the voucher program will benefit the wealthy, providing another tax benefit for wealthy parents and organizations that invest in private schools, while further reducing available tax dollars to fund public education.

Institutions that could potentially receive funding under voucher programs will still, in many cases, not be held accountable to federal/state laws prohibiting discrimination. For instance, in Georgia, the tax voucher program is being used to fund more than 400 schools that refuse, on religious principles, to enroll gay and/or lesbian students.[8] Private schools in general are less diverse and place less emphasis on promoting or fostering ethnic and racial diversity. A study from the Southern Education Foundation found that 43 percent of the nation's private schools were 90 percent or more white, compared with 27 percent of public schools.[9] While proponents argue that the voucher program may change this, such a change would be unlikely without a massive expansion of private school startups in ethnically diverse areas.

As voucher programs have been in place for more than 20 years, economists and researchers have had ample time to study the results. A 2017 review by the Economic Policy Institute found that students participating in voucher programs exhibited little to no improvement in academic performance and that heightened competition has not improved public schools in regions that employ tax vouchers.[10] In some cases, studies indicate that students who transfer to private schools tend to decline in performance compared to students who remain in public school.[11] Even when it comes to the issue of educational quality, there is little reason to believe that private schools provide a measurable benefit for many students. Contrary to popular belief, students from similar socioeconomic environments perform about the same on tests whether they attend private or public schools. On the most basic level, therefore, the influence of socioeconomic environment, such as parental level of education and access to resources and assistance, has a far larger impact on educational outcomes than the choice of public or private schooling.[12]

Educational reform is a complex goal and there has been little agreement on the best way to achieve a stronger education system. As Trump and DeVos have committed to the privatization option, there will likely be little emphasis on alternative proposals. Progressives like Bernie Sanders, favor a more or less opposite approach that increases tax funding for public schools and would create a system of free higher education. In education, as in many other facets of American public discourse, approaches depend on perspective. With a highly conservative president and legislature, and tax proposals that primarily benefit corporations and the wealthy, education reform is likely to align with these interests. It therefore remains to be seen if this investment will have any net positive effect for the majority of Americans or whether the elite class will be the primary beneficiaries until future electoral change creates a new direction in reform.

Micah L. Issitt

Works Used

Braun, Henry, Jenkins, Frank, and Wendy Grigg. "A Closer Look at Charter Schools Using Hierarchical Linear Modeling." *IES*. National Center for Education Statistics. Aug 2006. Web. 25 Apr 2017.

Braun, Henry, Jenkins, Frank, and Wendy Grigg. "Comparing Private Schools and Public Schools Using Hierarchical Linear Modeling." *IES*. National Center for Education Statistics. Jul 2006. Web. 28 Apr 2017.

Broussard, Meredith. "Why Poor Schools Can't Win at Standardized Testing." *The Atlantic*. The Atlantic Monthly Group. Jul 15 2014. Web. 5 May 2017.

Carnoy, Martin. "School Vouchers Are Not a Proven Strategy for Improving Student Achievement." *EPI*. Economic Policy Institute. Feb 28 2017. Web 28 Apr 2017.

"Charter School Financial Impact Model." *MGT of America*. MGT of America, Inc. Sep 11 2014. Web. 25 Apr 2017.

"Evaluation of the Public Charter Schools Program." *PPSS*. Policy and Program Studies Service. US Department of Education. 2004. Web. 25 Apr 2017.

Figlio, David and Krzysztof Karbownik. "Evaluation of Ohio's EdChoice Scholarship Program: Selection, Competition, and Performance Effects." *Thomas B. Fordham Institute*. July 2016. Web. 28 Apr 2017.

Hiaasen, Scott and Kathleen McGrory. "Florida Charter Schools: Big Money, Little Oversight." *Miami Herald*. Miami Herald Media Company. Sep 19 2011. Web. 28 Apr 2017.

Keller, Jared. "Did Massachusetts Just End the Country's Charter School Debate?" *PSMAG*. Pacific Standard. Nov 8 2016. Web. 25 Apr 2017.

Le Miere, Jason. "It's Not Just Trump: Poll Says His Cabinet and Other Republican Leaders Are Unpopular Too." *Newsweek*. Mar 20 2017. Web. 25 Apr 2017.

"Race and Ethnicity in a New Era of Public Funding for Private Schools." *Southern Education*. Southern Education Foundation. Mar 2016. Web. 28 Apr. 2017.

Resmovits, Joy. "Betsy DeVos Says It's 'Possible' Her Family Has Contributed $200 million to the Republican Party." *Los Angeles Times*. Los Angeles Times. Jan 17 2017. Web. 25 Apr 2017.

Strauss, Valerie. "Welfare for the Rich? Private School Tax Credit Programs Expanding." *The Washington Post*. Nash Holdings. Feb 28 2013. Web. 30 Apr 2017.

Strauss, Valerie. "Why the Movement to Privatize Public Education Is a Very Bad Idea." *The Washington Post*. Nash Holdings. Jul 14 2016. Web. 30 Apr 2017.

Notes

1. Le Miere, "It's Not Just Trump: Poll Says His Cabinet and Other Republican Leaders Are Unpopular Too."
2. Strauss, "Why the Movement to Privatize Public Education Is a Very Bad Idea."
3. Braun, Jenkins, and Grigg, "A Closer Look at Charter Schools Using Hierarchical Linear Modeling."
4. "Evaluation of the Public Charter Schools Program," *PPSS*.
5. "Charter School Financial Impact Model," MGT of America.
6. Hiaasen and McGrory, "Florida Charter Schools: Big Money, Little Oversight."
7. Keller, "Did Massachusetts Just End the Country's Charter School Debate?"
8. Strauss, "Welfare for the Rich? Private School Tax Credit Programs Expanding."
9. "Race and Ethnicity in a New Era of Public Funding for Private Schools," *Southern Education*.
10. Carnoy, "School Vouchers Are Not a Proven Strategy for Improving Student Achievement."
11. Figlio and Karbownik, "Evaluation of Ohio's EdChoice Scholarship Program: Selection, Competition, and Performance Effects."
12. Braun, Jenkins, and Grigg, "Comparing Private Schools and Public Schools Using Hierarchical Linear Modeling."

Tax Credits, School Choice and "Neovouchers": What You Need to Know

By Kevin Welner
The Conversation, April 14, 2017

As Republican lawmakers craft a tax reform bill, there's speculation on the import taxes, value-added taxes and tax cuts it may usher in. Meanwhile, it's likely that the bill will also include a major education policy initiative from the Trump administration: a tax credit designed to fund private school vouchers.

A decade ago I started researching this new kind of voucher—funded through a somewhat convoluted tax credit mechanism—that appears to have particular appeal to President Trump and other Republicans.

These new vouchers (or "neovouchers") are similar to conventional vouchers in many ways, but there are some important differences. It's those differences that neovoucher advocates most care about and that everyone should understand.

Conventional Vouchers

What exactly is a school voucher? Typically, a voucher is direct financial support that helps families pay for the cost of private K-12 schooling. Proponents see vouchers as a way to help children attend nonpublic schools. Detractors see vouchers as undermining funding and support needed by public education.

All vouchers subsidize tuition with tax dollars. This can be accomplished in many ways, and the nuances matter.

Conventional voucher policies use the relatively straightforward method of allocating state money to give vouchers directly to eligible parents. The parents, in turn, give the vouchers to a private school of their choice. These schools are sometimes secular, but are usually religious.

The private schools then redeem these vouchers to obtain money from the state. In the 16 states where conventional voucher policies exist, they produce about 175,000 vouchers annually. This amounts to 3.3 percent of the nation's private school population.

Yet, these direct vouchering programs present four major problems for school choice advocates.

First, they're typically available only to lower-income families; wealthier families are usually not eligible.

Second, when governments directly provide voucher money, participating schools are generally required to comply with a variety of guidelines, such as accreditation requirements, anti-discrimination regulation, minimum teacher qualifications, financial reporting and/or the administration of a standardized test to students receiving the voucher.

Third, vouchers are simply not politically popular—which is why the more palatable term "opportunity scholarships" (courtesy of messaging guru Frank Luntz) has become increasingly popular.

Finally—and importantly—state constitutions often prohibit the channeling of state money to religious institutions. In many states, this means that conventional voucher programs cannot exist if the program includes religious schools. Although the Supreme Court has ruled that vouchers don't violate federal law, state constitutions can create legal obstacles that are more formidable than those under the U.S. Constitution.

Vouchers on Steroids

To sidestep these issues, many state lawmakers have embraced a new kind of voucher policy that gets essentially the same result but changes the state's role from paying for vouchers to issuing tax credits.

This approach was first adopted in Arizona, in 1997, where the legislature passed a law setting up a system in which any taxpayer could "donate" money to a special, private nonprofit corporation. That corporation then issues vouchers to parents, who use them to pay for private school tuition. The taxpayers then get the money back from the state in the form of a tax credit.

Arizona's constitution—typical of language in state constitutions—requires that "No public money or property shall be appropriated for or applied to any religious worship, exercise, or instruction, or to the support of any religious establishment." But Arizona's elaborate mechanism keeps the specific dollars out of state coffers. Consequently, state funding only indirectly supports religious institutions. The Arizona Supreme Court found this distinction sufficient, ruling that the tax credits did not violate the state's constitutional prohibition against spending public money for religious support.

Beyond this legal advantage, advocates favor this sort of tax-credit-voucher method because it appears less likely to be regulated. It's also likely to be open to a wider range of parents—not just lower-income or special needs families. And the complexity of the neovoucher approach obscures the fact that it's really a voucher program, making it less of a political lightning rod.

Some wealthy taxpayers can even receive tax benefits exceeding the value of their donations. This baffling outcome is because of a loophole tied to the Alternative Minimum Tax (AMT), an extra tax imposed on some wealthier taxpayers to ensure that they pay their fair share. The AMT limits certain tax breaks, such as the ability to deduct state tax payments from federal taxes. However—and here's the twist—these AMT taxpayers can deduct charitable contributions. And so, these wealthier taxpayers can shift their state tax payment into a "charitable" contribution

These new vouchers (or "neovouchers") are similar to conventional vouchers in many ways, but there are some important differences.

and instantly transform the payment into a federal deduction. In the six states that give a full tax credit for voucher donations, those taxpayers can get back the full value of their voucher plus a deduction for the donation.

A decade ago when I wrote a book explaining these tax credit policies and labeling them "neovouchers," they existed in only six states and generated about 100,000 vouchers. Today, 17 states have tax-credit policies similar to Arizona's on their books, generating a quarter-million vouchers and growing every year.

These New Vouchers Aren't Likely to Help Kids

Do these vouchers improve student achievement? The research suggests that we shouldn't expect children's learning to be affected.

An evaluation of Florida's neovoucher law—which the Trump administration appears to be using as its model—found that students receiving these neovouchers had a nonsignificant (-0.7 percentile points) loss in math and nonsignificant (+0.1 percentile points) gain in reading on standardized test scores.

Similarly, research focused on conventional vouchers has tended to reach this same conclusion, finding no significant change in student test scores. More recent studies, looking at conventional vouchers in Louisiana, Ohio and Indiana actually find that test scores have declined—in some cases, by surprisingly large margins.

What to Expect

While, thus far, neovoucher policies have existed only on the state level, proposals are now appearing at a federal level.

In February of 2017, Rep. Todd Rokita of Indiana and three Republican colleagues introduced a bill (H.B. 895) that sets forth the basic structure for a federal neovoucher policy.

But the particulars of the neovoucher policy that ultimately emerges in the Republicans' tax reform bill are up for grabs. Based on the wide variety of existing state neovoucher policies, it is possible that the federal proposal will provide a full 100 percent credit (as does H.B. 895) or a credit of only 50 or 65 percent. It might limit eligibility to children in families at the poverty level, or it might have expanded or even universal eligibility.

It also remains to be seen whether federal neovouchers would be allocated only in states with existing programs or might be distributed in all states, including those with no such laws.

Interestingly, some of the staunchest advocates of state-level neovouchers have expressed concern and even opposition to a federal initiative. Beyond general conservative resistance to federal overreach in education policy, they voice familiar concerns about the likelihood of regulations following money, particularly from future Democratic leadership in Washington, DC.

And, of course, a federal neovoucher program would face significant fiscal obstacles as well. Absent large cuts elsewhere, these policies would strain the federal budget, requiring some creative work on the part of lawmakers—particularly since the tax reform bill will have to be revenue neutral. The cost of vouchers for even a fraction of the nation's 57 million K-12 students could easily cost tens of billions.

This daunting price tag, however, probably won't deter President Trump or Education Secretary Betsy DeVos, who have stated their opposition to the "public" part of public schools, with Trump even denigrating them as socialistic "government schools" that are part of the "American carnage" that "leaves our young and beautiful students deprived of all knowledge."

It seems unlikely that they will forego their chance to give tax dollars to private education.

Print Citations

CMS: Welner, Kevin. "Tax Credits, School Choice, and 'Neovouchers': What You Need to Know." In *The Reference Shelf: Education Reform*, edited by Betsy Maury, 43–46. Ipswich, MA: H.W. Wilson, 2017.

MLA: Welner, Kevin. "Tax Credits, School Choice, and 'Neovouchers': What You Need to Know." *The Reference Shelf: Education Reform*. Ed. Betsy Maury. Ipswich: H.W. Wilson, 2017. 43–46. Print.

APA: Welner, K. (2017). Tax credits, school choice, and "neovouchers": What you need to know. In Betsy Maury (Ed.), *The reference shelf: Education reform* (pp. 43–46). Ipswich, MA: H.W. Wilson. (Original work published 2017)

It's Not What Trump's Education Department Will Do That Should Worry Critics; It's What It Won't Do

By Conor Williams
the74million.org, April 11, 2017

Much of the public concern about Education Secretary Betsy DeVos has consisted of folks burning themselves up speculating at the damage she'll actively do to public schools.

When she was nominated, the education media wondered whether she would make good on then-President-elect Trump's campaign promise to convert the federal government's funding for high-poverty public schools into a voucher system. In March, liberals read Trump's proposed budget and found confirmation of their fears: As written, it would cut billions from teacher training in favor of significant new spending on school choice. In a recent talk at Brookings, DeVos hinted that her department might use its authority to encourage states to expand school choice programs.

Is there a there there? In the Trump era, when every new, suspicious fact just gets more concerning upon further investigation, when outwardly disconnected events seem to keep stubbornly linking up into nefarious conspiracies, it's easy to survey DeVos's record and short time in office and see the groundwork for a steady campaign against public education.

But much of this sort of hand-wringing about DeVos is misplaced. Given the limits that Congress placed on the Department of Education at the tail end of the Obama administration, her ability to make states hew to her agenda is limited. What's more, the public's general disinterest in education as a political issue will also limit DeVos's room to maneuver. Specifically, while Americans often express concern about the state of public education, they're generally comfortable with their own schools. This means that any dramatic changes to American schooling usually come with greater risks than rewards.

Put it this way: Critics looking for major activism from DeVos are likely to be disappointed. It's far more likely her "sins" against public education will be sins of omission than of commission.

Here's a handy way to keep the two clear in your head. Let's say you have a really nice set of wine glasses. They're beautiful keepsakes, family antiques handed down by your partner's dear great-grandmother, perfect in every way—except that they're way too fragile to put in the dishwasher. Late one night, after a particularly long, rowdy dinner party, you decide to clean up the mess and chuck them in there anyway. The next morning, you awake to find the heirlooms—and your relationship—in pieces.

That, my friend, is a sin of commission. Like a massive, fundamental adjustment to how the federal government distributes school funding to support underserved kids, sins of commission are easy to spot. You knew what you were doing, but you did it anyway.

Sins of omission, by contrast, are tougher to see. Imagine that after huzzah-ing the last guest out the door after the aforementioned rowdy party, you turn around, survey the bacchanalian wreckage, and stump off to bed. The next morning, you awake to find the mess still there, along with a grumpy partner chasing your new-found rodent roommates out of the kitchen.

That sort of dereliction of duty is a sin of omission. You didn't do anything wrong—indeed, you didn't do anything—but you failed at an opportunity to do something right.

As far as DeVos is concerned, critics ought to spend less time (and cortisol) worrying whether she is trying to "advance God's kingdom" via U.S. public schools and pay more attention to the consequential things she isn't doing. In a February interview with Axios, after her confirmation, DeVos expressed skepticism about the federal role in overseeing public education. While she suggested that government involvement made sense "when we had segregated schools and when ... girls weren't allowed to have the same kind of sports teams," she couldn't think of any current issues that might warrant attention from her department.

With limited authority, DeVos can't do much harm. But beware of what she doesn't do.

This is either supremely cynical or gobsmackingly naive. Folks who spend their lives working in education are aware that U.S. school segregation is a present-day plague, not some conquered problem of the past. And they know that, absent oversight, states routinely use federal education dollars for purposes that do not help underserved students succeed.

That's why DeVos's hypothetical sins of commission warrant much less anxiety than they're generating. If she follows Trump's budget roadmap and tries to eliminate major federal funding streams, the education world will be ablaze—creating new headaches for an administration that already generates at least a half-dozen daily migraines for itself.

But if DeVos sticks to her public position that the federal government's civil rights authority is obsolete and unnecessary, there will be a steady stream of sins of omission.

During the Obama administration, the department's Office for Civil Rights struggled to keep up with the number of complaints it received. How will that office perform its function effectively under a secretary of education who is skeptical of its purpose? And how will the Trump administration's proposed budget cuts affect its capacity?

That's where DeVos's critics should be looking. Sure, sins of omission are harder to see. It's not as easy to find out that the Department of Education didn't act as it is to scream bloody murder when it does. If the department doesn't investigate claims that English-language learners are being systematically denied access to educational opportunities in Arizona (or in Cincinnati, or in Charleston, etc.), will that spark national outrage? If the department allows states to weaken oversight of and accountability for persistently failing schools, will anyone complain?

What's more, it's harder to ignite controversies around DeVos's inaction on civil rights or federal accountability, since any critique will have to begin by articulating a convincing alternative version of what she should have done. That is, if DeVos advocated for a national transgender bathroom policy, there would be massive pushback. If her department never really gets around to doing anything about current and future transgender civil rights complaints, it'll be hard to generate an opposition movement.

So, will Secretary DeVos "destroy public education"? She seems to be committing herself to a sustained crusade against it: DeVos almost never misses an opportunity to denigrate public school performance. She dismissed teachers at a D.C. middle school she visited as passive, in "receive mode." During her talk at Brookings, she complained that it would be hard for U.S. public education "to get a lot worse."

But it's far more likely that the real harm will come from what DeVos doesn't do.

Print Citations

CMS: Williams, Conor. "It's Not What Trump's Education Department Will Do That Should Worry Critics; It's What It Won't Do." In *The Reference Shelf: Education Reform*, edited by Betsy Maury, 47–49. Ipswich, MA: H.W. Wilson, 2017.

MLA: Williams, Conor. "It's Not What Trump's Education Department Will Do That Should Worry Critics; It's What It Won't Do." *The Reference Shelf: Education Reform*. Ed. Betsy Maury. Ipswich: H.W. Wilson, 2017. 47–49. Print.

APA: Williams, C. (2017). It's not what Trump's education department will do that should worry critics: It's what it won't do. In Betsy Maury (Ed.), *The reference shelf: Education reform* (pp. 47–49). Ipswich, MA: H.W. Wilson. (Original work published 2017)

Dismal Voucher Results Surprise Researchers as DeVos Era Begins

By Kevin Carey
The New York Times, February 23, 2017

The confirmation of Betsy DeVos as secretary of education was a signal moment for the school choice movement. For the first time, the nation's highest education official is someone fully committed to making school vouchers and other market-oriented policies the centerpiece of education reform.

But even as school choice is poised to go national, a wave of new research has emerged suggesting that private school vouchers may harm students who receive them. The results are startling—the worst in the history of the field, researchers say.

While many policy ideas have murky origins, vouchers emerged fully formed from a single, brilliant essay published in 1955 by Milton Friedman, the free-market godfather later to be awarded a Nobel Prize in Economics. Because "a stable and democratic society is impossible without widespread acceptance of some common set of values and without a minimum degree of literacy and knowledge on the part of most citizens," Mr. Friedman wrote, the government should pay for all children to go to school.

But, he argued, that doesn't mean the government should run all the schools. Instead, it could give parents vouchers to pay for "approved educational services" provided by private schools, with the government's role limited to "ensuring that the schools met certain minimum standards."

The voucher idea sat dormant for years before taking root in a few places, most notably Milwaukee. Yet even as many of Mr. Friedman's other ideas became Republican Party orthodoxy, most national G.O.P. leaders committed themselves to a different theory of educational improvement: standards, testing and accountability. That movement reached an apex when the No Child Left Behind Act of 2001 brought a new focus on tests and standards to nearly every public school nationwide. The law left voucher supporters with crumbs: a small demonstration project in Washington, DC.

But broad political support for No Child Left Behind proved short-lived. Teachers unions opposed the reforms from the left, while libertarians and states-rights conservatives denounced them from the right. When Republicans took control of more governor's mansions and state legislatures in the 2000s, they expanded vouchers to an unprecedented degree. Three of the largest programs sprang up in Indiana,

Louisiana and Ohio, which collectively enroll more than a third of the 178,000 voucher students nationwide.

Most of the new programs heeded Mr. Friedman's original call for the government to enforce "minimum standards" by requiring private schools that accept vouchers to administer standardized state tests. Researchers have used this data to compare voucher students with similar children who took the same tests in public school. Many of the results were released over the last 18 months, while Donald J. Trump was advocating school choice on the campaign trail.

The first results came in late 2015. Researchers examined an Indiana voucher program that had quickly grown to serve tens of thousands of students under Mike Pence, then the state's governor. "In mathematics," they found, "voucher students who transfer to private schools experienced significant losses in achievement." They also saw no improvement in reading.

The next results came a few months later, in February, when researchers published a major study of Louisiana's voucher program. Students in the program were predominantly black and from low-income families, and they came from public schools that had received poor ratings from the state department of education, based on test scores. For private schools receiving more applicants than they could enroll, the law required that they admit students via lottery, which allowed the researchers to compare lottery winners with those who stayed in public school.

Until about a year ago, however, few if any studies had shown vouchers causing test scores to decline drastically.

They found large negative results in both reading and math. Public elementary school students who started at the 50th percentile in math and then used a voucher to transfer to a private school dropped to the 26th percentile in a single year. Results were somewhat better in the second year, but were still well below the starting point.

This is very unusual. When people try to improve education, sometimes they succeed and sometimes they fail. The successes usually register as modest improvements, while the failures generally have no effect at all. It's rare to see efforts to improve test scores having the opposite result. Martin West, a professor at the Harvard Graduate School of Education, calls the negative effects in Louisiana "as large as any I've seen in the literature"—not just compared with other voucher studies, but in the history of American education research.

There's always the chance that a single study, no matter how well designed, is an outlier. Studies of older voucher programs in Milwaukee and elsewhere have generally produced mixed results, sometimes finding modest improvements in test scores, but only for some subjects and student groups. Until about a year ago, however, few if any studies had shown vouchers causing test scores to decline drastically.

In June, a third voucher study was released by the Thomas B. Fordham Institute, a conservative think tank and proponent of school choice. The study, which was financed by the pro-voucher Walton Family Foundation, focused on a large voucher program in Ohio. "Students who use vouchers to attend private schools have fared worse academically compared to their closely matched peers attending public schools," the researchers found. Once again, results were worse in math.

Three consecutive reports, each studying one of the largest new state voucher programs, found that vouchers hurt student learning. Researchers and advocates began a spirited debate about what, exactly, was going on.

Mark Dynarski of the Brookings Institution noted that the performance gap between private and public school students had narrowed significantly over time. He argued that the standards, testing and accountability movement, for all its political shortcomings, was effective. The assumed superiority of private schools may no longer hold.

Some voucher supporters observed that many private schools in Louisiana chose not to accept voucher students, and those that did had recently experienced declining enrollment. Perhaps the participating schools were unusually bad and eager for revenue. But this is another way of saying that exposing young children to the vagaries of private-sector competition is inherently risky. The free market often does a terrible job of providing basic services to the poor—see, for instance, the lack of grocery stores and banks in many low-income neighborhoods. This may also hold for education.

Others have argued that standardized test scores are the wrong measure of school success. It's true that voucher programs in Washington and some others elsewhere, which produced no improvements in test scores, increased the likelihood of students' advancement and graduation from high school. One study of a privately financed voucher program in New York found positive results for college attendance among African-Americans.

But research has also linked higher test scores to a host of positive outcomes later in life. And voucher advocates often cite poor test scores in public schools to justify creating private school vouchers in the first place.

The new voucher studies stand in marked contrast to research findings that well-regulated charter schools in Massachusetts and elsewhere have a strong, positive impact on test scores. But while vouchers and charters are often grouped under the umbrella of "school choice," the best charters tend to be nonprofit public schools, open to all and accountable to public authorities. The less "private" that school choice programs are, the better they seem to work.

The new evidence on vouchers does not seem to have deterred the Trump administration, which has proposed a new $20 billion voucher program. Secretary DeVos's enthusiasm for vouchers, which have been the primary focus of her philanthropic spending and advocacy, appears to be undiminished.

Print Citations

CMS: Carey, Kevin. "Dismal Voucher Results Surprise Researchers as DeVos Era Begins." In *The Reference Shelf: Education Reform*, edited by Betsy Maury, 50–53. Ipswich, MA: H.W. Wilson, 2017.

MLA: Carey, Kevin. "Dismal Voucher Results Surprise Researchers as DeVos Era Begins." *The Reference Shelf: Education Reform*. Ed. Betsy Maury. Ipswich: H.W. Wilson, 2017. 50–53. Print.

APA: Carey, K. (2017). Dismal voucher results surprise researchers as DeVos Era begins. In Betsy Maury (Ed.), *The reference shelf: Education reform* (pp. 50–53). Ipswich, MA: H.W. Wilson. (Original work published 2017)

Education for Sale? School Choice and the Future of American Education

By Linda Darling-Hammond
The Nation, March 9, 2017

On February 7, Betsy DeVos was confirmed as the nation's new education secretary after a contentious 50-50 vote in the Senate, with Vice President Mike Pence breaking the tie. Coming to the job with no experience in public education—either as a student, parent, educator, or board member—DeVos's only stated commitment is to expand "choice" nationally through charter schools and private-school vouchers, as she worked to do in her home state of Michigan.

There, DeVos was a key player in expanding a free-market system that features the largest number and percentage of for-profit charter schools in the nation: 79 percent of Michigan's charters are for-profit. This is highly unusual, as more than 80 percent of charters nationwide are nonprofit. DeVos has also owned shares in K12 Inc., the nation's largest operator of for-profit charter schools. In 2000, she helped fund an unsuccessful effort to change the state constitution in order to permit private-school vouchers.

In a recent interview about her goals as education secretary, DeVos stated that she intends to expand on this vision of choice, saying: "I expect there will be more public charter schools. I expect there will be more private schools. I expect there will be more virtual schools. I expect there will be more schools of any kind that haven't even been invented yet."

"Choice" has become a popular mantra in education-reform circles, used primarily to describe initiatives to increase the number of charter schools, which are publicly funded but privately operated, and to increase funding for private schools through voucher systems. The presumption in both of these instances is that they will expand high-quality options for parents and students.

Yet even among ardent charter-school supporters, DeVos's approach to choice is controversial. In an unexpected twist, the Massachusetts Charter Public School Association opposed her nomination because of concerns about the low quality of many charters under Michigan's lax accountability rules. In addition, one of the nation's leading proponents and funders of charter schools, billionaire Eli Broad, sent a strongly worded letter to Senate majority leader Mitch McConnell and Senate minority leader Chuck Schumer stressing his opposition to DeVos. "At the risk of stating the obvious," Broad wrote, "we must have a secretary of education who believes in public education and the need to keep public schools public."

Clearly, the issues surrounding school choice are more complex than the typical pro-charter/anti-charter battle lines might suggest. The central question for a public-education system in a democratic society is not whether school options should exist, but whether high-quality schools are available to all children. The fact that choice doesn't guarantee quality should be clear each time we flick through 500 cable-TV channels without finding a single good viewing option. In public education, this kind of choice is not an acceptable outcome.

The key question, therefore, is whether we can create a system in which all schools are worth choosing and all children are chosen by good schools. How might DeVos's agenda affect these goals?

The State of Educational Choice

Despite the association of choice with privately operated charter schools and voucher programs, the vast majority of schools of choice are operated by public-school districts. Since the 1960s, districts have sponsored alternatives like magnet schools, themed schools (e.g., schools dedicated to the arts, law, or health professions), language-immersion schools, and networks of innovative school models, such as the Internationals Network for Public Schools, the New Tech Network, and California's Linked Learning Academies. Many cities—including New York, San Francisco, and Cambridge, Massachusetts—have pioneered choice systems in which parents are able to choose among the different public schools in their neighborhoods.

The first modern voucher program, in which public funds are provided to students to offset tuition at private schools, was pioneered in Milwaukee in 1990. Since then, vouchers have been hotly contested in the courts and at the ballot box. Although there are now 25 voucher programs operating across 14 states and Washington, DC, the estimated 178,070 recipients represent far less than 1 percent of all school-age students. Most vouchers are for small amounts and do not cover a full tuition, so most recipients are students who were already attending private school.

The idea of "chartering" schools was initially proposed in 1988 by teachers' union leader Albert Shanker and embraced by progressive educators, who saw such schools as places where teachers could innovate. Minnesota passed the first charter law in 1991; by 2013, 42 states had enacted similar legislation. Federal incentives began during the George W. Bush administration, were increased in the Obama years, and were augmented by substantial investments from philanthropies like the Broad, Gates, and Walton foundations. There are now about 6,500 public charter schools serving 2.5 million students—or about 5 percent of the K–12 population.

Although their overall numbers are small, there are also some communities where initiatives to close district-run schools have left many or most students in charter schools. The most extreme case is New Orleans, where, as of this coming school year, all students will need to enroll in a charter or private school, as the last district-run schools will have been closed or transformed into charters. Ironically, given Shanker's early vision, a major goal for many charter supporters has been to dismantle teachers' unions. Louisiana fired all of New Orleans's 7,000 public-school teachers after Hurricane Katrina and replaced them with nonunionized charter-school teachers. By the time the courts declared the move illegal, it was too late to restore the teaching force.

Over time, the charter movement has grown from individual schools created by groups with innovative education ideas to chains operated by charter-management organizations, some of them for-profit companies. The number of for-profit education-management companies running charter schools increased from five to 99 between 1995 and 2012, and the number of schools they operate from six to 758.

These education companies exert substantial influence on US policy-making. As *Education Week* reported in 2013, K12 Inc., the publicly traded online-charter company in which DeVos had been an investor, deployed 39 lobbyists in 2012 "to work for state and local policies that would help expand the use of virtual learning." And between 2004 and 2012, the for-profit charter operator White Hat Management and its employees poured more than $2 million into the campaigns of Ohio politicians. At the time, *Education Week* reported, White Hat was "under fire for poor performance."

The Consequences of "Choice"

After 25 years of charter-school efforts, there are clearly some innovative charter schools that promote high-quality education. Some offer unique philosophies of teaching, including the Montessori and Waldorf methods, and some offer new school models, like High Tech High in San Diego, which is project-based and technology-oriented. Other charters look little different from traditional neighborhood public schools in their curricula and offerings.

Some successful charters serve high-need students without "creaming and cropping"—a now-common practice by which schools admit only the most promising students and push out those who struggle to learn. For many schools, however, selectivity has become one of the major ways they sustain positive outcomes. In a system of accountability in which schools are evaluated by test scores and threatened with closure if they don't continually improve them, the easiest way to appear successful is to keep out, or push out, low-performing students.

Both charters and district-run schools have engaged in these practices, but it's easier for charters that manage their own admissions and expulsion policies to do so. In some states, like Louisiana, charters are allowed to set admissions policies just like private schools. In others, like California, this practice is illegal, but a recent study found that one in five California charters violate state law by restricting access for high-need students. Most studies have found that charters underserve English learners and special-education students relative to the public schools in their districts. They are also more racially and economically segregated than public schools generally.

While the promise of choice sounds tantalizing, the reality has proved to be much more complex. It turns out that in many systems of choice, a relatively small number of good schools are available to a small number of children—usually the most advantaged. In New Orleans, for example, the Southern Poverty Law Center had to sue to ensure that charter schools would accept special-education students, which most refused to do. Even after the lawsuit was resolved, researchers at Stanford University found that special-education students and other vulnerable young people have little actual choice, as they are often assigned, against their will, to failing schools. The successful charters in New Orleans disproportionately serve white and financially secure students in a highly stratified system that confines most poor black students to schools rated "D" or "F" by the state.

A similar dynamic has played out in more than 20 other cities in recent years, as state and local governments have taken advantage of a combination of fiscal crises and federal incentives under the No Child Left Behind Act to close district-run schools and replace them with privately run charters. In Detroit, for instance, the last state-appointed emergency manager aimed to replace the entire school district with charters. And in Pennsylvania, then-Governor Tom Corbett cut Philadelphia's budget by hundreds of millions of dollars, throwing it into fiscal distress. Hundreds of educators were fired and a manager installed who carved up the school district and turned over large sections to private operators.

A new organization called Journey for Justice, comprising civil-rights and grassroots groups in 24 cities, has set out to halt this trend, demanding "community-driven alternatives to the privatization of and dismantling of public schools systems." The coalition notes that in every one of its districts, school closings disproportionately affect African-American and Latino students and communities. As a consequence, many have filed complaints under Title VI of the Civil Rights Act demanding that the Department of Education investigate the racial impact of public-school closings in these cities.

The Price of "Choice"

Despite the rush to trade district-run public schools for privately managed options, the research has found mixed results for both voucher programs and charter schools, with some charters doing better and others doing worse than public schools. For example, a large-scale study of student data from 16 states by Stanford's Center for Research on Education Outcomes found that only 17 percent of charters produced academic gains that were better than those at traditional public schools, while 37 percent performed worse than their public-school counterparts. Most showed no difference.

Outcomes vary across states, which have very different laws. In California, where charters have been regulated relatively carefully to ensure fair access, a thoughtful curriculum, and qualified staff, they generally perform comparably with other public schools, although those focused on home schooling or distance learning do worse. Students in charter high schools did worse in mathematics and better in English-language arts. However, in Ohio and Arizona, where unregulated market strategies have created a huge range of for-profit and nonprofit providers with few public safeguards, most charter schools have low ratings, and charter-school students perform at consistently lower levels than their demographically similar public-school counterparts.

Scandals abound, especially with online charters, which have consistently negative outcomes yet reap the highest profits, since operators don't have to buy buildings and often hire few teachers at low salaries. For example, over the course of nearly a decade, The Columbus Dispatch reported on the cyber-school ECOT (The Electronic Classroom of Tomorrow) in Ohio, which in one month received $932,030 in taxpayer money for 2,270 students, but could provide evidence that only seven had logged on.

In DeVos's home state of Michigan, critics say that unaccountable charter-school policies have produced a large number of failing schools in the poorest communities. Although one study by Stanford's Hoover Institution found better outcomes for Michigan charter students than similar students coming from their "feeder schools," the study did not compare charter outcomes to those of the two-thirds of Michigan's schools that students didn't leave—likely the stronger schools in the state.

The central question is not whether school options should exist, but whether high-quality schools are available to all children.

Some Michigan officials argue that the effects of the choice plan and simultaneous cuts in public-school budgets have been negative statewide. John Austin, the president of the State Board of Education, noted that the expansion of choice is "destroying learning outcomes." And indeed, the state's overall performance has sunk like a stone in the last decade. Until the early 2000s, Michigan reliably ranked above the national average and often in the top tier of states on the National Assessment of Educational Progress, especially in math. However, by 2015, it lagged behind most other states. Only seven states scored lower than Michigan in measurements of fourth-grade reading, and no state scored lower for black students in reading or math. While eighth graders did a bit better, they also scored below the national average, and African-American students underperformed their peers in nearly all other states in reading and math. Detroit's students scored below those in every other major US city.

An International Perspective

These outcomes are similar to those my colleagues and I found in our investigation of several countries that had adopted privatization initiatives without safeguards. In our 2016 book Global Education Reform, we tracked what happened in Chile, beginning under the dictator Augusto Pinochet in 1980, and later in Sweden, starting in 1992, when these countries adopted widespread voucher and charter-like policies, including pouring public funding into private for-profit schools while disinvesting from their public-school systems. Both are now trying to reverse course after their systems became more segregated and unequal, and dropped dramatically in achievement in comparison to their international counterparts.

Sweden, once the educational jewel of high-achieving Scandinavia, now performs well below most European and Asian countries on the Program for International Student Assessment. It stands in sharp contrast to Finland, once the least-educated Scandinavian country, which made substantial investments in a high-quality public system beginning in the 1970s and now consistently performs near the top of the international rankings.

Meanwhile, Chile performs even lower than Sweden, closer to the ranks of the developing nations, and it has only one-third as many high-performing students as Cuba, which leads the rankings in Central and South America. Like Finland, Cuba invested in its public schools with a highly prepared teaching force, an inquiry-oriented curriculum, and strong relationships with families.

It may be that, in countries like Sweden and Chile, a tipping point occurs when the number of private schools proliferates and for-profit providers sacrifice quality for greater profits, producing negative results. The same thing may be happening in some states in this country as they approach a tipping point in privatized choice. For example, three studies of voucher programs in Louisiana and Indiana found large negative effects on student achievement compared to similar students in public schools.

Clearly, there are some excellent private and charter schools. But there are also some that fail badly and exploit the most vulnerable students. A public-education system cannot leave choice to chance: It must ensure equitable access to high-quality schools for all children.

Can Choice and Democracy Coexist?

Are there ways the United States can get the benefits of choice without the downsides that have accompanied initiatives like Michigan's? At the heart of the challenge is creating a system of schools worth choosing, and in which all children are chosen by a good school.

The poor outcomes found in some states and nations stand in contrast with those of Massachusetts, our highest-performing state. Massachusetts has many district-run schools of choice, along with a small number of high-performing charter schools—just 81—that operate under a cap on the total number of charters. These schools are held to rigorous expectations not only for curriculum, staffing quality, and academic performance, but also for the admission and retention of high-needs students.

Massachusetts demonstrates some of the principles that might support a democratic system that incorporates productive choice. Rather than creating a competitive marketplace of successes and failures, such a system would increase educational quality and equity by encouraging innovation and allowing diversity among schools, including public schools run by districts. It would maintain a commitment to equity and access through regularly monitored open-admissions policies and would prohibit selective admissions or the pushing out of students. School funding would be based on student needs and pose no burdens to families in terms of tuition, fees, or transportation. Allowing for-profit entities to operate schools would be recognized as creating an inherent conflict of interest. In short, the system would need to operate like a public system.

At the end of the day, the public welfare is best served when investments in schools enable all young people to become responsible citizens prepared to participate effectively in the political, social, and economic life of their democracy. As John Dewey wrote in *The School and Society*, "What the best and wisest parent wants for his own child, that must the community want for all of its children. Any other ideal for our schools is narrow and unlovely; acted upon, it destroys our democracy.... Only by being true to the full growth of all the individuals who make it up, can society by any chance be true to itself."

Print Citations

CMS: Darling-Hammond, Linda. "Education for Sale? School Choice and the Future of American Education." In *The Reference Shelf: Education Reform*, edited by Betsy Maury, 54–60. Ipswich, MA: H.W. Wilson, 2017.

MLA: Darling-Hammond, Linda. "Education for Sale? School Choice and the Future of American Education." *The Reference Shelf: Education Reform*. Ed. Betsy Maury. Ipswich: H.W. Wilson, 2017. 54–60. Print.

APA: Darling-Hammond, L. (2017). Education for sale? School choice and the future of American education. In Betsy Maury (Ed.), *The reference shelf: Education reform* (pp. 54–60). Ipswich, MA: H.W. Wilson. (Original work published 2017)

Massachusetts Charter Cap Holds Back Disadvantaged Students

Sarah Cohodes and Susan M. Dynarski
The Brookings Institute Report, September 15, 2016

This November, Massachusetts voters will go to the polls to decide whether to expand the state's quota on charter schools. The ballot initiative would allow 12 new, approved charters over the current limit to open each year.

Would the ballot proposal be good for students in Massachusetts? To address this question, we need to know whether charter schools are doing a better job than the traditional public schools in districts where the cap currently limits additional charter school seats.

There is a deep well of rigorous, relevant research on the performance of charter schools in Massachusetts. This research exploits random assignment and student-level, longitudinal data to examine the effect of charter schools in Massachusetts.

This research shows that charter schools in the urban areas of Massachusetts have large, positive effects on educational outcomes. The effects are particularly large for disadvantaged students, English learners, special education students, and children who enter charters with low test scores.

In marked contrast, we find that the effects of charters in the suburbs and rural areas of Massachusetts are not positive. Our lottery estimates indicate that students at these charter schools do the same or worse than their peers at traditional public schools. Notably, the charter cap does not currently constrain charter expansion in these areas. The ballot initiative will therefore have no effect on the rate at which these charters expand.

Massachusetts' charter cap currently prevents expansion in precisely the urban areas where charter schools are doing their best work. Lifting the cap will allow more students to benefit from charter schools that are improving test scores, college preparation, and college attendance.

This November, Massachusetts voters will go to the polls to decide whether to expand the state's quota on charter schools. The "Lift the Cap" referendum has generated enormous controversy, with supporters and opponents canvassing neighborhoods, running ads, and blitzing social media.

As is true with many policy debates, the back-and-forth about the referendum has generated a lot of heat but not much light. There is a deep well of rigorous, relevant research on the performance of charter schools in Massachusetts. In fact,

From *The Brookings Institute Report* September 15 © 2016. See charts and data at https://www.brookings.edu/research/massachusetts-charter-cap-holds-back-disadvantaged-students/

it is hard to think of an education policy for which the evidence is more clear. As policies are debated, we often have to rely on research that is ill-suited to the task. Its methodology is frequently too weak to form a firm foundation for policy. Or, the population, design, and setting of the research study are so different from the policy in question that the findings cannot be easily extrapolated. This is not one of those times. We have exactly the research we need to judge whether charter schools should be permitted to expand in Massachusetts. This research exploits random assignment and student-level, longitudinal data to examine the effect of charter schools in Massachusetts.

To preview the results: Charter schools in the urban areas in Massachusetts have large, positive effects on educational outcomes, far better than those of the traditional public schools that charter students would otherwise attend. The effects are particularly large and positive for disadvantaged students, English learners, special education students, and children who enter charters with low test scores. By contrast, the effects outside the urban areas (where the current cap does not constrain charter expansion) are zero to negative.

This pattern of results accords with research at the national level, which finds positive impacts in urban areas and among disadvantaged students.[1]

Massachusetts' charter cap currently prevents expansion in precisely the urban areas where charter schools are doing their best work. Lifting the cap will allow more students to benefit from charter schools that are improving test scores, college preparation, and college attendance.

Massachusetts' Charter School Ballot Question

Before we turn to a detailed discussion of the research, let's summarize the ballot proposal and how it would alter the state's charter law.

Current law sets a cap on the number of charter schools statewide, as well as the share of each district's funds that can flow to charters. Massachusetts now has 78 charter schools.

Since 2010, a "smart cap" has given priority to applications from charter providers with a proven track record that seek to expand in low-performing districts.[2] Even with the additional expansion permitted under the current smart cap, the charter cap constrains expansion in many urban areas, including Boston, Springfield, Malden, and Lawrence. Tens of thousands of students are on waiting lists for charter schools in these districts.[3] The state's low-income, immigrant, Hispanic, and Black students are concentrated in these cities.

The ballot initiative would raise the cap, allowing 12 new, approved charters over the current limit to open each year.[4] New and expanding charters would have to go through the current application and review process, which is one of the most rigorous in the country.[5] An indicator of the robustness of the state's oversight: since 1997, 17 charter schools that the state deemed ineffective or mismanaged have closed.

The state's board of education would review any applications that seek to go above the current cap, as it does all charter applications. In contrast, in Ohio (where presidential candidate Donald Trump recently made a visit to a charter school), the state has 69 authorizers, including school districts, higher education institutions, and nonprofit organizations.[6] Each authorizer has its own standards for approval, renewal, and revocation.

Ohio's arrangement, in comparison to that in Massachusetts, makes it difficult for the state to set consistent, high standards for charter schools. We suspect that the robust system of accountability in Massachusetts underpins the strong performance of its charter sector.

Estimating Charter School Impacts

Would the ballot proposal, which allows the expansion of charter schools in low-performing districts, be good for students in Massachusetts? To address this question, we need to know whether charter schools are doing a better job than the traditional public schools in districts where the cap currently limits additional charter school seats.

In short, the answer is "Yes." In urban, low-income districts of Massachusetts, charter students are learning more than children in the traditional public schools.

We base this statement on rigorous, peer-reviewed research. Since 2007, when we were both researchers at Harvard, we have collaborated with researchers at Harvard and MIT, including professors Joshua Angrist, Thomas Kane, Parag Pathak, and Chris Walters (who is now at Berkeley). In cooperation with the state's department of education, which provided the student-level, longitudinal data necessary for this research, we have evaluated the effect of charter schools on student achievement, high school graduation, preparation for college, and college attendance.

The test-score gains produced by Boston's charters are some of the largest that have ever been documented for an at-scale educational intervention.

Measuring the effectiveness of any school is challenging. Parents choose their kids' schools, either by living in a certain school district or sending them to a private or charter school. As a result, some schools are filled with children of parents who are highly motivated and/or have extensive financial resources. This is selection bias, the key challenge in evaluating the effectiveness of schools.

Charters are required to run lotteries when they have more applicants than seats. And since many charter schools in Massachusetts have long waiting lists, there are many lotteries each year across the state.

The charter school lotteries are "natural experiments," each their own randomized trial. Randomization is the gold standard for social-science research, allowing an "apples-to-apples" comparison. At the time of application, there are no differences (on average) between those who win and lose the admissions lottery. Should we observe differences in student outcomes after the lottery, we can be confident this is due to charter school attendance.[7]

The Evidence on Massachusetts Charter Schools

So what have we learned from our research?

Charter schools in Boston (where charter enrollment has almost reached the cap) produce very large increases in students' academic performance.[8] Education researchers often express test score differences in standard deviations, which allow for comparison across different tests, populations, and contexts. According to the most recent estimates, one year in a Boston charter middle school increases math test scores by 25 percent of a standard deviation. The annual increases for language arts are about 15 percent of a standard deviation.[9] Test score gains are even larger in high school.

These differences for middle school and high school can be seen with the results disaggregated for subgroups of students. Values above zero indicate that charter school students score higher than their traditional public school counterparts. A shaded bar indicates a statistically significant positive effect.

How big are these effects? The test-score gains produced by Boston's charters are some of the largest that have ever been documented for an at-scale educational intervention. They are larger, for example, than the effect of Head Start on the cognitive outcomes of four-year-olds (about 20 percent of a standard deviation).[10] The effect of one year in a Boston charter is larger than the cumulative effect of the Tennessee STAR experiment, which placed children in small classes for four years (17 percent of a standard deviation).[11]

Another gauge of magnitude: the gap in test scores between Blacks and Whites nationwide (and in Boston) is roughly three-quarters of a standard deviation. One year in a Boston charter therefore erases roughly a third of the racial achievement gap.

One concern is that charter schools are just "teaching to the test." To stay open, charter schools need to demonstrate they are effective, and performance on the MCAS (Massachusetts Comprehensive Assessment System, the statewide test) is an important part of that assessment. If the charter schools are simply coaching students on the skills they need to succeed on the MCAS, they may have little impact on real, lasting learning.

But we found positive effects of Boston's charters beyond the MCAS test,[12] and no evidence that they "inflate" MCAS scores.[13] These effects comparing the percent of charter vs. noncharter students attaining particular outcomes.[14] For example, the lottery studies show Boston charters substantially increase SAT scores. This is not explained by differential selection into this optional test, since charter students are just as likely as their peers in traditional public schools to take the SAT.

Boston charters double the likelihood of taking an Advanced Placement (AP) exam. They substantially increase the AP exam pass rate, with ten percent of charter students passing the AP calculus test, compared with just one percent of students in Boston's other public schools.

Students at Boston's charters are just as likely as their peers at traditional public schools to graduate high school, though they are more likely (by 14 percentage points) to take five years rather than four years to do so. Boston charter students enter high school with scores far below the state mean, and even further below the typical scores in the wealthy suburbs where AP courses are the norm. It is therefore unsurprising that it takes some students five years in high school to successfully complete AP courses (which are required by some Boston charters).

Boston charter students are far more likely to attend a four-year college than their counterparts in traditional public schools. This is likely due, at least in part, to their better academic preparation, as just explained. The difference is large: 59 percent attend a four-year college as compared to 41 percent for their counterparts who did not attend charters.

Reminder: All of these results are based on comparisons of applicants who randomly won or lost admission to charter schools. The estimates are therefore not biased by demographic differences between students at charters and traditional public schools.

Some might be concerned that the charter students have unusually motivated parents, as demonstrated by their willingness to apply to charters. But by this metric, all of the children in our lottery studies have motivated parents. Yet the students who don't win admission to charters (and so are more likely to go to the traditional public schools) do far worse than those who win.

It's also important to note here that more than a third of students in Boston Public Schools apply to charters, so any "cream skimming" goes pretty deep. As charters have expanded in Boston, differences between applicants and non-applicants in the city have narrowed considerably, and are now quite small.[15]

Beyond Boston, charters in the other urban areas of Massachusetts also boost test scores.[16] Most of these schools are young compared to the Boston charters, and we have not yet evaluated their effects on long-term outcomes such as college attendance.

Across the board, we find that urban charters produce the biggest boosts for students who most need help. Score effects are largest for students who enter charters with the lowest scores. Urban charters are particularly effective for low-income and non-white students. The score gains for special education students and English learners are just as large as they are for students who are not in these specialized programs.[17]

In marked contrast, we find that the effects of charters in the suburbs and rural areas of Massachusetts are not positive. Our lottery estimates indicate that students at these charter schools do the same or worse than their peers at traditional public schools.

Many students in these non-urban districts have access to excellent schools, so it is not surprising that charters don't produce better outcomes than the traditional public schools. In fact, the excellent schools are a draw for families who have the financial resources to move to high-performing, wealthy districts like Newton, Wellesley, and Weston. Low-income families can't afford homes in these districts. Their choice is the local charter school.

Importantly, the charter cap does not constrain charters in the suburbs where they appear to have zero to negative effects. Current law allows charter schools to expand in these districts. The cap, if lifted, would expand choice in the urban areas where charters have been highly successful with disadvantaged students who most need access to better schools.

No one (including social scientists!) can predict the future. There is no guarantee that new charter schools will be as successful as existing charter schools. The research we have summarized here, and the state's track record in carefully vetting schools, strongly suggest that if allowed to grow the charter schools in the urban areas of Massachusetts will continue to improve learning, especially among disadvantaged children.

The Voters' Decision

The research we have summarized here is irrelevant to the decisions of some voters. Some oppose charter schools on principle, because they prefer the governance and structure of traditional public schools. That's their prerogative.

What we find distressing, and intellectually dishonest, is when these preferences are confounded with evidence about the effectiveness of charter schools. The evidence is that, for disadvantaged students in urban areas of Massachusetts, charter schools do better than traditional public schools.

Voters are free to decide that the proven benefits that Massachusetts charter schools provide for disadvantaged students are outweighed by a principled opposition to charters. It's our job as researchers to make clear the choice that voters are making.

Notes

1. See, for example, Gleason, Philip, Melissa Clark, Christina Clark Tuttle, Emily Dwoyer, and Marsha Silverberg. 2010. *The Evaluation of Charter School Impacts: Final Report. NCEE 2010-4029.* Washington, DC: U.S. Department of Education, National Center for Education Evaluation and Regional Assistance, Institute of Education Sciences.
2. Massachusetts General Laws, *An Act Relative to the Achievement Gap*, 2010.
3. Massachusetts Department of Elementary and Secondary Education. *Massachusetts Charter School Waitlist Updated Report for 2015-2016 (FY16).* See attached spreadsheet for location-specific waitlist numbers.
4. https://ballotpedia.org/Massachusetts_Authorization_of_Additional_Charter_Schools_and_Charter_School_Expansion,_Question_2_(2016).
5. National Association of Charter School Authorizers: Massachusetts.
6. National Association of Charter School Authorizers: Ohio.
7. The lottery analyses are conducted using two-stage least-squares (2SLS). Winning the lottery is used as an instrument for attending a charter school. Throughout, when we refer to "the effect of charter school attendance," we mean the 2SLS estimate of the effect of charter attendance, with winning the lottery used to instrument for attendance.
8.

9. Abdulkadiroglu, Atila, Joshua D. Angrist, Susan M. Dynarski, Thomas J. Kane, and Parag A. Pathak. 2011. "Accountability and Flexibility in Public Schools: Evidence from Boston's Charters and Pilots." *Quarterly Journal of Economics* 126(2): 669–748.
10. Cohodes, Sarah R., Elizabeth M. Setren, Christopher R. Walters, Joshua D. Angrist, and Parag A. Pathak. 2013. "Charter School Demand and Effectiveness: A Boston Update." The Boston Foundation.
11. Puma, Mike, Stephen Bell, Ronna Cook, Camilla Heid, Pam Broene, Frank Jenkins, Andrew Mashburn, and Jason Downer. 2012. *Third Grade Follow-up to the Head Start Impact Study Final Report, OPRE Report # 2012-45,* Washington, DC: Office of Planning, Research and Evaluation, Administration for Children and Families, U.S. Department of Health and Human Services.
12. Dynarski, Susan, Hyman, Joshua. and Schanzenbach, Diane. W. 2013. "Experimental Evidence on the Effect of Childhood Investments on Postsecondary Attainment and Degree Completion." *Journal of Policy Analysis and Management* 32: 692–717.
13. Angrist, Joshua D., Sarah R. Cohodes, Susan M. Dynarski, Parag A. Pathak, and Christopher R. Walters. 2016. "Stand and Deliver: Effects of Boston's Charter High Schools on College Preparation, Entry, and Choice." *Journal of Labor Economics* 34(2).
14. Cohodes, Sarah. 2016. "Teaching to the Student: Charter School Effectiveness in Spite of Perverse Incentives." *Education Finance and Policy* 11(1): 1-42.
15. In the graph, the percentages for charter students are the 2SLS estimates of effect of charter attendance added to relevant noncharter mean. The percentages for the noncharter students are the proportion who attain each outcome, for students in the sample who do not attend a charter school.
16. Cohodes, Sarah R., Elizabeth M. Setren, Christopher R. Walters, Joshua D. Angrist, and Parag A. Pathak. 2013. "Charter School Demand and Effectiveness: A Boston Update." The Boston Foundation.

    Setren, Elizabeth. 2015. "Special Education and English Language Learners in Boston Charter Schools: Impact and Classification." *School Effectiveness and Inequality Institute (SEII) Discussion Paper 2015.05.*
17. Angrist, Joshua D., Parag A. Pathak, and Christopher R. Walters. 2013. "Explaining Charter School Effectiveness." *American Economic Journal: Applied Economics* 5(4): 1–27.
18. Setren, Elizabeth. 2015."Special Education and English Language Learners in Boston Charter Schools: Impact and Classification." *School Effectiveness and Inequality Institute (SEII) Discussion Paper 2015.05.*

Print Citations

CMS: Cohodes, Sarah, and Susan M. Dynarski. "Massachusetts Charter Cap Holds Back Disadvantaged Students." In *The Reference Shelf: Education Reform*, edited by Betsy Maury, 61–68. Ipswich, MA: H.W. Wilson, 2017.

MLA: Cohodes, Sarah, and Susan M. Dynarski. "Massachusetts Charter Cap Holds Back Disadvantaged Students." *The Reference Shelf: Education Reform*. Ed. Betsy Maury. Ipswich: H.W. Wilson, 2017. 61–68. Print.

APA: Cohodes, S., & S. M. Dynarski. (2017). Massachusetts charter cap holds back disadvantaged students. In Betsy Maury (Ed.), *The reference shelf: Education reform* (pp. 61–68). Ipswich, MA: H.W. Wilson. (Original work published 2016)

An Education Leader with One Big Idea

By Dan Currell

The National Review, January 26, 2017

Betsy DeVos is the focused campaigner American schools need. Big institutions aren't easy to change, and American public education is big: Over 3 million teachers were employed in American public schools in 2016. Walmart, the world's largest employer, has 1.4 million U.S. employees; the American military has 1.3 million people on active duty. Since American public education needs to change, as everyone seems to agree, what would it take to turn around an institution that's bigger than Walmart and the U.S. military combined?

A technocrat who knows many things will never turn around a massive organization. Subtlety and complexity are quickly lost in a sea of 3 million people. The focused leader who knows one big thing at least stands a chance of turning around even the largest organization: One big message, driven home relentlessly, can get through.

Betsy DeVos's one big idea is school choice, and that big idea brings a secondary effect, which is institutional competition. While her big idea is not guaranteed to fix America's failing public schools, at least it has a chance—and that's more than can be said for everything else that has been tried. Indeed, DeVos would be worse off if she had the kind of extensive in-school experience that liberals so angrily attack her for lacking. If she had been a teacher, administrator, and political campaigner, she would be the fox that knows many things. Thankfully, she's not. Instead she has stuck with one big idea over a long philanthropic career: school choice. She's the hedgehog that knows one big thing. And this hedgehog is about to wander into a very complicated situation.

The United States has the best public schools in the world. The top public high schools send nearly all their graduates on to college, and many to the most selective colleges. Faculty and parents are dedicated to the educational task, and most students graduate with college credit already in hand. The quality of these schools supports high housing prices within the district, generating property-tax revenues to fund the schools. Even a whiff of weak school performance will draw the ire not only of parents but of every homeowner with something to lose. It's a positive feedback loop. We also have the worst public schools in the developed world. In 1,200 American high schools, a third or more of the students don't graduate. In 2013, 66 percent of U.S. fourth graders and 64 percent of eighth graders could not read at their grade level, according to the National Assessment of Education Progress (NAEP) reading test. In 2013 the United States spent more per student than all Organisation for Economic Co-operation and Development OECD countries except Austria, Luxembourg, Norway, and Switzerland—yet our educational outcomes have hovered around 20th place among OECD's 34 (now 35) nations. Our worst high schools are essentially prisons with poor security and lots of overhead.

Parents see all of this, and most would rather not be trapped in a bad system. According to a 2013 Luntz Global Public Opinion Survey, 64 percent of American parents said they would send their children to a different school if they could. What that means in practice is that most American parents want—and lack—the option to enroll their child in a better charter, magnet, or private school than the public school they now attend. Into this complex picture walks Betsy DeVos, a relentless school-choice advocate. The daughter of a public-school teacher, she has never taught professionally and never attended public schools. Her philanthropic career has never strayed from the issue of school choice. She has campaigned in her home state and across the country to give lower-income families the chance to choose the right schools for their children. Can her big idea fix American public education?

Consumer choice has been a basic tenet of American law since at least 1890. At that time, the field of economics was still evolving, but competition was one of its tenets as well, and it would turn out to be its most enduring. Competitive markets were known to improve products, prevent corruption, encourage adequate supply, and keep prices moderate. And competition happens only when consumers have a meaningful choice between different products or services. This point was enshrined in the Sherman Anti-Trust Act of 1890, a statute that remains a cornerstone of American commercial law. Theodore Roosevelt and his successor as president, William Howard Taft, were the original trust-busters, doggedly prosecuting over 100 companies under the Sherman Act in what seemed at the time an uphill battle against large, entrenched interests. Today such high-profile prosecutions are less frequent and arguably less necessary because our society is so committed to the basic principle of consumer choice.

She has campaigned in her home state and across the country to give lower-income families the chance to choose the right schools for their children.

But consumer choice suddenly becomes controversial—and somehow emotional—when it comes to public schools. The local monopoly of the public school went unquestioned until Milton Friedman suggested a free-market voucher system in 1962. His idea didn't take root right away, but in 1991 some left-leaning reformers in Minnesota passed a charter-school law, creating for the first time the possibility of school choice. Now 43 states and the District of Columbia have passed charter-school laws and 17 states have some form of voucher system.

Still, change is hard. Powerful institutional forces keep millions of American students in poorly performing public schools with no meaningful alternatives. As Betsy DeVos said in her confirmation hearing, "The human tendency is to guard what is because change is difficult." She appears to know, after a few decades dedicated to this issue, that most failing schools won't improve on their own, because teachers, administrators and even parents fear change. To change, the worst schools need exposure to a force more powerful than their own incentives and inertia.

DeVos knows that competition is a force powerful enough to change a sector as big and change-resistant as American education. Perhaps nothing else is. The best evidence that competition might actually be powerful enough to work is the unearthly shrieking now emanating from those who fear change the most: teachers' unions. Their shrieking is probably justified. Competition always brings on change, and change within large institutions hurts like hell. Michigan, DeVos's home state, is familiar with that kind of pain. By the 1980s it was clear that Detroit's signal industry was ceding ground to foreign competition—Toyota in particular. It would have been sensible for a company like General Motors to seek out Toyota's recipe for success and start to replicate it. W. Edwards Deming, an American well known in Detroit, was the inspiration for Toyota's quality revolution. In fact, Toyota shared Deming's playbook with General Motors through a joint venture begun in California in 1984.

Deming's approach was initially rejected by GM, Ford, and Chrysler because it involved massive change, and change hurts. But competition is powerful enough to change even the biggest institutions, given enough time to do its work. Toyota didn't just give us great Toyotas; it eventually gave us better Fords.

American education in 2017 looks a lot like American cars did in 1987. Average quality is low by international standards. The largest school districts (e.g., Chicago) fear competition the most because, like the Big Three, they know how much pain it will bring. For unions and management alike, the great enemy is not one another; it's the spectre of competition.

Which is why school choice is the only remaining hope for parents and children caught in America's failing schools. The Bush administration's effort to achieve higher public-school performance through the No Child Left Behind Act was finally abandoned in late 2015 after broadly failing to achieve its goals. As reported this week, the Obama administration's effort to improve America's worst high schools with $7 billion in federal cash has been judged by the Department of Education itself to have had no effect. School choice has the power to be different. It may be that some of the worst schools can't be fixed. For some children, school choice will mean a chance to attend a private or charter school that performs better—or is just a better fit for their needs. For others, the competition brought on by school choice will mean that their local public school will begin to make some painful changes, the way GM, Ford, and Chrysler all eventually did. Either path is far better than the status quo. Mrs. DeVos's confirmation hearing saw Democratic senators concede that charter schools could be acceptable as long as they had no effect on public schools. (Senator Murray asked DeVos to commit that she would "not

Competition is powerful enough to change even the biggest institutions.

cut a penny" from public schools.) But having an effect on public schools is half the point of school choice. We don't just want to be able to buy Toyotas. We want the fact that we could buy a Toyota to make our Chevrolets better.

Betsy DeVos will continue to be characterized by her critics as an opponent of public schools. She is no more against American public schools than W. Edwards Deming was against American cars or Theodore Roosevelt was against American railroads. In all three cases, the success of the whole sector required a hedgehog with one big idea: competition. For American schools, Betsy DeVos is that hedgehog, and in 2017 her time has come.

Print Citations

CMS: Currell, Dan. "An Education Leader with One Big Idea." In *The Reference Shelf: Education Reform*, edited by Betsy Maury, 69–72. Ipswich, MA: H.W. Wilson, 2017.

MLA: Currell, Dan. "An Education Leader with One Big Idea." *The Reference Shelf: Education Reform*. Ed. Betsy Maury. Ipswich: H.W. Wilson, 2017. 69–72. Print.

APA: Currell, D. (2017). An education leader with one big idea. In Betsy Maury (Ed.), *The reference shelf: Education reform* (pp. 69–72). Ipswich, MA: H.W. Wilson. (Original work published 2017)

3
In the Classroom—Skills, Knowledge, Climate

Credit: Victor J. Blue/Bloomberg via Getty Images

Employees assist kids with building a video game using code on an Apple Inc. iPad Mini during the Hour of Code workshop at an Apple store in New York, U.S., on Thursday, Dec. 10, 2015. Hour of Code, a free one-hour introduction to the basics of computer programming, is a special event for kids ages six and up hosted by Apple Inc. in conjunction with Computer Science Education Week.

The Modernization of Education

In each generation, some industries dwindle while others grow and expand and the education system must evolve to prepare students for the career environment of the present *and* future. In 2017, vocational and personalized educational options are among the most popular education trends, and both are aimed at expanding educational options for students who have difficulty in traditional educational environments. While digital classroom tools and alternative, career-based training show promise for reaching underserved students, each new development reveals new difficulties as well.

Schooling for Work

Vocational schools and programs provide an alternative to traditional education, by providing students with direct training in career skills. Vocational schools have been around for more than a century, but did not receive federal or state support until the 1917 Smith-Hughes Act, when the growth of manufacturing stimulated programs aimed at attracting laborers for factory jobs. At the time, the philosophy behind vocational education was essentially what would today be called "tracking," which is the process of separating students according to their perceived academic ability. Some students would therefore be filtered into academic programs, while others were sent to vocational programs where they would learn job skills in place of traditional subjects. While many nations openly track students from an early age, the practice has fallen out of favor due to studies showing how tracking deepens inequality between social classes. Social scientists found that educators were more likely to separate students according to race and class prejudice than by legitimate academic potential and this meant that tracking essentially deepened existing class and racial inequality.[1]

Vocational programs were traditionally seen as an inferior educational option and studies in the 1990s and 2000s revealed that students at vocational high schools and colleges fell behind the general population in terms of reading and mathematics. In the 2000s, a new wave of legislation threatened vocational programs by requiring that all educational programs receiving tax funding must meet minimum requirements in teaching basic subjects like math, science, and literacy. In addition, educators had been finding that rapid changes in the job marketplace meant that students with vocational education, who did not receive sufficient basic educational training, were at a disadvantage when market changes increased competition in the marketplace. This led to a reform movement within the vocational education industry as educators struggled to enhance the value of vocational programs. Since the 2010s, the reputation of vocational education has begun to change and more vocational programs and schools now offer higher-quality training in basic subjects, in addition to direct career training, thus meaning that graduates are not only prepared for jobs in specific fields, but also have the potential to pursue higher education or change career paths after graduation.[2] Another way that vocational programs have become more relevant in the modern education market is by offering classes aimed at careers in emerging, digital technology markets. Electrical and computer repair courses, in addition to a new trend in offering coding, programming, and digital design courses as vocational options, are helping to make vocational education a competing alternative to standard academia that broadens, rather than limits, the career and educational options available to students.

Everything Goes Digital

Another innovative movement within education seeks to make computer science part of the basic educational curriculum, beginning with early childhood education. Many secondary schools already offer classes in computer literacy, which amounts to basic training in using computers and understanding technological terminology. By contrast, computer science can be considered a branch of math and science education and focuses on introducing students to computer engineering, programming, and design.[3]

The movement to embrace computer science as a core subject is partially based on the economics of the current job market. There are more than 1.5 million computer-related jobs in the United States and computer-related career fields are among the fastest growing in the world. This means that computer technology is, and is likely to remain, an essential tool for job seekers. Experts note that computer science instruction also teaches critical thinking and problem solving, which are essential intellectual skills that can greatly improve student performance on tests in all subjects. In addition, integrating computer science lessons into standard math and science curricula helps to make education more relevant for students who can connect the skills they learn to real-world applications and job skills.[4] Though the computer science education movement has only begun, an increasing number of primary and secondary schools are adding computer science classes to their curricula and a number of tech companies are investing in basic computer education programs out of the belief that this effort will create a stronger field of applicants for the next generation of tech jobs.

Achievement Versus Enrichment

The goal of public education is to provide essential knowledge to the greatest number of students possible, but this is a difficult feat as centuries of experience have demonstrated that each student is unique and not all students learn in the same way. Lecture-style teaching is still the norm in many fields and is considered most appropriate when the subject involves the memorization of facts. The 1920s saw a philosophical revolution in the classroom based on the writings and research of educational philosopher John Dewey. Dewey initiated a new era in American education known as "progressivism," in which teachers embraced the idea that the purpose of education, and the basic structure of education, should be built around encouraging students to solve problems.[5]

Out of progressivism, teachers and researchers began developing more collaborative, interactive teaching methods. This shift, towards a more participatory learning system, helped a larger number of students to succeed by making learning more integrative and engrossing and by shifting emphasis from rote memorization to critical thinking and problem solving.

Beginning in the early 2000s, education reforms began to adopt an intense focus on holding schools accountable for what many saw as a failure to improve educational quality. To do this, legislation forced schools to adopt an intense focus on teaching "core" subjects, like reading and math, and subjects students to years of standardized testing in an effort to measure student ability and judge the quality of schools. Unfortunately, this intense focus on testing has created a situation in which more and more schools focus on training students to pass standardized tests and deemphasize subjects and programs that contribute to a more well-rounded education. Additionally, the core curriculum and standardized testing system has not been effective. In 2015, a study from the National Assessment of Educational Progress (NAEP) the focus on standardized testing and on teaching essential core subjects had not led to any overall improvement in literacy or mathematics.[6]

The very idea of using a single, quantifiable system to judge students is flawed, as generations of research and observation have demonstrated that all students are unique and that no single measure is effective at accurately measuring a student's intelligence or ability. This was, after all, one of the observations that led to the progressivist movement in education. There are many other ways of assessing students that have been proposed, including performance or portfolio-based assessments, collecting data from game-based software that can automatically measure skills in key areas, and using tests similar to the current standardized tests, but through sampling rather than mass testing, a system that would mean less testing for each child and a reduced focus on preparing for tests overall.[7]

Another emerging trend in education, known as personalized or adaptive learning, seeks to return to the tenets of progressivism by individualizing education to the interests of individual students or certain groups. There are many ways to individualize education, such as designing programs that integrate core curriculum subjects with real-world situations and project-based learning so as to create more interesting, relevant programs that better appeal to certain types of students. In Deer Isle-Stonington Maine, a small community centered around the lobster fishing industry, the local high school increased its graduation rate from 58 to 91 percent between 2009 and 2014, by blending subjects like mathematics and composition with activities like boat building and studying the global fishing industry.[8]

In other cases, technology may be the key to opening up the potential of personalized education for more students. One example, the Reading Plus program, allows students to log onto a Web-based reading system that assesses the student's relative ability and provides lessons tailored to that student. Adaptive software like Reading Plus can provide teachers with multiple advantages by automatically measuring student progress while engaging students in the learning process, helping students to gain familiarity and skill operating digital tools, and providing lessons tailored for each student, rather than forcing students with different levels of skill to struggle through the same lessons. A related trend, known as gamification, integrates lessons into video games that allow students to learn while they play.[9]

Trends like adaptive learning software and educational games may become ubiquitous educational tools in the future, and such programs can provide personalized lessons in ways that individual teachers cannot. Some teachers have begun to wonder how this technological revolution may redefine the role of the teacher and whether the teachers of the future will focus more on classroom management and less on providing lessons.[10] Writing in the *Atlantic*, teacher Michael Godsey described his role, as a kindergarten teacher, as shifting from "content expert" to "curriculum facilitator." Godsey imagines that in the future, classes might be taught by virtual teachers, using digital footage of current events, relevant excerpts of expert lectures, and interactive games to deliver lessons while teachers like Godsey function more as managers, guiding students through the automated programs and making sure that the class stays on track.[11]

Though some worry that technology could eventually make classroom teachers obsolete, the failure of online education demonstrates that many, if not most students, from primary school to higher education, still learn more effectively with the personal guidance of a skilled teacher. In the future, a hybrid of digital classroom tools and virtual connectivity may become the norm in education, but teachers have always done more than simply deliver information. Teachers observe students in ways that automated programs cannot, not only measuring progress, but protecting, nurturing, and guiding students in their work. Much of this guidance is not, and never has been, a matter of expertise in a certain subject, but rather is about connecting and helping people to meet challenging goals. This aspect of the teacher's role will be far more difficult to replicate with technology and is arguably among the most important functions in any society.

Micah L. Issitt

Works Used

Barnwell, Paul. "Are Teachers Becoming Obsolete?" *The Atlantic*. The Atlantic Monthly Group. Feb 15 2017. Web. 28 Apr 2017.

Godsey, Michael. "The Deconstruction of the K-12 Teacher." *The Atlantic*. The Atlantic Monthly Group. Mar 25 2015. Web. 28 Apr 2017.

Hanford, Emily. "The Troubled History of Vocational Education." *American Radio Works*. American Public Media. Sep 9 2014. Web. 28 Apr 2016.

Kamenetz, Anya. The Test: Why Our Schools Are Obsessed with Standardized Testing—But You Don't Have to Be. New York: PublicAffairs, 2015.

Kohli, Sonali. "Modern-Day Segregation in Public Schools." *The Atlantic*. The Atlantic Monthly Group. Nov 18, 2014. Web. 28 Apr 2017.

Miller, Alison Derbenwick. "Why We Must Have Computer Science in More Schools and Classrooms." *Forbes*. Forbes Inc. Nov 14 2014. Web. 28 Apr 2017.

"Moving Beyond Computer Literacy: Why Schools Should Teach Computer Science." *NCWIT*. National Center for Women & Information Technology. 2016. Web. 28 Apr 2017.

Oakes, Jeannie. *Keeping Track: How Schools Structure Inequality*. New Haven, CT: Yale University Press, 2005.

Paperny, Tanya. "How Lobsters Are Keeping Students in School." *The Atlantic*. The Atlantic Monthly Group. Oct 11 2016. Web. 28 Apr 2017.

Radu, Lucian. "John Dewey and Progressivism in American Education." *Bulletin of the Transilvania University of Brasov*. Vol. 4, No. 53 (2011), 85–90.

Savitz, Eric. "5 School Technologies to Watch: Pesonalized Learning Is Here." *Forbes*. Forbes Inc. Oct 22 2012. Web. 28 Apr 2017.

Singer, Alan. "Results Are In: Common Core Fails Tests and Kids." *Huffington Post*. Huffington Post. May 2 2016. Web. 28 Apr 2017.

Notes

1. Kohli, "Modern-Day Segregation in Public Schools."
2. Hanford, "The Troubled History of Vocational Education."
3. "Moving Beyond Computer Literacy: Why Schools Should Teach Computer Science," *NCWIT*.
4. Miller, "Why We Must Have Computer Science in More Schools and Classrooms."
5. Radu, "John Dewey and Progressivism in American Education."
6. Singer, "Results Are In: Common Core Fails Tests and Kids."
7. Kamentz, *The Test: Why Are Schools Are Obsessed with Standardized Testing—But You Don't Have to Be*.
8. Paperny, "How Lobsters Are Keeping Students in School."
9. Savitz, "5 School Technologies to Watch: Personalized Learning Is Here."
10. Barnwell, "Are Teachers Becoming Obsolete?"
11. Godsey, "The Deconstruction of the K-12 Teacher."

What We're Missing in Measuring Who's Ready for College

By Mikhail Zinshteyn
Fivethirtyeight.com, March 23, 2015

Who's ready for college? At first blush, not a lot of us. By most measures, far less than half of those taking college entrance exams could tread water at our nation's colleges and universities.

That's not too surprising. College enrollment rates are higher than completion rates, suggesting that while the draw of a post-secondary degree is strong and growing, something goes awry once a student kicks off her college career.

At the same time, the pressure is on to send even more students to college, with President Obama challenging the nation to reclaim the title of being the country with the highest percentage of adults who have a post-secondary degree by 2020. The Lumina Foundation, an influential nonprofit that supports efforts to increase the number of college graduates in the U.S., is committed to raising the portion of the U.S. workforce that has a post-secondary degree to 60 percent by 2025. Today that figure hovers at 42 percent for those age 25 and over, according to U.S. Census data released this year.

A more educated workforce would be a great boon to the economy: Scholars say more employees would earn higher wages, which leads to more taxes being collected and fewer Americans grappling with the challenges of poverty, among other benefits.

Before we can implement policies designed to shepherd more of this country's residents toward a college degree, we must actually know what makes a student college-ready. But what if our definitions of college readiness are incomplete, or worse, painting an unreasonably dour picture of how prepared U.S. students are for the rigors of college?

"Everyone has their own definition of college readiness, which makes it a little tricky," said Jack Buckley, the head of research at the College Board, who previously led the Department of Education's research arm.

So tricky, in fact, that there's sharp disagreement over whether test scores or high school grades are better predictors of college readiness.

Resolving that disagreement may help underprepared students avoid financial distress: Enticing high schoolers and adults to enroll in college without gauging their ability to complete a degree can saddle them with debt they'll struggle to repay if they don't graduate. Identifying the factors that make someone ready for college can also steer nontraditional students—those who otherwise wouldn't attend college or would enroll in a weak institution—toward a degree.

That U.S. colleges could do a better job of finding talent is hardly a secret. Shaun Harper, a researcher at the University of Pennsylvania, found that in numerous instances, college recruiters tend to concentrate on high schools with an established track record of talented students, overlooking schools with predominantly black and Latino students, regardless of whether those students are ready for the rigors of college.

A 2013 report issued by the Center on Education and the Workforce at Georgetown University found that white students tend to enroll at the nation's leading colleges while black and Latino students largely attend schools with lower admissions standards. Though the number of black and Latino freshmen enrolling at colleges greatly increased (by 73 and 107 percent, respectively) between 1995 and 2009, the majority of those students have entered open-enrollment institutions—schools that are considered academically weaker than flagship public universities and elite private colleges. A small slice—about a tenth—enrolled at one of the 468 most-selective colleges in the U.S.; of the freshmen representing the increased enrollment by white students in the same period, 82 percent wound up at one of those elite schools.

In many cases, black and Latino students who have the potential to enroll at better schools aren't doing so. Black and Latino students with an A average in high school matriculated at a community college 30 percent of time, while the same was true for 22 percent of white students with A averages, the report's authors found. They note that "each year, there are 111,000 high-scoring African-American and Hispanic students who either do not attend college or don't graduate."

Think about that: Since 1995, the U.S. has missed out on about 2 million black and Latino students completing a post-secondary degree.

The College Board argues that college readiness can be measured by how well a student scores on the SAT, one of the many standardized tests it produces. A student who earns a 1550 on the SAT out of a possible 2400, the College Board says, has a 65 percent chance of achieving a B- average in her first year of college. Students who clear this threshold graduate from college after six years 69 percent of time, while those who score below 1550 graduate in six years just 45 percent of the time, according to the College Board. In 2014, more than half of SAT test-takers earned scores lower than 1550, a sign to the College Board that they're unlikely to be college-ready. By this metric, only 16 percent of black students and 23 percent Hispanic students were considered ready for college.

The other major player in college entrance exams is the ACT, which is the name of both the organization and its flagship test. ACT maintains that students who meet its college-readiness benchmarks have a 50 percent chance of earning a B average in select courses during their first year of college. So a student scoring a 22 out of a possible 36 on the math section has a 50 percent chance of earning a B in college-level algebra. Close to 40 percent of ACT test-takers in 2014 hit the college-ready benchmarks in three or all four of the tested subjects. One-third of test-takers didn't meet the benchmarks in any subject.

There's also something called the "hidden curriculum": those non-academic skills, like scheduling meetings with academic advisers and forging relationships with tutors, that are less familiar to low-income and first-generation college students.

The makers of the nation's gold standard for measuring how much K-12 students know, the National Assessment of Educational Progress (NAEP), seem to find value in the college entrance exams. In a bid to transform its 12th-grade assessments into a national benchmark for college readiness, the governing board overseeing the NAEP linked its scores to the SAT to create its own college-readiness indicator. The latest version shows that nearly 4 in 10 seniors have the math and reading skills needed to perform reasonably well in college—quite similar to the college readiness findings from the ACT and the College Board.

Not so fast, says William Hiss, a former admissions dean at Bates College in Maine, who argues that college entrance exams do not accurately foretell student performance in post-secondary settings. He and a co-author made the case in a 2014 paper that high school GPAs are much better at predicting a student's college grades and likelihood of graduating.

"What we have found is that in a significant number of cases, the students who have perfectly sound high school records, but much less impressive SAT scores, do fine in college," Hiss said in a phone interview.

In the study, Hiss and his co-author broke down the high school transcripts and college performances of 123,000 students in 33 colleges and universities of various sizes and statures that did not require test scores as part of the admissions process. The authors compared students who did submit ACT or SAT scores to those who did not, granting the institutions anonymity in exchange for access to student admissions data.

Overall, students who didn't submit their ACT or SAT scores posted high school GPAs that were similar to students who did. The report also found that among the accepted students, those with strong GPAs in high school performed reasonably well in college, while students with relatively strong ACT or SAT scores but lower high school GPAs finished with slightly lower college GPAs and graduated less frequently. To Buckley, tests like the SAT complement GPAs and provide a standard by which to judge the millions of students who submit report cards from tens of thousands of high schools, each with its own definition of what makes an A or a B.

For Hiss, "the SAT and ACT are acting as what any statistician would call a false negative," identifying students as lacking the qualities to perform well in college when in fact they can graduate with solid GPAs.

The debate over how much to value test scores versus GPAs gives way to a larger question of what high school transcripts and SAT results are telling us about students. In many ways, these numbers serve as proxies for other qualities that contribute to college-readiness but are much harder to measure.

An increasing number of scholars have begun looking at the nonacademic factors that enable students to work their way through the challenges of college and careers. David Conley at the University of Oregon created the Four Keys to College and Career Readiness, which include not only testing acumen but also thinking and reasoning skills, familiarity with the college-attendance process, the ability to self-motivate and assess one's progress, and other attributes.

But what if our definitions of college readiness are incomplete, or worse, painting an unreasonably dour picture of how prepared U.S. students are for the rigors of college?

Other researchers have set their sights on "noncognitive" attributes like grit, motivation and perseverance. Decades of research in psychology suggests that there's power in helping students develop growth mind-sets—in other words, if educators change the way disadvantaged students think about their own abilities, the students might perform better academically.

There's also something called the "hidden curriculum": those non-academic skills, like scheduling meetings with academic advisers and forging relationships with tutors, that are less familiar to low-income and first-generation college students. Missing out on the hidden curriculum can be the difference between completing one's studies and dropping out entirely.

Even Buckley acknowledged, "There are other things that you need to know to be prepared for college. You've got to have actual knowledge of the college process itself; you need to have the study skills and other noncognitive skills that are necessary."

"It's not enough to look at anyone's test scores," he added.

Maybe a longitudinal data system that tracked every student's K-12 and college performance—something the Obama administration has encouraged states to develop—would lend more clarity to how we measure college readiness. With that data in hand, would we need college entrance exams like the ACT or SAT?

"Even that data system is not going to have all the key elements of readiness," Buckley said. "I need assessments of their noncognitive skills; I need to know about their maturity. To really have a very strong estimate, broadly defined, you just need data that we don't have, or don't have on everyone."

Print Citations

CMS: Zinshteyn, Mikhail. "What We're Missing in Measuring Who's Ready for College." In *The Reference Shelf: Education Reform*, edited by Betsy Maury, 81–85. Ipswich, MA: H.W. Wilson, 2017.

MLA: Zinshteyn, Mikhail. "What We're Missing in Measuring Who's Ready for College." *The Reference Shelf: Education Reform*. Ed. Betsy Maury. Ipswich: H.W. Wilson, 2017. 81–85. Print.

APA: Zinshteyn, M. (2016). What we're missing in measuring who's ready for college. In Betsy Maury (Ed.), *The reference shelf: Education reform* (pp. 81–85). Ipswich, MA: H.W. Wilson. (Original work published 2015)

It's Time for Vocational Schools to Get Some Respect

By Deborah Halber
The Boston Globe, September 28, 2016

On a Monday morning in late spring, city buses arrive like clockwork on Malcolm X Boulevard, disgorging students hunched over cellphones, earbud wires trailing down the fronts of hoodies. They file toward Madison Park Technical Vocational High School, where executive director Kevin McCaskill, in a suit and pin-striped shirt with matching pocket square, and two other administrators greet them as if part of a receiving line. "Good morning! Good morning! Good morning!" McCaskill booms at bleary-eyed kids moving as if they are battling a stiff wind.

Among those passing through the metal doors is Reno Guerrero, who emigrated several years ago with his mother, older sister, and younger brother from the Dominican Republic to Dorchester. Guerrero, 19, wears a white T-shirt, jeans, and white socks with soccer sandals. His hair is close-cropped, and a shadow of a beard is shaved to precision points at his temples. Clear stone studs sparkle in each earlobe. He is feeling nervous about his senior presentation on engine repair, the culmination of three years of course work plus intensive training in automotive technology. But the nerves are tempered by excitement. He's learned he's been accepted to MassBay Community College, and he already has a job lined up for after graduation at a garage that services Boston's city-owned vehicles. "Cars, for me, is everything right now," he says. "It's what I know how to do, and I'm going to do it for life."

Guerrero is a success story, but his school, one of the most beleaguered in the state, fits a different stereotype: the vocational school as a place where "you stuck people who had nothing going for them," says Katherine S. Newman, a social scientist at UMass Amherst. In 2014, Madison Park had a four-year graduation rate of 63 percent (the statewide average is 86), and on the 2015 math Massachusetts Comprehensive Assessment System MCAS, only 24 percent of its students scored at least proficient (the statewide average is 79). Almost 60 percent of its students are economically disadvantaged, nearly triple the statewide rate, and it has almost double the rate of students with disabilities of the Boston Public Schools overall.

Madison Park's widely known designation as one of the state's underperforming schools has obscured what's happening across the rest of the Commonwealth: rising interest in vocational schooling. Students want into vocational schools for the job opportunities. The Commonwealth's 55 vocational schools claim some 48,000 students, but more than 3,000 others are wait listed at schools without seats to accommodate them. Massachusetts vocational schools are stretched thin at a time when local employers anticipate the majority of jobs they'll create in the next few years will be well suited to vocational school grads. Business owners and others fear not enough is being done to address the problem.

"We're turning away work because we don't have the people to do it," says Michael Tamasi, CEO of Avon-based AccuRounds Inc. His company, which makes precision-machined parts for industries, including medicine and aerospace, recruits heavily from the voc-ed schools in southeastern Massachusetts and Greater New Bedford.

"Employers are clamoring for training," says Barry Bluestone, a professor of public policy at Northeastern University, who has co-authored two recent studies on vocational education in Massachusetts. The October 2015 report, "Meeting the Commonwealth's Workforce Needs," analyzed 675 occupations, from journalist to bank teller, and found state employers anticipate having 1.2 million relevant job openings between 2012 and 2022. In the January 2016 report, "The Critical Importance of Vocational Education in the Commonwealth," 90 percent of employers surveyed wanted a larger pool of vocational-school graduates and nearly the same percentage agreed the schools themselves should have more modern equipment. Of respondents, 75 percent said they prefer to hire voc-ed graduates for entry-level positions and 61 percent for higher-level jobs.

Massachusetts employers depend on their graduates and say more must be done to address long wait lists and out-of-date facilities.

Despite that interest, vocational schools have a long history of disfavor to overcome. Bluestone says public opinion about them started to trend negative after the 1963 federal Vocational Education Act required the schools to educate all comers, including prisoners and adults who needed retraining. With US manufacturing becoming a smaller part of the economy and automation replacing workers, a perception emerged that these were schools of last resort.

Unlike many industrialized countries, the United States "pushed the blue-collar training agenda into an educational corner and virtually assured that anyone who ventured there would be tarred by stigma," UMass's Newman and coauthor Hella Winston argue in their new book, *Reskilling America: Learning to Labor in the Twenty-First Century*.

This national notion that vocational education tracked students toward dead-end, non-white-collar professions also took root in Massachusetts. Former lieutenant governor Tim Murray, an ardent advocate of vocational ed who is now president and CEO of the Worcester Regional Chamber of Commerce, says that while the 1993 Massachusetts Education Reform Act pumped more than $80 billion into schools to enhance academic standards, accountability, and school choice, it eliminated the position of associate commissioner of vocational technical education. After that, voc-tech programs "were treated as second-class citizens, because [state education overseers] were just so focused on MCAS," Murray says about the standardized test that has been a high school graduation requirement since 1993.

In fact, many of the state's vocational schools, or "vokes," as they're called, now see higher MCAS pass rates than the state's comprehensive schools, have average dropout rates of below 1 percent, and send 57 percent of their students to postsecondary schools. Vokes offer the same core academic courses as comprehensive schools and many even offer Advanced Placement courses, along with vocational training.

Brendan O'Rourke, a lanky 18-year-old from Arlington with a shock of dark hair, shows me around Minuteman Regional Vocational Technical High School in Lexington one day last spring. "My parents thought voke schools were for knuckleheads," he confides as we walk through the underground "trade floor" where students in football field-size rooms bend over car engines, measure and cut PVC pipe, blast sheet metal with blowtorches, and fashion electrical circuits on pegboard walls.

O'Rourke explains that his middle school wood-shop teacher saw him struggling in English and math and suggested Minuteman as an alternative to Arlington High School. O'Rourke and his parents drove the 3 miles to the school, nestled on 66 wooded acres in Lexington just off Interstate 95, and after touring it, decided he should apply. He was admitted on the strength of his grades, attendance record, discipline history, recommendations, and an interview.

In the office of Minuteman's superintendent-director, Edward A. Bouquillon, a rendering of a sleek new $144.9 million school building sits on an easel. In September, after an eight-year battle, voters in the towns that make up the Minuteman regional school district green-lighted the building. The school is refashioning itself into a "career academy" where students follow individualized educational tracks with access to state-of-the-art equipment relevant to potential careers in the state's booming biotech and engineering industries. It will also continue to offer more traditional vocational pursuits like plumbing and cosmetology. Such a facility, Bouquillon says, will generate "a robust pipeline of qualified, joyful individuals to work in the region."

Minuteman's 87 percent graduation rate, like that of many Massachusetts vocational schools, is better than the state average for the nearly 950,000 students in the public schools. This is so even though almost half the students come into the school with an Individualized Education Program for a range of educational challenges such as autism spectrum disorders; intellectual, developmental, visual, or hearing impairments; and anxiety or depression. The data suggest vocational education's mix of academic classwork with hands-on training helps these kids excel, and parents are noticing—one reason for the wait lists at many schools.

"The problem we found is, because the waiting lists are so long and they have so many applicants, to some extent these vocational schools are 'creaming,' " Barry Bluestone says. "They're taking the best students, not the worst. They've set the standards pretty high."

Wearing white lab coats, hair tucked under protective caps, seven of O'Rourke's classmates sit at a long table, pipettes in hand. Small class sizes are not unusual in vokes; as one administrator puts it, teacher-student ratios need to be smaller in classrooms where kids are wielding blowtorches or wiring transformers. O'Rourke and his classmates in the biotech track have to create an unadulterated bacteria culture in a petri dish.

Minuteman's academics and opportunities clearly suit O'Rourke. "I got to work at Boston College's research lab the summer of my sophomore year and the summer of my junior year, and that was such a great influence on me wanting to go to college," he says. "Because some of the research I did was so out of this world, I couldn't think I wanted to be anywhere but in a college lab."

O'Rourke would go on to achieve his goal; he graduated in May and now is a biology major at the University of Massachusetts Lowell.

When Tim Murray was a Boy Scout growing up in Worcester, he recalls earning part of a merit badge by visiting Worcester Vocational High School. Built in 1909, the school was funded by local industrialists intent on turning the influx of Irish, French, and Swedish immigrants into a trained workforce. Today, Worcester's immigrants come from Iraq, Burma, Bhutan, Burundi, Somalia, Liberia, and Vietnam. Like other "gateway cities"—New Bedford, Springfield, Brockton, Fall River—with high unemployment and large minority communities, skill building is in demand. Worcester Technical, which replaced the old voke in 2006, has some 1,400 students. There were 500 students wait listed for the class of 2019.

The data suggest vocational education's mix of academic classwork with hands-on training helps these kids excel, and parents are noticing—one reason for the wait lists at many schools.

Murray is a driving force behind the Alliance for Vocational Technical Education coalition, which brings together the Massachusetts Association of Vocational Administrators, chambers of commerce around the state, and the Massachusetts Competitive Partnership, a public policy group of CEOs that aims to promote job growth. One of AVTE's primary goals is to get thousands of students off wait lists and into the metal shops and industrial kitchens.

To do so requires "a new level of thinking," Murray says. "It's about better utilizing the dollars right now that are allocated in the education world and in the workforce training world. It's about more flexibility of funding. It's thinking in some new ways about after-school and summer programs to get these skills for those kids on waiting lists.

"We can do this," he says. "We wouldn't necessarily have to build new $100 million schools."

David J. Ferreira, executive director of the Massachusetts Association of Vocational Administrators, says that "ideally, we would build another two or three schools" to get at least some of the kids off waiting lists. But, statewide, the overall number of high school students is stagnant, and in areas such as Western Massachusetts and

Cape Cod, enrollment is actually dropping. "When the existing buildings aren't full, it's hard to make a case to build new schools," Ferreira says. With the biggest waiting lists generally in gateway cities that can't share the tax load with wealthy towns like Lexington or Dover, "the state's got to pick up a bigger piece of the action," he says, never an easy proposition.

Like Murray, Ferreira believes that regional vocational school staff offering after-hours programs for local high school students could be part of the solution. For instance, at Greater Lowell Technical High School in Tyngsborough, the state's largest voke with 2,250 students, superintendent-director Roger Bourgeois says the school has turned away a hundred qualified students each year since 2013. At the same time, the school has completed a $65 million renovation, adding a new cafeteria, a cyber cafe, and 13 new science labs. Grant money is available to schools for innovative proposals, and Bourgeois pictures offering four of Greater Lowell's 24 vocational programs (one each from the personal service, construction, technology, and manufacturing/transportation clusters) as a half-day session. Wait-listed students would attend academic classes in their local high schools in Dracut, Dunstable, Lowell, and Tyngsborough from late morning through mid-afternoon, then get bused to Greater Lowell for shop classes.

Ideas like Bourgeois's may have merit, Ferreira says, but "Massachusetts tends to be very parochial. . . . It's hard to get partnerships going. Even if you're able to start them, money gets tight, and those programs disappear."

Unlike Murray, Bourgeois believes the 1993 Reform Act has actually helped vocational education. Being held to the same standards as comprehensive high schools busted the myth that if you go to voc school, you can't go to college. "That was the number one question that we got for 20 years," Bourgeois says. " 'Can they go?' Yes, they can, because we're still giving them quality academics in addition to the training."

A case in point is Greater Lowell student Alvin Tran. In a computer-aided design/computer-aided manufacturing class last spring, Tran works on the design of a water purification device. He shows off a plastic prototype he generated on a 3-D printer. Tran's parents emigrated from Southeast Asia. His brother, older by one year, is a senior at Greater Lowell and hopes to be the first in the family to attend college. Tran, a junior honors student and tennis standout, also plans to go to college, possibly at UMass Lowell. He is thinking about pursuing civil engineering. "I like math," he says, "so this suits me."

But vocational students also come out of high school with a real skill. They could, as Murray puts it, "earn and learn" their way through college. "They're generally more serious students, and they're work-ready," he says.

Tim Murray says Madison Park's "underperforming" school label is partly to blame for vocational education's tarnished reputation in Massachusetts. "Public policy leaders at the State House and others—the Boston media, the business community—saw voc-tech education and the issues surrounding it simply through the prism of Madison Park," Murray says. "They said, 'This is what's happening at Madison Park. This is what must be happening around the state. It's not working,' when in fact, Madison Park is the outlier." Northeastern's Barry Bluestone says we may need to scrap Madison Park and "start over again."

Kevin McCaskill, who became Madison Park's first-ever executive director in April 2015, disagrees with Bluestone. There is no waiting list at his school, designed for 1,500 students, but enrollment is up to 930 from 800 last year. "I think it's just a matter of putting the right people in the right spot and making some great things happen," McCaskill says. "The word in other segments of the Commonwealth is that [vocational ed] is the wave. We've really got to get Boston in tune that this is one of the hottest things going. Vocational education has been big for a long time. Why not be big in Boston?"

Like other voke schools, Madison Park is enormous, more than a million square feet of 1970s Brutalist-style concrete architecture. After the morning rush on that day back in May, Madison Park's wide halls seemed eerily quiet. But in a room smelling of raw lumber, senior Kayla Colon, thick black ponytail falling to her waist over a Roxbury Community College T-shirt, maneuvered a plank through a table saw. At a break, she showed off a meticulously crafted toy chest with a hinged top, a present for her then 4-month-old daughter. Colon spent three years in the facilities-management program at Madison Park. She knew as soon as she tried out the program—which encompasses carpentry, electricity, plumbing, painting, papering, and landscaping—that it was right for her. "I like to work with my hands," she said.

Colon graduated from the program this year. She considered joining the carpenters' union but plans instead to study criminal justice at Roxbury Community College, which is close to her home in the South End and has a day-care center for her child.

Colon's classmate at Madison Park, Reno Guerrero, who graduated with her, is now taking classes at MassBay. His Madison Park teachers had assured him that with the skills he learned in high school—and the city garage job that will cover his college tuition—he's likely set for life. He hopes they're right. His older sister has married and moved out of their Dorchester home. It's all on him and his brother, he says, to "return all that happiness" that his mother has provided the family in the challenging years since they emigrated. He sees other teens doing drugs and joining gangs, but he doesn't want that for himself. "I love cars," he says simply. "This is my passion. I have to do what I love to do, and if I want to do this in the future, even if it's not easy at first, I have to study hard and work hard." He hopes, now that he is earning a salary, his mom will be able to quit her job as a taxi driver.

"Madison taught me how great it is to have an education and about being a professional in life," he writes me via text. "I just can't ask for anything better. Madison Park saved my life."

Print Citations

CMS: Halber, Deborah. "It's Time for Vocational Schools to Get Some Respect." In *The Reference Shelf: Education Reform*, edited by Betsy Maury, 86–92. Ipswich, MA: H.W. Wilson, 2017.

MLA: Halber, Deborah. "It's Time for Vocational Schools to Get Some Respect." *The Reference Shelf: Education Reform*. Ed. Betsy Maury. Ipswich: H.W. Wilson, 2017. 86–92. Print.

APA: Halber, D. (2017). It's time for vocational schools to get some respect. In Betsy Maury (Ed.), *The reference shelf: Education reform* (pp. 86–92). Ipswich, MA: H.W. Wilson. (Original work published 2016)

Forget Welding: The Hottest New Vocational Schools Do Digital Design

By Margaret Rhodes
Wired, March 6, 2017

When Ella Nance graduated college with a bachelor's in advertising, she landed a job as an analyst helping hospitals decide what equipment to purchase. Her company generated a lot of reports, and built digital tools to help hospital administrators keep track of inventory and contracts. Untangling that information required user research, prototypes, and usability tests. Nance's company didn't need analysts—it needed designers. So, last fall, she left her job to enroll in Center Centre.

Center Centre is a new, small user experience design school in Chattanooga, Tennessee. Launched October 2016, its founders modeled it after traditional vocational programs, in which students receive hyper-focused training in, say, welding or radio engineering, to meet the needs of hiring managers. And right now, hiring managers need UX designers. That's what happens when your company has a digital presence. The way a website flows, the placement of buttons on a mobile interface, the clarity and readability of the accompanying language—all of these things and more affect a user's experience of a brand and its products. A UX designer's job is to make sure that experience is as pleasant as possible.

The field is growing and evolving quickly, and so is demand for its practitioners. "Ten years ago no one even knew what user experience design was, and five years ago it was still a pretty difficult thing to nail down," says John Paul Rowan, vice president at the Savannah College of Art and Design. No longer. Like coding, UX design has become integral at any company with a digital component. In a recent survey of 500 department heads, Adobe found that most of them expect to double the number of UX designers they employ in the next five years. But until recently, people didn't explicitly choose experience design as a career path, so much as they stumbled into it through a side door.

Center Centre wants to be the front door. The curriculum skews pragmatic, not scholarly, and simulates life at work. For two years students arrive in the morning, depart in the evening, and tackle projects that stretch out for three to five months. One early project tasked the six 1-person inaugural class with building an online resource bank for designers, akin to Hacker News. Outside companies, such as Capital One, which donated to Center Centre's student loan fund, will suggest future projects. Students learn how to sketch, wireframe, and prototype. Guest lecturers from companies like Etsy and the Center for Civic Design dip into Chattanooga to speak on those topics. User research factors in heavily. Students display competency through projects. There are no tests.

Real projects and real schedules will, Center Centre hopes, prepare students for future jobs. "That doesn't happen in a traditional academic environment, where I put in 90 minutes of class, and now I can go play frisbee," says Leslie Jensen-Inman, one of the school's founders. "That doesn't really help a hiring manager." Center Centre will also aim for real demographics; it aspires for each class to represent women and people of color, and that students be recruited through unusual avenues—via relationships with local churches and volunteering events, instead of bus-stop advertisements—to reach people outside the design and tech world.

In a recent survey of 500 department heads, Adobe found that most of them expect to double the number of UX designers they employ in the next five years.

Center Centre's creators say its curricula and policies will distinguish it from similar programs that have emerged in recent years, which range from 10-week "bootcamps" to extension classes at major universities. The Savannah College of Art and Design added a UX design degree just last year. General Assembly, a coding academy, created a UX design track in 2013, a year after opening its Bay Area campus. "We were in San Francisco, starting to hear this zeitgeist talk of UX, UX," says Anna Lindow, who oversees campus education for General Assembly. "I remember feeling that we were at the beginning of the wave." To date, 3,200 students have gone through the 10-week-long course. Of those, General Assembly says 99 percent found design jobs within six months. Recently, IBM Design and InVision offered input on curriculum updates.

Corporate partners help, but General Assembly's impressive placement rate has mostly to do with the changing needs of companies. American interest in vocational schools tends to fluctuate in response to socioeconomic shifts. "There's a long history behind this ambivalence," says UMass Amherst sociologist Katherine Newman, citing the uptick in white-collar jobs following WWII and cultures' wavering biases towards and against four-year education. Countries like Germany and Austria, Newman says, make good use of government-funded apprenticeship programs, in order to maintain a strong, relevant workforce. The US follows a boom-and-bust pattern, and is currently, slightly, booming. "There's growing interest right now, in part from coming out of the Great Recession." Vocations evolve with the times, so this go-around there's heightened focus on television, engineering, and tech jobs.

The challenge for schools like Center Centre will be keeping curriculums relevant to a market that's evolving faster than ever. "That is exactly the most difficult thing about being in UX design," says Khoi Vinh, principal designer at Adobe. "The technology is changing, and it changes every 5 to 7 years, that's the cycle where things get radically different. We're completing the mobile cycle and moving into this new cycle of chatbots, AI, conversational interfaces." By that logic, any skills acquired in a two-year program come with a looming expiration date.

That hardly renders them useless. Programs will do well to future-proof curriculums, but Vinh says the fact that they exist helps hiring managers. "In the first decade of this profession, a lot of it was improvised," he says of the UX design career path. "We might start to see more straightforward paths into the trade." Take Nance, for instance. Only recently, she says, did she appreciate design's ability to dictate online experiences. Now she does, and intends to wield that knowledge at a company—maybe a bank, perhaps another healthcare outfit—that needs to make its platforms clear to customers. Once companies have a reliable workforce available to do that, the real creativity can begin.

Print Citations

CMS: Rhodes, Margaret. "Forget Welding: The Hottest New Vocational Schools Do Digital Design." In *The Reference Shelf: Education Reform*, edited by Betsy Maury, 93–95. Ipswich, MA: H.W. Wilson, 2017.

MLA: Rhodes, Margaret. "Forget Welding: The Hottest New Vocational Schools Do Digital Design." *The Reference Shelf: Education Reform*. Ed. Betsy Maury. Ipswich: H.W. Wilson, 2017. 93–95. Print.

APA: Rhodes, M. (2017). Forget welding: The hottest new vocational schools do digital design. In Betsy Maury (Ed.), *The reference shelf: Education reform* (pp. 93–95). Ipswich, MA: H.W. Wilson. (Original work published 2017)

A Plan to Teach Every Child Computer Science

By Emily Deruy
The Atlantic, October 19, 2016

More and more jobs are requiring some knowledge about how computers work. Not just how to start one up and surf the web, but how they actually run, how—at the simplest level—a series of inputs leads to a series of particular outputs.

Yet, across the United States, few children are being taught even the basics of computer science. It's a discipline left largely to the self-motivated YouTube watchers and the kids lucky enough to be born into tech-minded families with resources.

According to a new national survey from Google and Gallup, just more than half of seventh- through 12th-grade students attend a school that offers a dedicated computer-science class. Black students are less likely than their white peers to have access to such courses, and teachers and parents are more likely to tell boys that they would be good at computer science than they are girls. That a disproportionate number of technical workers at companies like Google, Apple, and Facebook are white and male is no surprise.

But a group of nonprofits, educators, tech companies, states, and districts want to change that. And after more than a year of work, a carefully crafted yet adaptable framework for what computer-science education should look like at each grade level went live this week. The writers hope it will help more states craft standards and ultimately bring the subject to classrooms across the country.

The K-12 Computer Science Framework is a "response to the history of inequity in computer science," said Pat Yongpradit, the chief academic officer at Code.org, one of the organizations steering the initiative.

People had different motivations for participating. Some wanted to make sure their states have a strong pipeline of workers to fill local tech jobs. Others think basic coding is up there with reading and writing as a skillset that 21st-century American students need to possess. And still others hope that creating a framework will help roll back the mindset that computer science is for a select few, and begin to diversify what is a largely white, male space.

Yongpradit sees computer science as "a literacy for the modern age." Right now, many people use dating apps with no idea how the algorithm that could literally help them meet their future spouse works, he pointed out. It's hard to understand what all the talk around Hillary Clinton's emails means without a basic understanding of a server, he added. Equipping young people with a fundamental understanding of computer science will provide them with a "richer experience as a citizen in this modern age," he said.

According to the groups involved, this is the first time that people from across the computer-science spectrum have come together for such a broad task. Perhaps contrary to other disciplines where teachers aren't exactly clamoring for someone to tell them how and what to teach, most educators don't have a background in computer science, and states and districts seem to be welcoming the input.

Mark Saunders is the director of the Office of Technology and Virtual Learning at the Virginia Department of Education, one of just a handful of states actively working to develop K-12 computer-science standards. The state plans to use the framework as the basis for its own standards.

"It's bigger than just preparing students for potential jobs," Saunders said. "At the core of computer science is computational thinking, and, to me, computational thinking and that algorithmic process is a key skill that every student should have, that they can use in a lot of different professions and in everyday life."

And the framework will help the state's teachers, particularly at the elementary level, where computer science will likely be integrated into the day and not framed as a pull-out class, think through how to teach concepts.

Most of those concepts don't even require a computer to learn at the early stages, said Rebecca Dovi, the director of education at the Virginia nonprofit CodeVA, which works with teachers and students to improve computer-science education. At a recent camp, Dovi, whose group reviewed the framework, said, her team worked the programming concept of a loop—which essentially hinges on repetition—into a cheer routine a group of young girls was planning for fun. On a piece of paper, the girls drew symbols to describe different movements. Two lines for a clap. A dot for a foot stomp. Then, they learned that they could use those symbols to describe the routine on paper. "That's very, very algorithmic," Dovi said, "but not necessarily needing to be on a computer."

"Others think basic coding is up there with reading and writing as a skillset that 21st-century American students need to possess."

States and nonprofits like Dovi's are working to train more teachers in how to teach computer science. But there's general acknowledgement that the lack of computer-science savvy among those who will be asked to teach the subject as more states work it into standard curriculum presents a significant hurdle. "I think it's a low supply right now," Saunders said. While a number of states, including Virginia, and nonprofits provide teacher training for existing teachers, there are still few pathways in most states to computer-science certification for teachers. Yongpradit pointed out that few new teachers come in prepared to teach computer science, so the pipeline is still sparse. There's also, he acknowledged, the challenge of losing teachers who are highly qualified to teach computer science to the tech industry, where salaries are often higher. (Some districts offer signing bonuses to certain teachers, but they're generally pretty small.)

But Leigh Ann DeLyser, the co-chair of the national CS for All consortium and the director of education and research at the New York City Foundation for Computer Science Education, characterized the idea that computer-science teachers are more likely to leave the classroom than other teachers as "complete mythology." And in the last six months, she said, around 600 teachers in the city have been trained to teach the basics of computer science.

One of the trickier challenges is getting parents and, more broadly, communities on board with the idea that computer science is for everyone. For many years, the only computer-science education that was broadly codified was the AP course at the high-school level. There was an assumption, DeLyser said, that students "had to be special or smarter to do computing." She hopes the framework will help change that.

But there's work to do. According to the Google-Gallup survey, while a whopping 93 percent of parents say they see computer science as a good use of resources, just 28 percent have told a teacher or other school official they feel that way. And parents often cite a lack of interest in the subject as a key reason women are underrepresented in computer science, yet they are perhaps unconsciously less likely to tell girls they would be good at it.

Saunders, at the Virginia Education Department, also said that some counselors may be more likely to think students with high math aptitude will succeed in computer science, which he thinks is too limited a view.

Sepi Hejazi Moghadam, the head of research and development for K-12 education at Google, which supports the new framework, finds that mindset concerning because it masks the fact that there are very real differences in access and encouragement both at school and at home that are creating those gaps. "It's kind of suggesting that there's not higher representation because they're just not motivated," he said.

Moghadam thinks more school principals are beginning to look at incorporating computational skills into lessons, though, and he hopes the framework will accelerate the pace.

That a framework was developed at all is something of a minor miracle, given that there were more than 25 writers and hundreds of people on the periphery offering different opinions. They didn't always agree. DeLyser, who was one of the framework writers, said, for instance, that very technical things about routing protocols were included early on and then simplified when it was pointed out that the minute details weren't necessarily things every child needs to know.

But now the framework is here and computer science is maybe having "a moment"—heavy emphasis on the maybe because even the people who want desperately for it to happen say it's too early to tell. Last year, President Obama said every student should have the opportunity to learn computer science. He called on the federal government to approve funding for states to make that goal a reality. The nation's new K-12 education law names computer science as a core subject, up there with writing. And in the last several years, Yongpradit said, there has "definitely been a wave of activity at the federal and state levels." Arkansas, Indiana, and Florida have made major computer-science pushes at the K-12 level, as have major cities like New York and Chicago. California is moving, albeit slowly, toward its own standards. So are Virginia, South Carolina, and Washington state.

What they're designing isn't necessarily ideal. Activists think some states are too focused on cranking out programmers instead of teaching every student to think computationally. But ultimately, said Dovi at CodeVA, the framework is a chance to show teachers how they can introduce every child at every grade level to computer science. "We have this really beautiful opportunity to really disrupt some of the inequity that's been in place," she said. That, she hopes, will draw all students and not just a select few into conversations and lessons about big data and cybersecurity and privacy, critical issues that today's children will have to grapple with as adults. "We have," she said, "to prepare."

Print Citations

CMS: Deruy, Emily. "A Plan to Teach Every Child Computer Science." In *The Reference Shelf: Education Reform*, edited by Betsy Maury, 96–99. Ipswich, MA: H.W. Wilson, 2017.

MLA: Deruy, Emily. "A Plan to Teach Every Child Computer Science." *The Reference Shelf: Education Reform*. Ed. Betsy Maury. Ipswich: H.W. Wilson, 2017. 96–99. Print.

APA: Deruy, E. (2017). A plan to teach every child computer science. In Betsy Maury (Ed.), *The reference shelf: Education reform* (pp. 96–99). Ipswich, MA: H.W. Wilson. (Original work published 2016)

Inside Silicon Valley's Classrooms of the Future

By Hannah Kuchler
The Financial Times, February 3, 2017

In chalets scattered across the snow in California's ski country, a school of the future is taking shape. Warm inside a classroom, teenage twins Laurel and Bryce Dettering are part of a Silicon Valley experiment to teach students to outperform machines.

Surrounded by industrial tools, Bryce is laying out green 3D-printed propellers, which will form part of a floating pontoon. The 15-year-old is struggling to finish a term-long challenge to craft a vehicle that could test water quality remotely.

So far, the task has involved coding, manufacturing and a visit to a NASA contractor who builds under-ice rovers. "I suck at waterproofing. I managed to waterproof one side, did a test of it, it proved waterproof. I made sure the other side was waterproof, put both sides on and both of them leaked!" he laughs. Laurel, already adept in robotics, chose a different kind of project, aimed at developing the empathy that robots lack: living on a reservation with three elderly women from the Navajo tribe. "The experience was just, honestly, it was really..." she trails out, her navy nails fiddling with her dark-blonde hair. "They didn't have running water, didn't have electricity, they had 54 sheep and their only source of income was weaving rugs from wool." The Detterings have embraced personalised education, a new movement that wants to tear up the traditional classroom to allow students to learn at their own pace and follow their passions with the help of technology. Mark Zuckerberg, the founder of Facebook, and his wife Priscilla [Chan] are leading the push to create an education as individual as each child, aiming to expand the experiments beyond the rarefied confines of Silicon Valley.

Tahoe Expedition Academy uses software developed by Facebook and Summit Public Schools, a free charter chain 200 miles south in the Bay Area. Every morning, Laurel and Bryce log on to their "personalised learning platform," which looks like a website, and progress through a "playlist" of reading material, videos and tests. They decide which modules to learn next based on what they enjoy or have yet to master. By focusing on what they need and want to learn, rather than following a class-wide curriculum, the platform frees up time for additional projects that encourage taking risks and solving problems. Having disrupted the world, the tech community now wants to prepare children for their new place in it. Leading venture capitalist Marc Andreessen predicts a future with two types of job: people who tell computers what to do, and people who are told what to do by computers.

Silicon Valley wants to equip young people to rule the machines by focusing on what makes them individuals. But how far can this reinvention of learning be extended from the wealthy environs of northern California to the broader US education system, where some state schools struggle to provide up-to-date textbooks, let alone personalised, digital tutoring? The Detterings' parents signed up for an alternative education after Laurel became frustrated at her private girls' school in San Francisco. She was ahead of her peers and not content with drawing on her shoes—which is what her mother had done when she was bored in class. "I was really good at looking like I was listening and dreaming in my head," Sue Dettering smiles. "This generation does not tolerate that very well." Tahoe Expedition Academy combines academic teaching with what it calls "constructive adversity"—adventures that push kids to the edge to build character. Like an endless educational gap year, each high-school senior has spent 130 days away in the past three years.

One group went to Greece to work with Syrian refugees, while a class of 13-year-olds drove and kayaked to the Mexican border to interview border patrols and immigrants and see how Donald Trump's wall could shape the region.

"Rote learning is done—computers can do that," says Sue Dettering. "The kids are going to have to have the interpersonal skills to work in groups, to communicate well, be creative, arrive at an answer in many different ways." Their father Bill, who runs a tech company, says other parents think they are brave—but believes this new education is sensible. "It really is the human-oriented jobs that are going to be the opportunity."

The uncertain future facing the next generation of workers is partly Silicon Valley's fault. Tech companies have stripped out jobs as they transform industries, from retail to media to cars. Artificial intelligence will accelerate the shift, with Accenture predicting that AI will increase labour productivity by up to 40 per cent by 2035, when Bryce and Laurel turn 33. Fewer workers will be needed for the jobs we have now, so kids must be prepared for the jobs we cannot imagine. Silicon Valley is, as ever, optimistic. It wants to move on from a 19th-century, artisanal model of education—where knowledge resides with each classroom teacher—to a 21st-century personalised experience that technology can replicate on a global scale. The new model focuses on skills, not knowledge you can Google, and social abilities that will be needed, whatever the workplace.

When Zuckerberg and Chan's daughter Max was born in 2015, they announced they would donate 99 per cent of their Facebook shares, worth $45bn at the time, to the Chan Zuckerberg Initiative (CZI). Penning an open letter to their firstborn, they focused on the prospects for personalised education. "You'll advance quickly in subjects that interest you most, and get as much help as you need in your most challenging areas. You'll explore topics that aren't even offered in schools today. Your teachers will also have better tools and data to help you achieve your goals," they wrote. More than a year later, Zuckerberg is posting Max's toddling attempts on Facebook to his 85 million followers, and CZI is looking to make education investments. Personalised education is not new: in 1926, Sidney Pressey created a "teaching machine," where students could read material and complete multiple-choice tests at their own pace, pulling down levers and receiving sweets for correct responses.

The personalised education movement combines a testing machine for the big-data age with a key idea taken from Maria Montessori, who developed her approach more than a century ago: that each child should drive their own learning. Silicon Valley hopes new technology will help personalisation finally succeed at scale. Today's teaching machines look like data dashboards, which teachers monitor as each child works through tasks and tests. This instant data speeds up teachers' decisions—they don't have to wait until a child hands in homework or for the results of an end-of-term test. In class, they can spot who needs help and assemble impromptu tutoring groups, while others steam ahead, taking on honours units in subjects they love. A moving line on the student's dashboard shows the term ticking away, prompting them to stay on top of units where they are slower. Final tests are only taken when a child is ready.

> **Rote learning is done—computers can do that. Kids will need to be able to work in groups, be creative.** —*Sue Dettering, parent*

The problem Silicon Valley is trying to solve can be summed up by a 1984 study by educational psychologist Benjamin Bloom. Cited by every personalised-education advocate including Zuckerberg, it found students who received one-on-one attention performed better than 98 per cent of their peers. The challenge is to achieve the benefits of that one-on-one tutoring in a class of 30 or more.

Personalisation is so popular in the Bay Area that parents can pick their experiment: public, private or funded by non-profits. The Tahoe Expedition Academy is a private school, charging up to $17,000 a year, with a focus on the outdoors. The AltSchool combines a start-up filled with engineers and product managers, funded by CZI and venture capitalists including Andreessen Horowitz and Peter Thiel's Founders Fund, with a chain of private "lab schools," where parents pay about $27,000 a year. The Emerson Collective, established by Steve Jobs' widow Laurene Powell Jobs, has invested in existing schools, including one for low-income students in San Jose, where some high-schoolers work a day a week as product managers at Cisco. Chan, a paediatrician and teacher, started The Primary School, combining education and healthcare for an underprivileged community in East Palo Alto.

Many of these private schools want to contribute their technology and lesson plans to state schools now or in the future. But the original personalisation Petri dish was Summit Public Schools, a charter chain that has germinated from one school in Silicon Valley to a learning platform that is now used by 20,000 students across 27 states. Summit Tamalpais, the chain's newest school, opened last August in Richmond, the poor, post-industrial and heavily Hispanic end of the Bay Area. Driving up to the school, opposite a grey-box Walmart, my car is flagged down by a woman begging for money for a motel room for her and her three-year-old. Inside, the children are rambunctious, celebrating break time as if it were a birthday. Self-portraits line the walls, with each 12-year-old illustrating their identity inside silhouetted profiles: one child has painted a pizza, a French flag, YouTube and a fighter plane; another Lake Tahoe, September 11 and a rainbow. When kids return to class, a Summit teacher's job is to turn these interests into a personalised curriculum that keeps every child engaged in learning through class, college and career.

Diane Tavenner, the founder and chief executive of Summit, believes technology addresses this challenge. As a child in the 1970s, her progressive teacher experimented with different levels of spelling tests, distributed on cards in wooden pigeon holes. But the teacher gave up because it was impossible to mark each test at the right pace. "We went back to the same spelling book and did the same list. It wasn't really self-directed," she says. Summit's personalised-learning platform uses technology to make these tasks easier. At Tamalpais, Dajana, 12, is preparing for a debate on whether Roman society was just. After finishing the reading and videos in her playlist, she decides that it was hugely unjust, because men could sell their wives and sons. She uses a traffic-light system to assess what she needs to do next: she is "yellow," needing more practice ahead of her speech at the debate. "It is harder because we are doing it by ourselves, but it is good practice for the future," she says.

In a silent neighbouring classroom, where each 12-year-old works on his or her own computer, Fernando Torres' screen shows he has completed most of the core courses, depicted by coloured blocks, and several advanced units. "I find the easy ones and then I start on the hard ones after. I'm really excited by science, so I did the science ones first," he explains. Next week he'll spend every morning working on a video-games project.

Zuckerberg hails Tavenner as a personalisation pioneer. Live streaming on Facebook from his couch on CZI's anniversary, he spoke excitedly about how Chan, sitting next to him, urged him to visit the school. "You go in and it feels like the future, it feels like a start-up to me," he says. To hear about life pre-Zuckerberg from Tavenner and the other half of the Summit double act, engineer Sam Strasser, it sounds like the tech was held together with sticky tape. Strasser, then the only engineer, tried persuading friends to help build the software: "That didn't work out logistically. They have day jobs, they can't just do your job for you," he grins. Zuckerberg lent them the technical talent. "There were three of us—which is a tiny, tiny team at Facebook but was 300 per cent growth for me. So I was like, this is huge!" Summit plans to expand to hundreds more schools. Tavenner now meets with Zuckerberg about once a month, Strasser works at Facebook, and the senior management team spend every Monday there. Everyone contributes ideas to develop the platform, even the kids, though they don't have the direct line they had when Strasser was in school. "They literally would, like, chase him through the school, [shouting] 'Hey, hey, hey—Mr Strasser, we have an idea!'" laughs Tavenner, mimicking the children's high-pitched voices. The day before we met, Tavenner discovered another assumption she had yet to question. "Yesterday afternoon we stopped and said: wait, why do we assume that every teacher has to grade their own kids' performance tasks?" She points out that the dual coaching and testing role of a teacher can potentially create grade inflation, as teachers fail to be objective with students they know. "With technology, it literally doesn't have to be true," she says. Tests could be sent instantly to be marked by another teacher in the school or even elsewhere. Tavenner's next challenge is more political: convincing universities of the value of Summit's own data, so her students no longer have to sit standardised tests. She is pushing deans of admissions to abandon the current "hoops for college" in favour of a more detailed, nuanced picture of a child.

At the AltSchool in San Francisco's start-up district, a few streets away from the offices of companies such as Dropbox, Pinterest and Airbnb, four-year-olds are advised to be "mindful" as they cut up painted paper for a puppet show; the project was devised by one of the kids in class.

One floor up, 12- to 14-year-old children run election campaigns, designing websites and playing TV anchors on video. On another floor, a teacher photographs children listening to an expert on how to design their own Olympic stadiums; the picture is uploaded to AltSchool's app to share with parents instantly. Ernesto, 12, is passionate about cooking: he runs a website making $20 cakes to order and argues with his teacher about the best kind of Italian baking chocolate. Given a project where he had to prove or disprove a myth, he tested his hypothesis that drying pasta at a high heat caused it to lose its taste. He made an entertaining YouTube video about the experiment, including a cameo from a local artisanal pasta producer, concluding that high temperatures did indeed hamper flavour. "I got better at video editing and coming up with an experiment, following the scientific process," he says. AltSchool's classrooms are considered "labs" because the teachers and engineers are hoping to spread what they learn here beyond the chain in Silicon Valley and New York. Like tech inventions from the iPhone to Uber, the personalised-education movement intends to go global. For funders, the size of the market is both tempting and terrifying. Josh Kopelman, a venture capitalist at First Round Capital, says its investment in AltSchool is a financial, not philanthropic decision. "Would I rather fund this or another photo-sharing app? There's no question for me," he says.

He holds forth on the vastness of the education industry: "It's an industry that is measured in trillions of dollars, not billions; it's multiple percentage points of gross domestic product. "The consumption of this product is required for a meaningful portion of our population. And you have tens of thousands of fractured competitors that all spend collectively less than 1 per cent of their budget on R&D and don't innovate in terms of process and software." But Jim Shelton, charged by Zuckerberg and Chan to invest in personalised education, believes that even with billions, it will take clever decision-making to change such a large industry. "In philanthropic terms, these are a tremendous amount of resources. But in the US alone we spend $650bn in K12 [primary and secondary] education every year, so the investments we make will need to be very strategic." Shelton has the pedigree: he was deputy secretary in the US education department, directed programmes for the Bill & Melinda Gates Foundation and worked at education technology companies. Chatting with Zuckerberg and Chan during their Facebook Live broadcast, it is clear they regularly swap notes. "It is something we are very much doing together," he says. "Priscilla is there engaged daily—and nightly—and Mark is there a surprising amount. They want to understand deeply what is going on and they have perspectives on most of what we do." The couple learnt a hard lesson from their first foray into education philanthropy—a donation of $100m to schools in Newark, New Jersey in 2010. The effort, led by Cory Booker, then mayor of the city, and Chris Christie, the Republican governor, failed to win over a wary community. Dale Russakoff, who wrote a book called *The Prize* about the turnaround attempt, says Zuckerberg did not realise the scale of the challenge he faced. "He was 26 when he made that gift, Facebook was young and he was still called the 'Toddler CEO,'" she says. "I think he learnt a lot about politics and just how hard it is to change an education system." CZI will focus on what Zuckerberg knows well: using technology to personalise, and investing in research and development. But it plans to progress more slowly than the social network, investing in the US before expanding globally and, says Shelton, being sensitive to community needs, perhaps taking on a "different flavour" for local cultures.

Shelton believes personalised learning can grow where other educational movements have failed: "Ideas are easy to spread, [but] practices are very hard to spread with fidelity, especially when they are not supported by good tools." The key is to create demand. "Stimulate it in a way that is not so cumbersome for learners and teachers to implement. Then, when they try it, they can't imagine living without it. It's how the best innovations work."

While Shelton uses the word "humble" to describe Zuckerberg and Chan's approach, industry analyst Trace Urdan describes Silicon Valley's push into education as "hubris." Established education companies such as McGraw Hill and Pearson have been working on adaptive learning technologies for years, and younger ed-tech companies have sometimes found they are more excited about data than their potential customers. "There's a little bit of Silicon Valley hubris here: 'We've arrived, we're here and now we're going to create all these amazing changes,'" he says. The Bay Area is also an unrepresentative test market, filled with millennial parents "steeped in large amounts of wealth," Urdan says. And the enviable student-to-teacher ratio in some of the private schools experimenting with personalisation (Tahoe Expedition Academy has a 7:1 ratio overall) is far from the norm across America. The cost of technology is another challenge: a survey by the Consortium for School Networking found that only 68 per cent of US districts currently have schools that meet even the minimum internet bandwidth recommendations set by the regulator. And few kids outside of Silicon Valley can ask their parents' friends to help with virtual reality projects. Expanding beyond northern California could be tough, he argues.

There's a bit of Silicon Valley hubris here—we've arrived, and now we're going to create all these amazing changes.
—Trace Urdan, education market analyst

Technology is usually sold by district to superintendents who frequently move positions, often replaced by someone who brings in different software. Once they get beyond early adopters, unionised teachers are "very suspicious" of anything that could replace jobs. Russakoff says it will take a "lot of engagement" to convince unions that the technology will make teachers more powerful. "It will not be an easy road." Howard Gardner, a professor of cognition and education at the Harvard graduate school of education, cautiously welcomes the tailored approach, but fears the entrepreneurs could be exercising a certain "noblesse oblige" by advocating the organisation of one's life around one's personal passions or interests—something that is not always possible for everyone or their children. "It is the Bill Gates fallacy: you think everyone is a little Bill Gates," he says.

Silicon Valley parents are probably less concerned about privacy concerns than many and, so far, privacy campaigners have not slammed the most widespread tool—the Summit Personalised Learning Platform—despite it working with Facebook, which stands accused of not protecting users' privacy in the past. Instead, they give it good marks for asking parents' permission at the start of each school year and storing the data on their own servers. In Europe, personalised education may face resistance because privacy is considered a fundamental right. Everyone from marketers to credit scorers to governments are thirsty for data: a picture of an individual built up over years, tracking their test scores and what they read and watch, could prove deeply attractive. "Privacy issues are coming," says Elana Zeide, a scholar working on education, big data and privacy at Yale and Princeton. Critics have so far focused on problems with software vendors—for example, whether student data can be sold off after bankruptcy. But they have not yet considered the new data-driven model of education in schools. "The shift will cause a jolt," Zeide says. Technologies are certain to pull in more data in the future.

At AltSchool, cameras mounted on classroom walls are used by some teachers to review how their lessons are going down. Elsewhere, researchers are using facial recognition software to work out when a learner becomes frustrated or when the whole class switches off halfway through a lesson. Algorithms risk reaching a point like the Facebook news feed, where few understand why information is selected, argues Zeide. "Algorithms can be unwittingly biased, can have inadvertent, disparate effects, and those kinds of perpetuated inequalities are particularly sensitive in education," she says. Today, people are increasingly worried about filter bubbles — but what if your child is kept back a grade and no one knows why? The bigger question is how much power this hands to Silicon Valley companies that already dominate our work and social lives. "The tradition of localised control is because people in the local community know the needs of that economy or what is consistent with local values," Zeide says. "If instruction is based on a platform developed by engineers in Silicon Valley, parents and school officials don't have the same control."

Max Ventilla left his job as former head of personalisation at Google to pursue another Google-sized challenge. The AltSchool chief executive sits in a start-up-style office on the top floor of the school, and draws on the whiteboard when excited. AltSchool, he says, is not a school or a start-up, it is a "full-stack education company." In tech speak, this means it does everything: a third of the employees are engineers, a third are educators and a third run the business.

Parents pay fees, hoping their kids will get a better education as guinea pigs, while venture capitalists fund the R&D, hoping for financial returns from the technologies it develops. AltSchool started selling to select "alpha" partner-schools, who are contributing feedback, last year. Every industry began as artisanal, Ventilla says, but changed when people pooled resources. "We used to produce our clothes, our materials, our everything at the household level," he says. "Now you spend a million dollars of software-engineer time to write a program but once it is written, it is basically free to have a two-millionth person [use it]." Silicon Valley has not yet succeeded. Ventilla lists the challenges that a child in 2050 needs to be prepared for: the changes wrought by globalisation, the acceleration of technical change, longer life spans and the "tidal wave" of artificial intelligence. "The purpose of schools is to prepare kids for the future and that goal post is moving higher and higher, and faster and faster. The change is happening, it is just not happening fast enough," he says. What the technology industry can perhaps bring best to education is its methods. "Iterate" is a much-loved word in Silicon Valley, encapsulating the desire to pursue big changes (Facebook's famous motto: move fast and break things) and test rapidly to see which button works better (A/B testing). Ventilla knows education will not be one of Silicon Valley's classic success stories with a growth chart that looks like a hockey stick and overnight riches for founders. "Ultimately, our mission is to enable every child to reach their full potential. It is not every American child, it's not every child in an urban area," he says. "If you could do it quickly, it would have been done."

Print Citations

CMS: Kuchler, Hannah. "Inside Silicon Valley's Classroom of the Future." In *The Reference Shelf: Education Reform*, edited by Betsy Maury, 100–107. Ipswich, MA: H.W. Wilson, 2017.

MLA: Kuchler, Hannah. "Inside Silicon Valley's Classroom of the Future." *The Reference Shelf: Education Reform*. Ed. Betsy Maury. Ipswich: H.W. Wilson, 2017. 100–107. Print.

APA: Kuchler, H. (2017). Inside Silicon Valley's classroom of the future." In Betsy Maury (Ed.), *The reference shelf: Education reform* (pp. 100–107). Ipswich, MA: H.W. Wilson. (Original work published 2017)

It Takes a Suburb: A Town Struggles to Ease Student Stress

By Kyle Spencer
The New York Times, April 5, 2017

Small rocks from the beaches of eastern Massachusetts began appearing at Lexington High School last fall. They were painted in pastels and inscribed with pithy advice: Be happy.... Mistakes are O.K.... Don't worry, it will be over soon. They had appeared almost by magic, boosting spirits and spreading calm at a public high school known for its sleep-deprived student body.

Crying jags over test scores are common here. Students say getting B's can be deeply dispiriting, dashing college dreams and profoundly disappointing parents. The rocks, it turns out, were the work of a small group of students worried about rising anxiety and depression among their peers. They had transformed a storage area into a relaxation center with comfy chairs, an orange/peach lava lamp and a coffee table brimming with donated art supplies and lots and lots of rocks—to be painted and given to favorite teachers and friends. They called it the Rock Room.

"At first it was just us," said Gili Grunfeld, a senior who helped with the effort. "Then everyone was coming in."

So many rocks were piling up, they had to be stored in a display case near one of the cafeterias. The maxims seemed to call out to students as they headed to their classes in conceptual physics, computer programming, astronomy and Advanced Placement Music Theory.

And they became a visual reminder of a larger, communitywide initiative: to tackle the joy-killing, suicide-inducing performance anxiety so prevalent in turbocharged suburbs like Lexington. In recent years, the problem has spiked to tragic proportions in Colorado Springs, Palo Alto, California, and nearby Newton, Massachusetts, where stress has been blamed for the loss of multiple young lives. In January, a senior at Lexington High School, who had just transferred from a local private school, took her own life.

Residents in this tight-knit hamlet, with its high level of civic engagement, are hoping to stem the tide. Mary Czajkowski, the district superintendent, was hired in 2015 with the mandate of "tackling the issue head on."

Elementary school students now learn breathing exercises and study how the brain works and how tension affects it. New rules in the high school limit homework. To decrease competition, there are no class rankings and no valedictorians and salutatorians. In town, there are regular workshops on teen anxiety and college forums designed to convince parents that their children can succeed without the Ivy Leagues. Last October, more than 300 people crammed into the town hall for a screening of "Beyond Measure," a sequel to Vicki Abeles's documentary on youth angst, "Race to Nowhere."

"We want to be a model," said Jessie Steigerwald, a longtime school board member.

But it has not been easy.

Claire Sheth, a mother of four who had invited Ms. Abeles to town, describes Lexington students as "tired to the core." Students say depression is so prevalent that it affects friendships, turning teenagers into crisis counselors. "A lot of kids are trying to manage adult anxiety," said the principal, Laura Lasa.

The problem is not anecdotal. In a 2015 national health survey, 95 percent of Lexington High School students reported being heavily stressed over their classes and 15 percent said they had considered killing themselves in the last year. Thinking about it most often were Asian and Asian-American students—17 percent of them, as is the case nationally.

The town's growing Asian community has not been timid acknowledging the problem. Through college forums and chat rooms, a group of parents and leaders of the local Chinese-American and Indian-American associations have been working to lower the competitive bar and realign parental thinking. Others are pushing back. They don't want the workload reduced—they moved here for the high-rigor schools. At association meetings, where the tension is most pronounced, discussions about academic competition in the district have brought some to tears.

Indeed, reversing the culture is complicated in a town that prides itself on sending dozens of students to the Ivy Leagues: 10 went to Harvard last year and seven to the Massachusetts Institute of Technology. Young people are lauded at school board meetings and online for having published academic papers or performed at Lincoln Center. Last year, the varsity team placed second in the 2016 History Bowl nationals and fourth in the National Science Bowl. The robotics team has qualified for the FIRST Championship, an international technology and engineering competition, for five of the last six years.

After school recently at the public library, which was packed with students poring over textbooks, calculus work sheets, lab reports and term papers, a sophomore looked up from her world history textbook and said, "You see all these people? They want the same thing—that's really overwhelming." What they want: Entry into a top college when acceptance rates are at an all-time low.

Lexington looks and feels like a lot of other affluent suburbs: serene, stately, with a whiff of muted money. Minivans and aging Volvos are packed with violins and well-worn soccer gear. There are meticulously restored Colonials and Tudor revivals. Walk along the red brick sidewalks of Massachusetts Avenue, which cuts through the center of town, and Lexington's Brahmin past is evident: a statue on the Battle Green of a musket-toting Captain John Parker, who led the fight against the British in 1775.

In recent years, the problem has spiked to tragic proportions in Colorado Springs, Palo Alto, California, and nearby Newton, Massachusetts, where stress has been blamed for the loss of multiple young lives.

In evidence as well are signs of the burgeoning biotech industry, and the changing face of America's elite.

Since 2000, the Asian population has ballooned from 11 percent to an estimated 22 percent of Lexington's 32,000 or so residents, surpassing Newton (at about 13 percent) and Cambridge (15 percent). Today, more than a third of Lexington's students are Asian or Asian-American. The demographic mirrors the migration of Asian families to suburbs across the country.

In the Crafty Yankee or the Asian bakery across the street, you are likely to bump into electrical engineers from Seoul, physicists from Beijing and biochemists from Boston. They teach at Harvard (10 miles away) and run labs at MIT (11 miles). They hold top positions in the pharmaceutical companies that dot the Boston-area tech corridor. More than half of the adults in Lexington have graduate degrees. And many want their children to achieve the same.

In many ways, students in Lexington are the byproduct of the self-segregation that Enrico Moretti writes about in his book *The New Geography of Jobs*, which addresses the way well-educated, tech-minded adults cluster in brain hubs. For their children, that means ending up in schools in which everyone is super bright and hypercompetitive. It's hard to feel special.

Best-selling authors and child psychologists have long urged parents to divest themselves from their child's every accomplishment, thereby sending the message that mental health matters more than awards. In Lexington, the attack is more comprehensive, involving schools, neighborhoods, churches and synagogues. It is riffing off research that shows that resilience and happiness, reinforced by the entire community, can be just as contagious as stress and depression.

"You need to bring along everybody," said Ms. Abeles, whose campaign has taken her to towns with similar communitywide efforts, including Elkins Park, Pennsylvania, San Ramon and Burbank, California, and New Rochelle, N.Y.

Peter Levine, associate dean for research at the Jonathan M. Tisch College of Civic Life at Tufts, says that communities that bond to promote pro-social behavior can be powerful inoculators for young people.

"Family problems are often community problems," he said. "They need community solutions."

No one is more aware of this than Ms. Lasa, who grew up here, earned degrees from nearby Springfield College and Lesley University, and then returned to the district—watching all the while as the population morphed from relatively laid back to Type A. She often wakes to emotional emails from parents delivered to her inbox after midnight. Most, she says, are about their children's academic standing, and the tone is often disappointment.

Last fall, as 557 bright-eyed freshmen gathered in cushioned folding chairs in the auditorium for orientation, she gave a speech that over the last few years has come to focus more and more on stress reduction. She begged the students to make mistakes. "Do not believe that you must acquire straight A's to be a successful student," she said. "If you and/or your parents are caught up in society's picture of success, let us help you change the focus."

Students are now required to meet with counselors when choosing courses to talk about their academic loads. The practice is largely seen as a way of keeping students from overscheduling to beef up their college transcripts.

"We are trying to change a culture that is deeply rooted here," Ms. Lasa told me in a sunny Boston accent as she barreled through the school. She was showing off the 45-minute free period she instituted this year, allowing—or in some cases, forcing—students to take time to unwind. Some were playing basketball in the gym. Others were talking with teachers. A few hung out in classrooms, chatting with friends. An awful lot, though, were getting a head start on homework. Ms. Lasa says she is trying to "balance all the messages" they are getting about success and happiness. The one she wants to most impart is: "Slow down."

The paradox of Lexington High School is that while indicators of anxiety abound, so too does an obsession with happiness. A large banner from the town's newly formed suicide prevention group, a chapter of the national organization Sources of Strength, greets students as they enter the sprawling red brick building, proclaiming: "Be a Part of Happiness." There are close to 50 students in the group. Below the banner are remnants of their project to spread positivity. Students were asked to write down their sources of strength, which were then posted beneath the banner and on Facebook. Some named their pets or friends. One wrote: "My mom." Another: "Trip to Israel!" A girl with green hair: "Chicken curry."

One morning in February, students in "Positive Psychology: The Pursuit of Happiness," a popular elective, were following up on a discussion about the psychologist Barbara Fredrickson's "broaden and build" theory, which posits that negative emotions like anxiety and fear prompt survival-oriented behaviors, while positive emotions expand awareness, spurring new ideas, creativity and eventually building skills.

"Today, we are going to look at pretty simple ways to make it more likely that you experience positive emotions on a day-to-day basis," Matthew Gardner told his "Happiness" students as they pulled out notebooks and pencil cases. The class discussed the benefits of exercise and eating foods that release feel-good hormones. The students also learned that smiling and being smiled at releases dopamine, which has an uplifting impact. Mr. Gardner offered an alternative to smiling: "Our brains are not so perfect that, sometimes, if you hold a pen or pencil like this"—he held a pencil between his teeth— "you activate some of the same face muscles. You might get a little bit of a dopamine effect, too." Several students held pencils between their teeth to test the theory.

At one point, the class practiced laughter yoga, raising their arms slowly as they breathed in, then lowering them as they breathed out, and bursting into peals of laughter. Afterward, the students recorded changes in their pulse rate to demonstrate research from the HeartMath Institute that shows heart rates slow down and smooth out after bouts of good feeling. "It's not just that your heart rate goes down and you become very calm," Mr. Gardner explained. "It's that the shape of your heart rate is smooth and more controlled. Frustration is more jagged." Their homework assignment: Do laughter yoga or "smile at five people you wouldn't normally smile at."

The effects of smiling are also taught in the A.P. Psychology class that Gili Grunfeld is taking, and it has informed her thoughts on stress. On a winter afternoon, she and several classmates were uncoiling in the Rock Room, making friendship bracelets and sketching in fat coloring books. A Post-it that read "Unplug" was taped to the wall clock. The students were bemoaning how so many of their peers develop "tunnel vision," in Gili's words, about schoolwork and extracurricular activities, sacrificing sleep and time with friends.

"They isolate for academics," she said glumly.

Soon the students had changed topics, and were discussing the ice that had caked the school parking lot that morning and how to balance on it. The subtext, once again, was well-being: How much can friends support each other if both feel overwhelmed?

"Are we more likely to fall or are we more steady if we hold onto each other?" asked Jocelyn Geller, a junior.

"I feel like if you have a friend with you, you feel safer," said Millie Landis, a sophomore, pulling Jocelyn up and wobbling on the floor with her to demonstrate. "But you could pull each other down."

The district has increased the number of counselors and social workers, including those working in the district's elementary schools, and expanded the training they receive in identifying and supporting at-risk students.

Cynthia Tang, whose parents emigrated from Taiwan, has been a counselor at Lexington High for 12 years. Warm and well-liked, she organizes workshops addressing the pressure on Asian students to succeed, borrowing insights from the childhood discord she experienced with her own parents as well as research on biculturalism. Studies show that the less assimilated parents are to American culture, the more stressed the children.

Adding to the pressure, she says, are cultural differences in how parents, raised abroad, and their offspring, raised in the United States, are expected to process setbacks and strife: American educators routinely encourage students to share their feelings; not so in Asia.

"I really see a lot of this being bicultural conflict," Ms. Tang said. "When you have one side of the family holding one set of values and the other embracing a new set of valuesthat inherently creates a lot of misunderstanding and a lot of tension."

Ms. Tang says that the disconnect is compounded by a lack of knowledge about the various routes to success available in the United States. Last year, she was brought in by the vice president of the local Chinese-American Association, Hua Wang, to help plan the college forum, a three-hour event on Father's Day. Dr. Wang, an engineering professor at Boston University, wanted to shift the focus away from a guide on applying to top colleges.

Despite resistance from the organizers, he and Ms. Tang prevailed. At the forum, she presented a slide show celebrating the academic trajectories of respected Chinese-Americans: the fashion designer Vera Wang went to Sarah Lawrence College; Andrew Cherng, the founder of the fast-food chain Panda Express, went to Baker University in Kansas; the best-selling author Amy Tan, San José State University. Parents were surprised. But, Ms. Tang said, "I think a lot of parents felt like: 'What do I do with that information?'"

This year, organizers will delve deeper into the differences between the Chinese and American systems, and are planning to add another new element: a panel discussion on combating stress. Dr. Wang said they want to showcase families who have adopted a more "holistic view" of education. Selected parents of graduating seniors will be asked to talk about how they encouraged their children to get enough sleep, comforted them when they came home with B's and discouraged them from skipping ahead in math to be eligible for higher level classes earlier.

Ms. Tang says that the disconnect is compounded by a lack of knowledge about the various routes to success available in the United States.

This would not be the only time that Dr. Wang has engaged in this kind of dialogue. Using the Mandarin words "danding," which means to keep calm and steady, and "ruizhi," which means wise and farsighted, he has initiated conversations on WeChat, an online chat room popular among Chinese parents. Recently, he told them: "Calmness and wisdom from the parents are the Asian child's greatest blessings."

But the message was not well received by everyone. Among the posted responses: "If your child gets a C, how do you get to a point of calm? You think we should be satisfied because at least he didn't get a D?" And: "But my heart still whispers: Am I not just letting my child lose at the starting line?"

One parent, Melanie Lin, found herself, too, in a heated conversation on WeChat after early-admissions decisions arrived last school year. She urged the other parents to stop bragging on the site about acceptance letters to top-tier schools: "If it's only those students who are attending the big-name schools that are being congratulated, then the idea being passed on is that only those students are successful, and attending a big-name school is the only way to become the pride of your parents."

Dr. Lin, who works at a pharmaceutical company, emigrated in the 1990s from Beijing to get a Ph.D. in biochemistry from Arizona State University. She says her rebuttal annoyed even close friends, whose online responses accused her of trying to deny parents and their children their moments in the spotlight. Recounting the conversation with me brought Dr. Lin to tears. "There is just so much pressure," she said. For her, the struggles are not theoretical. On the home front, she too can be just as obsessed as her peers, she says.

Her daughter, Emily, would agree. During junior year, she dreaded car rides and family dinners—any time, really, that she was alone with her parents—because conversations routinely veered back to college. Now a senior, Emily has eight A.P. and 13 honors classes under her belt. She is also a violinist, choral singer, competitive swimmer and class vice president.

For a chunk of her high school career, Emily was one of those who "isolated for academics," working into the early morning hours on homework and waking up, sometimes before dawn, after only five or so hours of sleep. She skipped birthday parties and lunch to squeeze in more studying. "I was never doing anything for pure fun," she said. "I put my head down and I was always running somewhere with some purpose."

But as a member of a youth board for a teen counseling center in town, she realized that her study habits were unhealthy. To get support for herself and others, she helped launch the town's Sources of Strength chapter. She has assisted in planning student outreach events and spoke up at a town meeting about "the dog-eat-dog" competition that still persists at the high school. Homework remains heavy, students say, particularly in high-level classes. Class rankings may be gone but students have a pretty good sense of where they stand. And while there has been talk of a later start time to the day so students can get more sleep, the idea is on hold.

In December, when early decisions came in, Emily found out she was deferred to the regular admissions pool by Yale, her top choice. Parents on WeChat were more sensitive this time around, but accepted seniors still bragged on Facebook. Since then, Emily has been admitted to nine universities; rejected by three, including Yale; and waitlisted by Harvard and the University of Chicago. She is deciding between Columbia and Duke.

Through it all, she has wondered if it's worth it. "I lost out on a lot of high school," she had told me as she waited for college decisions. What she hopes is that students who come after her find some balance before their time at Lexington is up.

Print Citations

CMS: Spencer, Kyle. "It Takes a Suburb: A Town Struggles to Ease Student Stress." In *The Reference Shelf: Education Reform*, edited by Betsy Maury, 108–114. Ipswich, MA: H.W. Wilson, 2017.

MLA: Spencer, Kyle. "It Takes a Suburb: A Town Struggles to Ease Student Stress." *The Reference Shelf: Education Reform*. Ed. Betsy Maury. Ipswich: H.W. Wilson, 2017. 108–114. Print.

APA: Spencer, K. (2017). It takes a suburb: A town struggles to ease student stress. In Betsy Maury (Ed.), *The reference shelf: Education reform* (pp. 108–114). Ipswich, MA: H.W. Wilson. (Original work published 2017)

4
Equity and the Achievement Gap

Credit: Photo by Drew Angerer/Getty Images

Parents, schoolchildren and education activists rally during an event supporting public charter schools and protesting New York's racial achievement gap in education, in Prospect Park, September 28, 2016 in the Brooklyn borough of New York City. The #PathToPossible rally and march, organized by the Families for Excellent Schools, is calling for New York City to double its public charter school sector to 200,000 students by 2020. An estimated 25,000 people attended the rally.

The Achievement Class

In a 1963 article for the *Saturday Review*, author James Baldwin described a paradox in education in that the more educated and "conscious" an individual becomes, the more that individual begins to question the society in which he or she was educated.[1] Throughout most of history, education was not considered a human right, but was a privilege available only to the elite, creating a hierarchy of knowledge that perpetuated class and economic hierarchies. It is through education that oppressed individuals begin to understand the nature of their oppression and thus education has fueled the many great social movements and revolutions aimed at creating more egalitarian societies. The "founding fathers" of the United States, for instance, were not "ordinary people," as some political rhetoric would contend, but were, in fact, elite, revolutionary thinkers whose belief in the new system they struggled to create was fostered by their education and consequent understanding of the inequities of Europe's prevailing class hierarchies.[2]

To avoid having the new republic become a reflection of the British aristocracy, pioneering Americans like Thomas Jefferson created the idea for the "Common School," a government-funded, free education system that would be open to all Americans without regard to class. However, Jefferson also believed that higher education was not for every American and that most Americans in the laboring class, were essentially destined to remain in that class. Rather than extending the benefits of education equally, therefore, Jefferson imagined that schooling should be divided into two tracks, one for laborers and one for elites, but that, in an effort to avoid an stagnant hierarchy, a few laborers should be periodically chosen to join the elite. In 1784, Jefferson wrote that, "...twenty of the best geniuses will be raked from the rubbish each year and be instructed in Greek, Latin, geography, and the higher branches of arithmetic at the public expense, creating a new generation of leaders without regard to wealth, birth, or accidental origin."[3] More than 200 years later, despite the long campaign to expand education in the public interest, the hierarchy envisioned by Jefferson remains the reality for a majority of Americans.

An Imagined Meritocracy

At its foundation, the United States was intended to serve as a great political "disruptor," eschewing the old world aristocracy in favor of a meritocracy where talent and hard work would be more important than an individual's class at birth. Stories of individuals who, though born without resources or status, managed to build economic empires, spread around the world in the early twentieth century and remain a staple of American mythology. The reality of life in the United States never reached the idyllic depictions of the Gilded Age. Those who are fortunate enough to climb the economic ladder from the lowest levels to the upper levels are, and have always been, the exceptions rather than the rule.[4]

At the turn of the *last* century, economic advancement was far more attainable than it is a century later and this has increased economic inequality. By the 2000s, the United States had the highest level of income inequality of any advanced nation. Between 1980 and 2016, income for the top one percent of Americans increased from an average of $428,000 to $1.3 million, while income for the bottom 50 percent of the population remained unchanged. In other words, spending power for America's elite more than doubled over the past 40 years, as spending power for more than half of Americans remained exactly the same. Furthermore, whereas the top 1% earned an estimated 10 percent of all income in the 1970s, in the 2000s the top 1% doubled their share of wealth, accounting for a staggering 20 percent of all income. Millennials, those born in the 1980s, are expected to have only a 50 percent chance of earning more than their parents, while those born in the 1940s had a 90 percent chance of achieving more wealth than the previous generation.[5]

Though it is widely agreed, across political ideologies, that wealth inequality is a serious problem, there is little agreement about how to address the issue. In general, the conservative approach is to invest in the wealthy and corporations out of the belief that these are the most productive facets of society and that, by investing in the wealthy, income will trickle down through the rest of the population. Years of economic data clearly show that progressive, liberal leadership leads to economic growth, while conservative administrations leave the nation with higher government debt and poverty.[6] When given greater freedom from taxation and governmental regulation, corporations do not generally "share the wealth" with their workers, but rather, transfer their profits to their shareholders and upper management. In 2016, the average CEO of a S&P 500 corporation, for instance, earned 335 times more than the average worker.[7]

In 2016, with the progressive majority in the United States divided between a moderate progressive approach (represented by Hillary Clinton) and a more radical progressive approach (represented by Bernie Sanders), the conservative minority was able to elect billionaire real estate developer Donald Trump. Trump, who was born into the nation's elite 1% and has focused his life on building his personal wealth, promised a radically different approach if elected president, but, through policy proposals and cabinet appointments demonstrated his intention to follow a standard conservative economic model. For instance, Trump's April 2017 tax reform proposal reduced taxes on corporations from 35 percent to 15 percent, and extended the tax break to real estate conglomerates like the Trump Corporation that previously paid higher tax rates.[8]

Trump appointed billionaire education activist Betsy DeVos to serve as Secretary of Education. DeVos supports a "voucher" system that allows parents to use federal funding to pay for private school, thus alleviating some of the financial burden faced by families who prefer private education. The prohibitively high cost of private school has traditionally meant that private schools cater primarily to the wealthy. In 2015, for instance, many of the 50 most prestigious private high schools in the United States charged annual tuition of over $42,000.[9] While DeVos contends that the voucher program will make private education possible for a larger share of American families, critics, supported by a wealth of research, argue that the voucher program will primarily benefit the wealthy, while reducing resources (both human and economic) for public education.[10]

Top of the Socioeconomic Class

The "achievement gap" is the term social scientists use to refer to a measurable disparity in academic performance/achievement between various groups in American society. There is an achievement gap between white students and their African-American or Latino/Hispanic peers and also a gulf between individuals at different ends of the income spectrum. For instance, a study from the Department of Education found that about 68 percent of 12th graders in high-poverty schools graduated in 2008, compared to 91 percent of students in low-poverty schools. Researchers believe that class and ethnic achievement gaps are related to a variety of subtle factors that greatly influence an individual's chances of educational success. These include a lack of resources in the home, disparities in parental education, and access to educated peers. There are systemic factors at play as well, such as student tracking, test bias, and discrimination, that exacerbate educational inequality.[11] By contrast, children in high-income families enjoy a wealth of advantages that help to prepare them, intellectually, emotionally, and economically, for each stage of their education and propel them further in their later career goals.

In many ways, the effects of class inequality are compounded by race. In the United States, black children are more likely to be born into poverty than white children, and less likely to escape poverty than white peers. The reasons for this are pervasive and complex. For instance, African Americans fare worse in the job market, regardless of education level, and they are more likely to be incarcerated than white offenders charged with the same crimes, thus destabilizing African-American homes and further disadvantaging children. The effects of prejudice and inequality are also transmitted through generations. African Americans are less likely to own homes and so less likely to transmit the benefits of economic stability, through home ownership and other factors, to their children. While two out of every three white people achieve middle class income by middle age, only 3 in 10 African Americans achieve the same. In 2017, there is a sense that many white Americans no longer believe that racial inequality is an important factor in American society. This thinking is incorrect and pernicious and ignores the many subtle and obvious ways that race continues to play a major role in achievement and prosperity for Americans.[12]

Higher Costs for Higher Education

The achievement gap in primary and secondary education is further compounded by the rising cost of higher education. In 2017, the average cost at a four-year, private university was $33,479, while the cost as a public institution was closer to $9,648. Imagining four years at an average public institution, a student would need at least $38,592 to obtain a bachelor's degree.[13] Each year, students and parents borrow around $100 billion to fund higher education and student debt was estimated at over $1.2 trillion in 2017.[14]

While there are grants and scholarships available for low-income, minority, and disadvantaged students, the rising cost is a severe problem that prohibits many individuals in the middle and working class from pursuing higher education. Increasingly, bachelor's degrees have become a prerequisite for entry-level or mid-level jobs, but the bachelor's degree is, in many cases, no longer sufficient to compete for higher-level positions. This leaves the majority of Americans facing the need to assume large amounts of debt before beginning their professional careers, without the guarantee that their investment will translate into a career that will allow them to repay their debt. Studies indicate that at least 40 percent of student borrowers are not able to repay their loans and default, which then damages their credit and makes it increasingly unlikely for individuals to afford home ownership and other investments that contribute to an individual's economic stability.[15]

This phenomena, what some have dubbed the student debt "crisis," occurs within an environment of predatory lenders, debt collectors, and refinancing companies that profit by exploiting a system that essentially works against student interest. To make matters worse, students in many cases are too inexperienced to make the best decisions when borrowing, refinancing, or planning for the future and so make ill-advised decisions that lead to debt default after college. With rising college costs and little in the way of income growth for most of the population, students each year pay more to finance an uncertain future while private loan companies like Sallie Mae, earn over $600 million per year.[16]

Always Forward

Public schools, the evolution of the common school system, make it possible for some, in each generation, to climb through the social strata, occasionally even from abject poverty to the elite. Social mobility is a hallmark of American identity and yet, for most Americans, such mobility is improbable because the economic system, created and dominated by the elite class, functions to preserve and maintain power within the elite and to marginalize forces that might destabilize the system. However, education fosters potential above all in that, through education, Americans at every level begin to see the inequities of American society. Ultimately, this means that there is the potential for future revolutions and social movements that could challenge class hierarchies and bring America closer to becoming the land of opportunity imagined by the nation's founders.

Micah L. Issitt

Works Used

Ansell, Susan. "Achievement Gap." *Education Week*. Aug 3 2004. Web. 30 Apr 2017.

Carey, Kevin. "Dismal Voucher Results Surprise Researchers as DeVos Era Begins." *The New York Times*. The New York Times Co. Feb 23 2017. Web. 30 Apr 2017.

Danner, Christi and Melissa Stanger. "The 50 Most Expensive Private High Schools in America." *Business Insider*. Web. 30 Apr 2017.

Davis, Julie Hirschfeld, Rappeport, Alan, Kelly, Kate, and Abrams, Rachel. "Trump's Tax Plan: Low Rate for Corporations, and for Companies Like His." *The New York Times*. The New York Times Co. Apr 25 2017. Web. 30 Apr 2017.

"Epilogue: Securing the Republic." The Founders' Constitution. Chapter 18, Doc. 16. *University of Chicago*. 1987. Web. 30 Apr 2017.

Henderson, A. Scott and Paul Lee Thomas. *James Baldwin: Challenging Authors*. Boston: Sense Press, 2014.

Kertscher, Tom. "Were the Founding Fathers 'Ordinary People'?" *Politifact*. Politifact. Jul 2 2015. Web. 5 May 2017.

Long, Heather. "U.S. Inequality Keeps Getting Uglier." *CNN Money*. Cable News Network. Dec 22 2016. Web. 30 Apr 2017.

Lorin, Janet. "Who's Profiting from $1.2 Trillion of Federal Student Loans?" *Bloomberg*. Bloomberg. Dec 11, 2015. Web. 30 Apr 2017.

McEachin, Andrew, Stecher, Brian, and Grace Evans. "Not Everyone Has a Choice." *U.S. News*. U.S. News and World Report. Aug 31, 2015. Web. 30 Apr 2017.

McElwee, Sean. "These 5 Chards Prove That the Economy Does Better Under Democratic Presidents." *Salon*. Salon Media Group, Inc. Dec 28 2015. Web. 30 Apr 2017.

Mitchell, Josh. "More Than 40% of Student Borrowers Aren't Making Payments." *The Wall Street Journal*. Dow Jones & Co. Apr 7 2016. Web. 30 Apr 2017.

Nicks, Denver. "CEOs Make 335 Times What Workers Earn." *Money*. Time, Inc. May 17 2016. Web. 30 Apr 2017.

Reeves, Richard V. "The Other American Dream: Social Mobility, Race and Opportunity." *Brookings*. Brookings Institution. Aug 28 2013. Web. 5 May 2017.

Schoen, John W. "Why Does a College Degree Cost So Much?" *CNBC*. NBC. 2017. Web. 30 Apr 2017.

Stiglitz, Joseph. "Equal Opportunity, Our National Myth." *The New York Times*. The New York Times Co. Feb 16, 2013. Web. 28 Apr 2017.

"Tuition and Fees and Room and Board over Time," *CollegeBoard*. Trends in Higher Education. 2017. Web. 30 Apr 2017.

Notes

1. Henderson and Thomas, *James Baldwin: Challenging Authors*, 142–43.
2. Kertscher, "Were the Founding Fathers 'Ordinary People'?"
3. "Epilogue: Securing the Republic," The Founders' Constitution.
4. Stiglitz, "Equal Opportunity, Out National Myth."
5. Long, "U.S. Inequality Keeps Getting Uglier."

6. McElwee, "These 5 Charts Prove That the Economy Does Better under Democratic Presidents."
7. Nicks, "CEOs Make 335 Times What Workers Earn."
8. Davis, Rappeport, Kelly, and Abrams, "Trump's Tax Plan: Low Rate for Corporations, and for Companies Like His."
9. Danner and Stanger, "The 50 Most Expensive Private High Schools in America."
10. McEachin, Stecher, and Evans, "Not Everyone Has a Choice."
11. Ansell, "Achievement Gap."
12. Reeves, "The Other American Dream: Social Mobility, Race and Opportunity."
13. "Tuition and Fees and Room and Board over Time," *College Board*.
14. Schoen, "Why Does a College Degree Cost So Much?"
15. Mitchell, "More Than 40% of Student Borrowers Aren't Making Payments."
16. Lorin, "Who's Profiting from $1.2 Trillion of Federal Student Loans."

College Calculus: What's the Real Value of Higher Education?

By John Cassidy
The New Yorker, September 7, 2015

If there is one thing most Americans have been able to agree on over the years, it is that getting an education, particularly a college education, is a key to human betterment and prosperity. The consensus dates back at least to 1636, when the legislature of the Massachusetts Bay Colony established Harvard College as America's first institution of higher learning. It extended through the establishment of "land-grant colleges" during and after the Civil War, the passage of the GI Bill during the Second World War, the expansion of federal funding for higher education during the Great Society era, and President Obama's efforts to make college more affordable. Already, the cost of higher education has become a big issue in the 2016 Presidential campaign. Three Democratic candidates—Hillary Clinton, Martin O'Malley, and Bernie Sanders—have offered plans to reform the student-loan program and make college more accessible.

Promoters of higher education have long emphasized its role in meeting civic needs. The Puritans who established Harvard were concerned about a shortage of clergy; during the Progressive Era, John Dewey insisted that a proper education would make people better citizens, with enlarged moral imaginations. Recently, as wage stagnation and rising inequality have emerged as serious problems, the economic arguments for higher education have come to the fore. "Earning a post-secondary degree or credential is no longer just a pathway to opportunity for a talented few," the White House Web site states. "Rather, it is a prerequisite for the growing jobs of the new economy." Commentators and academic economists have claimed that college doesn't merely help individuals get higher-paying jobs; it raises wages throughout the economy and helps ameliorate rising inequality. In an influential 2008 book, *The Race Between Education and Technology*, the Harvard economists Claudia Goldin and Lawrence F. Katz argued that technological progress has dramatically increased the demand for skilled workers, and that, in recent decades, the American educational system has failed to meet the challenge by supplying enough graduates who can carry out the tasks that a high-tech economy requires. "Not so long ago, the American economy grew rapidly and wages grew in tandem, with education playing a large, positive role in both," they wrote in a subsequent paper. "The challenge now is to revitalize education-based mobility."

The "message from the media, from the business community, and even from many parts of the government has been that a college degree is more important than ever in order to have a good career," Peter Cappelli, a professor of management at Wharton, notes in his informative and refreshingly skeptical new book, *Will College Pay Off?* (PublicAffairs). "As a result, families feel even more pressure to send their kids to college. This is at a time when more families find those costs to be a serious burden." During recent decades, tuition and other charges have risen sharply—many colleges charge more than fifty thousand dollars a year in tuition and fees. Even if you factor in the expansion of financial aid, Cappelli reports, "students in the United States pay about four times more than their peers in countries elsewhere."

Despite the increasing costs—and the claims about a shortage of college graduates—the number of people attending and graduating from four-year educational institutions keeps going up. In the 2000-01 academic year, American colleges awarded almost 1.3 million bachelor's degrees. A decade later, the figure had jumped nearly forty per cent, to more than 1.7 million. About seventy per cent of all high-school graduates now go on to college, and half of all Americans between the ages of twenty-five and thirty-four have a college degree. That's a big change. In 1980, only one in six Americans twenty-five and older were college graduates. Fifty years ago, it was fewer than one in ten. To cater to all the new students, colleges keep expanding and adding courses, many of them vocationally inclined. At Kansas State, undergraduates can major in Bakery Science and Management or Wildlife and Outdoor Enterprise Management. They can minor in Unmanned Aircraft Systems or Pet Food Science. Oklahoma State offers a degree in Fire Protection and Safety Engineering and Technology. At Utica College, you can major in Economic Crime Detection.

In the fast-growing for-profit college sector, which now accounts for more than ten per cent of all students, vocational degrees are the norm. DeVry University—which last year taught more than sixty thousand students, at more than seventy-five campuses—offers majors in everything from multimedia design and development to health-care administration. On its Web site, DeVry boasts, "In 2013, 90% of DeVry University associate and bachelor's degree grads actively seeking employment had careers in their field within six months of graduation." That sounds impressive—until you notice that the figure includes those graduates who had jobs in their field before graduation. (Many

DeVry students are working adults who attend college part-time to further their careers.) Nor is the phrase "in their field" clearly defined. "Would you be okay rolling the dice on a degree in communications based on information like that?" Cappelli writes. He notes that research by the nonprofit National Association of Colleges and Employers found that, in the same year, just 6.5 per cent of graduates with communications degrees were offered jobs in the field. It may be unfair to single out DeVry, which is one of the more reputable for-profit education providers. But the example illustrates Cappelli's larger point: many of the claims that are made about higher education don't stand up to scrutiny.

It is certainly true that college has been life changing for most people and a tremendous financial investment for many of them," Cappelli writes. "It is also true that for some people, it has been financially crippling. . . .The world of college education is different now than it was a generation ago, when many of the people driving policy decisions on education went to college, and the theoretical ideas about why college should pay off do not comport well with the reality."

No idea has had more influence on education policy than the notion that colleges teach their students specific, marketable skills, which they can use to get a good job. Economists refer to this as the "human capital" theory of education, and for the past twenty or thirty years it has gone largely unchallenged. If you've completed a two-year associate's degree, you've got more "human capital" than a high-school graduate. And if you've completed a four-year bachelor's degree you've got more "human capital" than someone who attended a community college. Once you enter the labor market, the theory says, you will be rewarded with a better job, brighter career prospects, and higher wages.

There's no doubt that college graduates earn more money, on average, than people who don't have a degree. And for many years the so-called "college wage premium" grew. In 1970, according to a recent study by researchers at the Federal Reserve Bank of New York, people with a bachelor's degree earned about sixty thousand dollars a year, on average, and people with a high-school diploma earned about forty-five thousand dollars. Thirty-five years later, in 2005, the average earnings of college graduates had risen to more than seventy thousand dollars, while high-school graduates had seen their earnings fall slightly. (All these figures are inflation-adjusted.) The fact that the college wage premium went up at a time when the supply of graduates was expanding significantly seemed to confirm the Goldin-Katz theory that technological change was creating an ever-increasing demand for workers with a lot of human capital.

With rapid advances in processing power, data analysis, voice recognition, and other forms of artificial intelligence, computers can perform tasks that were previously carried out by college graduates, such as analyzing trends, translating foreign-language documents, and filing tax returns.

During the past decade or so, however, a number of things have happened that don't easily mesh with that theory. If college graduates remain in short supply, their wages should still be rising. But they aren't. In 2001, according to the Economic Policy Institute, a liberal think tank in Washington, workers with undergraduate degrees (but not graduate degrees) earned, on average, \$30.05 an hour; last year, they earned \$29.55 an hour. Other sources show even more dramatic falls. "Between 2001 and 2013, the average wage of workers with a bachelor's degree declined 10.3 percent, and the average wage of those with an associate's degree declined 11.1 percent," the New York Fed reported in its study. Wages have been falling most steeply of all among newly minted college graduates. And jobless rates have been rising. In 2007, 5.5 per cent of college graduates under the age of twenty-five were out of work. Today, the figure is close to nine per cent. If getting a bachelor's degree is meant to guarantee entry to an arena in which jobs are plentiful and wages rise steadily, the education system has been failing for some time.

And, while college graduates are still doing a lot better than nongraduates, some studies show that the earnings gap has stopped growing. The figures need careful parsing. If you lump college graduates in with people with advanced degrees, the picture looks brighter. But almost all the recent gains have gone to folks with graduate degrees. "The four-year-degree premium has remained flat over the past decade," the Federal Reserve Bank of Cleveland reported. And one of the main reasons it went up in the first place wasn't that college graduates were enjoying significantly higher wages. It was that the earnings of nongraduates were falling.

Many students and their families extend themselves to pay for a college education out of fear of falling into the low-wage economy. That's perfectly understandable. But how sound an investment is it? One way to figure this out is to treat a college degree like a stock or a bond and compare the cost of obtaining one with the accumulated returns that it generates over the years. (In this case, the returns come in the form of wages over and above those earned by people who don't hold degrees.) When the research firm PayScale did this a few years ago, it found that the average inflation-adjusted return on a college education is about seven per cent, which is a bit lower than the historical rate of return on the stock market. Cappelli cites this study along with one from the Hamilton Project, a Washington-based research group that came up with a much higher figure—about fifteen per cent—but by assuming, for example, that all college students graduate in four years. (In fact, the four-year graduation rate for full-time, first-degree students is less than forty per cent, and the six-year graduation rate is less than sixty per cent.)

These types of studies, and there are lots of them, usually find that the financial benefits of getting a college degree are much larger than the financial costs. But Cappelli points out that for parents and students the average figures may not mean much, because they disguise enormous differences in outcomes from school to school. He cites a survey, carried out by PayScale for Businessweek in 2012, that showed that students who attend MIT, Caltech, and Harvey Mudd College enjoy an annual return of more than ten per cent on their "investment." But the survey also found almost two hundred colleges where students, on average, never fully recouped the costs of their education. "The big news about the payoff from college should be the incredible variation in it across colleges," Cappelli writes. "Looking at the actual return on the costs of attending college, careful analyses suggest that the payoff from many college programs—as much as one in four—is actually negative. Incredibly, the schools seem to add nothing to the market value of the students."

To what purpose does college really serve for students and employers? Before the human-capital theory became so popular, there was another view of higher education—as, in part, a filter, or screening device, that sorted individuals according to their aptitudes and conveyed this information to businesses and other hiring institutions. By completing a four-year degree, students could signal to potential employers that they had a certain level of cognitive competence and could carry out assigned tasks and work in a group setting. But a college education didn't necessarily imbue students with specific work skills that employers needed, or make them more productive.

Kenneth Arrow, one of the giants of twentieth-century economics, came up with this account, and if you take it seriously you can't assume that it's always a good thing to persuade more people to go to college. If almost everybody has a college degree, getting one doesn't differentiate you from the pack. To get the job you want, you might have to go to a fancy (and expensive) college, or get a higher degree. Education turns into an arms race, which primarily benefits the arms manufacturers—in this case, colleges and universities.

The screening model isn't very fashionable these days, partly because it seems perverse to suggest that education doesn't boost productivity. But there's quite a bit of evidence that seems to support Arrow's theory. In recent years, more jobs have come to demand a college degree as an entry requirement, even though the demands of the jobs haven't changed much. Some nursing positions are on the list, along with jobs for executive secretaries, salespeople, and distribution managers. According to one study, just twenty per cent of executive assistants and insurance-claims clerks have college degrees but more than forty-five per cent of the job openings in the field require one. "This suggests that employers may be relying on a B.A. as a broad recruitment filter that may or may not correspond to specific capabilities needed to do the job," the study concluded.

It is well established that students who go to élite colleges tend to earn more than graduates of less selective institutions. But is this because Harvard and Princeton do a better job of teaching valuable skills than other places, or because employers believe that they get more talented students to begin with? An exercise carried out by Lauren Rivera, of the Kellogg School of Management, at Northwestern, strongly suggests that it's the latter. Rivera interviewed more than a hundred recruiters from investment banks, law firms, and management consulting firms, and she found that they recruited almost exclusively from the very top-ranked schools, and simply ignored most other applicants. The recruiters didn't pay much attention to things like grades and majors. "It was not the content of education that elite employers valued but rather its prestige," Rivera concluded.

If higher education serves primarily as a sorting mechanism, that might help explain another disturbing development: the tendency of many college graduates to take jobs that don't require college degrees. Practically everyone seems to know a well-educated young person who is working in a bar or a mundane clerical job, because he or she can't find anything better. Doubtless, the Great Recession and its aftermath are partly to blame. But something deeper, and more lasting, also seems to be happening.

In the Goldin-Katz view of things, technological progress generates an ever-increasing need for highly educated, highly skilled workers. But, beginning in about 2000, for reasons that are still not fully understood, the pace of job creation in high-paying, highly skilled fields slowed significantly. To demonstrate this, three Canadian economists, Paul Beaudry, David A. Green, and Benjamin M. Sand, divided the U.S. workforce into a hundred occupations, ranked by their average wages, and looked at how employment has changed in each category. Since 2000, the economists showed, the demand for highly educated workers declined, while job growth in low-paying occupations increased strongly. "High-skilled workers have moved down the occupational ladder and have begun to perform jobs traditionally performed by lower-skilled workers," they concluded, thus "pushing low-skilled workers even further down the occupational ladder."

Increasingly, the competition for jobs is taking place in areas of the labor market where college graduates didn't previously tend to compete. As Beaudry, Green, and Sand put it, "having a B.A. is less about obtaining access to high paying managerial and technology jobs and more about beating out less educated workers for the Barista or clerical job."

Even many graduates in science, technology, engineering, and mathematics—the so-called stem subjects, which receive so much official encouragement—are having a tough time getting the jobs they'd like. Cappelli reports that only about a fifth of recent graduates with stem degrees got jobs that made use of that training. "The evidence for recent grads suggests clearly that there is no overall shortage of stem grads," he writes.

Why is this happening? The short answer is that nobody knows for sure. One theory is that corporate cost-cutting, having thinned the ranks of workers on the factory floor and in routine office jobs, is now targeting supervisors, managers, and other highly educated people. Another theory is that technological progress, after favoring highly educated workers for a long time, is now turning on them. With rapid advances in processing power, data analysis, voice recognition, and other forms of artificial intelligence, computers can perform tasks that were previously carried out by college graduates, such as analyzing trends, translating foreign-language documents, and filing tax returns. In "The Second Machine Age" (Norton), the MIT professors Erik Brynjolfsson and Andrew McAfee sketch a future where computers will start replacing doctors, lawyers, and many other highly educated professionals. "As digital labor becomes more pervasive, capable, and powerful," they write, "companies will be increasingly unwilling to pay people wages that they'll accept, and that will allow them to maintain the standard of living to which they've been accustomed."

Cappelli stresses the change in corporate hiring patterns. In the old days, Fortune 500 companies such as General Motors, Citigroup, and IBM took on large numbers of college graduates and trained them for a lifetime at the company. But corporations now invest less in education and training, and, instead of promoting someone, or finding someone in the company to fill a specialized role, they tend to hire from outside. Grooming the next generation of leadership is much less of a concern. "What employers want from college graduates now is the same thing they want from applicants who have been out of school for years, and that is job skills and the ability to contribute now," Cappelli writes. "That change is fundamental, and it is the reason that getting a good job out of college is now such a challenge."

Obtaining a vocational degree or certificate is one strategy that many students employ to make themselves attractive to employers, and, on the face of it, this seems sensible. If you'd like to be a radiology technician, shouldn't you get a B.A. in radiology? If you want to run a bakery, why not apply to Kansas State and sign up for that major in Bakery Science? But narrowly focused degrees are risky. "If you graduate in a year when gambling is up and the casinos like your casino management degree, you probably have hit it big," Cappelli writes. "If they aren't hiring when you graduate, you may be even worse off getting a first job with that degree anywhere else precisely because it was so tuned to that group of employers." During the dot-com era, enrollment in computer-science and information-technology programs rose sharply. After the bursting of the stock-market bubble, many of these graduates couldn't find work. "Employers who say that we need more engineers or IT grads are not promising to hire them when they graduate in four years," Cappelli notes. "Pushing kids into a field like health care because someone believes there is a need there now will not guarantee that they all get jobs and, if they do, that those jobs will be as good as workers in that field have now."

So what's the solution? Some people believe that online learning will provide a viable low-cost alternative to a live-in college education. Bernie Sanders would get rid of tuition fees at public universities, raising some of the funds with a new tax on financial transactions. Clinton and O'Malley would also expand federal support for state universities, coupling this funding with lower interest rates on student loans and incentives for colleges to hold down costs. Another approach is to direct more students and resources to two-year community colleges and other educational institutions that cost less than four-year colleges. President Obama recently called for all qualified high-school students to be guaranteed a place in community college, and for tuition fees to be eliminated. Such policies would reverse recent history. In a new book, *Learning by Doing: The Real Connection between Innovation, Wages, and Wealth* (Yale), James Bessen, a technology entrepreneur who also teaches at Boston University School of Law, points out that "the policy trend over the last decade has been to starve community colleges in order to feed four-year colleges, especially private research universities."

Some of the discrepancies are glaring. Richard Vedder, who teaches economics at Ohio University, calculated that in 2010 Princeton, which had an endowment of close to fifteen billion dollars, received state and federal benefits equivalent to roughly fifty thousand dollars per student, whereas the nearby College of New Jersey got benefits of just two thousand dollars per student. There are sound reasons for rewarding excellence and sponsoring institutions that do important scientific research. But is a twenty-five-to-one difference in government support really justified?

Perhaps the strongest argument for caring about higher education is that it can increase social mobility, regardless of whether the human-capital theory or the signalling theory is correct. A recent study by researchers at the Federal Reserve Bank of San Francisco showed that children who are born into households in the poorest fifth of the income distribution are six times as likely to reach the top fifth if they graduate from college. Providing access to college for more kids from deprived backgrounds helps nurture talents that might otherwise go to waste, and it's the right thing to do. (Of course, if college attendance were practically universal, having a degree would send a weaker signal to employers.) But increasing the number of graduates seems unlikely to reverse the over-all decline of high-paying jobs, and it won't resolve the income-inequality problem, either. As the economist Lawrence Summers and two colleagues showed in a recent simulation, even if we magically summoned up college degrees for a tenth of all the working-age American men who don't have them—by historical standards, a big boost in college-graduation rates—we'd scarcely change the existing concentration of income at the very top of the earnings distribution, where CEOs and hedge-fund managers live.

Being more realistic about the role that college degrees play would help families and politicians make better choices. It could also help us appreciate the actual merits of a traditional broad-based education, often called a liberal-arts education, rather than trying to reduce everything to an economic cost-benefit analysis. "To be clear, the idea is not that there will be a big financial payoff to a liberal arts degree," Cappelli writes. "It is that there is no guarantee of a payoff from very practical, work-based degrees either, yet that is all those degrees promise. For liberal arts, the claim is different and seems more accurate, that it will enrich your life and provide lessons that extend beyond any individual job. There are centuries of experience providing support for that notion."

Print Citations

CMS: Cassidy, John. "College Calculus: What's the Real Value of Higher Education?" In *The Reference Shelf: Education Reform*, edited by Betsy Maury, 123–130. Ipswich, MA: H.W. Wilson, 2017.

MLA: Cassidy, John. "College Calculus: What's the Real Value of Higher Education?" *The Reference Shelf: Education Reform*. Ed. Betsy Maury. Ipswich: H.W. Wilson, 2017. 123–130. Print.

APA: Cassidy, J. (2017). College calculus: What's the real value of higher education? In Betsy Maury (Ed.), *The reference shelf: Education reform* (pp. 123–130). Ipswich, MA: H.W. Wilson. (Original work published 2015)

Skipping Class

The Economist, January 28, 2017

Reading John F. Kennedy's application to Harvard College is a study in mediocrity. The former president graduated from high school with middling marks and penned just five sentences to explain why he belonged at Harvard. The only bit that expressed a clear thought was also the most telling: "To be a 'Harvard man' is an enviable distinction, and one that I sincerely hope I shall attain." America's premier universities, long the gatekeepers for the elite, have changed greatly since their days as glorified finishing schools for scions. But perhaps not as much as thought.

New data on American universities and their role in economic mobility—culled from 30m tax returns—published by Raj Chetty, an economist at Stanford University, and colleagues show that some colleges do a better job of boosting poor students up the income ladder than others. Previously, the best data available showed only average earnings by college. For the first time, the entire earnings distribution of a college's graduates—and how that relates to parental income—is now known.

These data show that graduates of elite universities with single-digit admissions rates and billion-dollar endowments are still the most likely to join the top 1% (though having wealthy parents improves the odds). And despite recent efforts to change, their student bodies are still overwhelmingly wealthy.

Princeton University is the best at producing plutocrats—23% of its graduates end up as one-percenters, about the same as the share of its students who hail from equally wealthy households. Following closely are the University of Pennsylvania, Harvard and Stanford where this rich-in, rich-out model works well.

No matter their family income, students at America's most prestigious universities have a roughly equal chance of reaching the top 20% of the income distribution. Reaching the top 1% is a different story altogether. In this case, having a trust fund appears handy. Even if a student attends an elite university, the chances of eventually reaching the economic elite increase greatly with the wealth of parents. A rich student, hailing from a household in the top 5%, has about a 60% greater chance of reaching the income summit than a poor student, whose parents were in the bottom 5%, even if they both attended one of America's most esteemed universities. Elite financial and consulting firms, which often recruit for highly paid positions exclusively at Ivy League-calibre schools and rely on networking, may bear some of the blame.

Breaking into the upper-middle class is a good bit easier, our analysis of Mr Chetty et al's data shows. Three of the important factors in determining the average earnings of graduates are test scores, where the college is located and what subjects the alumni studied. Those who do not get into Yale should feel relieved that a clear path to the upper-middle still exists: study a technical subject like engineering or pharmacology, and move to a large city. Graduates from lesser-known colleges focusing on science, technology and maths like Kettering University and the Stevens Institute of Technology earn, on average, just as much as their Ivy League peers.

Such colleges however, host just a fraction of America's undergraduates. To identify which colleges are the best "engines of upward mobility," Mr Chetty and his collaborators rank universities on their ability to move large numbers of students from the poorest 20% of the income distribution to the top 20%. The best at this are mid-tier public universities like the City University of New York and California State systems.

Elite universities justify steep rises in tuition fees by pointing to their generous financial-aid programmes for poor students. Harvard's most recent fund-raising campaign passed the $7bn mark, partially by focusing on expanding financial aid. Parents with incomes under $65,000 are not expected to pay a cent. But the data show that, from 1999 to 2013, poor students' access to the university has stayed stubbornly low (more than half of Harvard students came from the richest 10% of households).

These data show that graduates of elite universities with single-digit admissions rates and billion-dollar endowments are still the most likely to join the top 1% (though having wealthy parents improves the odds).

Just 2% of Princetonians came from households at the bottom 20% of the income distribution, compared with 3.2% from the top 0.1% (corresponding to an annual income of more than $2.3m). Put another way, students from this zenith of the income scale are 315 times likelier to attend Princeton than those from the bottom 20%. Only Colby College, a small liberal-arts college in Maine, has a worse ratio.

The vast majority of talented low-income students do not apply to elite universities—despite the fact that they are often more affordable than their local colleges, one study shows. But the other problem is social. Poorer students tend to have worse test scores and thinner CV's—some must work or baby-sit instead of studying. Elite private universities—which already spend millions on outreach programmes—can only do so much to push against a public education system where quality and income go together.

Harvard and Princeton are not alone: the same trend held true for all elite universities in the country. "These numbers are not where we'd like them to be," says Stu Schmill, dean of admissions for the Massachusetts Institute of Technology (MIT).

Over the past decades, admissions offices' devotion to affirmative action brought an increase in black and Hispanic attendance at elite colleges and universities.

But legacy admissions, which give preferential treatment to family members of alumni, exacerbate the imbalance. Of Harvard's most recently admitted class, 27% of students had a relative who also attended. There's evidence that this system favours the already wealthy. MIT and the California Institute of Technology, two elite schools with no legacy preferences, have much fewer students who hail from the ranks of the super-rich.

"The dirty secret of elite colleges is that for all the positive talk about the importance of racial diversity, low-income students of all races are essentially shut out," says Richard Kahlenberg of the Century Foundation, a think-tank. Despite all the spending on financial aid, the Ivies are still doing a poor job of finding and educating bright, poor students.

Print Citations

CMS: "Skipping Class: New Data Show That Joining the 1% Remains Unsettlingly Hereditary." In *The Reference Shelf: Education Reform*, edited by Betsy Maury, 131–133. Ipswich, MA: H.W. Wilson, 2017.

MLA: "Skipping Class: New Data Show That Joining the 1% Remains Unsettlingly Hereditary." *The Reference Shelf: Education Reform*. Ed. Betsy Maury. Ipswich: H.W. Wilson, 2017. 131–133. Print.

APA: The Economist. (2017). Skipping class: New data show that joining the 1% remains unsettlingly hereditary. In Betsy Maury (Ed.), *The reference shelf: Education reform* (pp. 131–133). Ipswich, MA: H.W. Wilson. (Original work published 2017)

Student Debt Payback Far Worse Than Believed

By Andrea Fuller
The Wall Street Journal, January 18, 2017

Many more students have defaulted on or failed to pay back their college loans than the U.S. government previously believed. Last Friday, the Education Department released a memo saying that it had overstated student loan repayment rates at most colleges and trade schools and provided updated numbers.

When the *Wall Street Journal* analyzed the new numbers, the data revealed that the Department previously had inflated the repayment rates for 99.8% of all colleges and trade schools in the country. The new analysis shows that at more than 1,000 colleges and trade schools, or about a quarter of the total, at least half the students had defaulted or failed to pay down at least $1 on their debt within seven years.

The changes could have implications for federal policy. Some lawmakers have endorsed the idea of punishing colleges if enough students aren't paying back the loans.

A spokeswoman for the Education Department said that the problem resulted from a technical programming error. This isn't the first time data problems have affected the Education Department. A recent government report criticized how the department tracks information including the budgetary implications of student loan forgiveness.

"This is a quality control issue with a Department of Education that has been facing criticism already for other data issues," Robert Kelchen, an assistant professor of higher education at Seton Hall University. The department "needs to be regularly audited so these issues can be discovered sooner." The student loan repayment rates were originally released in 2015 as part of the Obama administration's College Scorecard, which followed an aborted attempt to rate colleges and tie federal funds to those ratings.

Revised Education Department numbers show at more than 1,000 schools, at least half of students defaulted or failed to pay down debt within 7 years.

At the time, the *Journal* reported that at 347 colleges and vocational schools, more than half of students had defaulted or failed to pay down their debt within seven years. Those figures were based on students who were supposed to start repaying loans in 2006 and 2007.

In September, the Department released data tracking students who should have begun repayment in 2007 and 2008, and that number rose to 477. But with the updated number released last week, that number grew to 1,029.

No college saw its repayment rate improve under the revision, and some schools saw their seven-year repayment rates fall by as much as 29 percentage points. The University of Memphis had one of the largest drops in its repayment rate following the recalculation. Previously, the Department said that 67% of its students were repaying loans within seven years of entering the repayment period. That number fell to 47% after the recalculation. In a statement, the school said it "was not contacted by or made aware of the data changes" from the Education Department.

"Given the magnitude of the numerical changes in the report released by the Department of Education, the University of Memphis will be challenging the accuracy of the newly adjusted data," the statement said.

Print Citations

CMS: Fuller, Andrea. "Student Debt Payback Far Worse Than Believed." In *The Reference Shelf: Education Reform*, edited by Betsy Maury, 134–135. Ipswich, MA: H.W. Wilson, 2017.

MLA: Fuller, Andrea. "Student Debt Payback Far Worse Than Believed." *The Reference Shelf: Education Reform*. Ed. Betsy Maury. Ipswich: H.W. Wilson, 2017. 134–135. Print.

APA: Fuller, A. (2017). Student debt payback far worse than believed. In Betsy Maury (Ed.), *The reference shelf: Education reform* (pp. 134–135). Ipswich, MA: H.W. Wilson. (Original work published 2017)

Sheila Bair's One Weird Trick to Make Her College Less White

By Shahien Nasiripour
Bloomberg, September 28, 2016

When former Federal Deposit Insurance Corp. chair Sheila Bair took over Washington College last year, she immediately started making changes. One of her goals was to find innovative ways to reduce her students' debt burden. But she also tackled a related and not insignificant problem: the overwhelming whiteness of her campus.

Three of every four students on the school's small rural campus in Maryland are white. It's not an unusual statistic at the nation's top schools, where black students in particular rarely make up more than 8 percent of undergraduates, Education Department data show.

But for students of color, life at a mostly white college like Washington can be profoundly isolating. "The way people of color process negative racial experiences is having family and friends to talk to about them," said Deborah Faye Carter, an associate professor at the School of Educational Studies at Claremont Graduate University. When there's no community, there's no support.

That makes students of color more likely to drop out: As many as 20 percent of college students from historically underrepresented communities who drop out of school do so because they feel like they don't belong, said Terrell Strayhorn, a professor and director of the Center for Higher Education Enterprise at the Ohio State University.

Washington College is located in Kent County, home to a public school system that was among the last in the nation to desegregate following the landmark Supreme Court ruling in *Brown v. Board of Education*, according to the C.V. Starr Center for the Study of the American Experience at Washington College. Vestiges of that past remain in Chestertown, where some black students have said they've felt like they're being watched while frequenting shops in town, said Alisha Knight, a professor at Washington College since 2004.

"My first year here I would commute to work, and every day I would see this huge rebel flag waving in front of a house," Knight said. "Every day, for the first year I was working here, I would think, Where am I going, where am I working, what are the attitudes of the people in this community, and what are they saying to me by having this flag?"

What if the school allowed certain students to apply as part of a group?

The Washington faculty and board spent years discussing ways to increase diversity on campus—in part because they thought a less homogeneous student body would make the school more appealing to prospective freshmen, said Larry Culp, chairman of the school's board.

Bair said she wanted to diversify the campus for its own sake. Making college more accessible to more students, particularly minority students from low-income households, was a "personal passion of mine," she said.

She remembered struggling as an undergraduate at the University of Kansas because she lacked a support network there. Perhaps she would've been less miserable had she attended with a friend from her hometown, she wondered.

Bair had spent five years chairing the FDIC, where she had gotten to know Senator Elizabeth Warren (D-Mass.), then a Harvard professor. Before starting her new job, Bair asked Warren for her thoughts on Washington College's diversity problem. What if the school allowed certain students to apply as part of a group?

Warren told Bair to check out the Manhattan-based Posse Foundation. Founded in 1989 by eventual John D. and Catherine T. MacArthur Foundation "genius grant" recipient Deborah Bial, Posse identifies disadvantaged students from urban public high schools who may be overlooked by top colleges—relatively low standardized test scores are often a culprit—but would succeed if they had more support.

Posse then organizes students in small groups—"posses"—that meet weekly for eight months during their senior year to help them get ready for college life. They're then placed at about 57 partner colleges across the country in groups of 10, with four-year scholarships that cover their tuition. Living expenses are covered if students' families can't afford it. Ninety percent graduate from college.

The program aims to diversify the nation's most prestigious schools so they're more representative of the country, Bial said. "The most selective colleges have made an incredible effort, especially over the past couple of decades, to focus on recruiting more diverse student bodies," Bial said. "But do I think we still have a long way to go? Yes."

Bial told Bair that if she were to implement her plan, she'd need to make sure that her campus didn't view these students as needing extra help. Rather, Bial told her, they're outstanding students who simply were born into challenging financial circumstances. The students would have to be celebrated as scholars, Bair recalled. Posse describes its students as future leaders.

Bair spoke with some high school seniors and college graduates who told her the group application plan was a good idea. Her board, while supportive, questioned her about whether the initiative—to be called "George's Brigade" after George Washington, the school's namesake—would increase the rate at which first-generation students end up graduating. Bair said it would.

The program, aimed at but not limited to students of color, went into action. Washington College recruited students from urban high schools, partnering with organizations such as the Simon Family Foundation and the federally funded Upward Bound to identify promising applicants. In some cases, Bair said, the school slightly eased its traditional admissions standards for certain students' friends, to allow them both to enroll.

This fall, 16 students enrolled as part of George's Brigade. Their average GPA is above 3.5, Bair said, and seven of them are from Baltimore. Ten of the 16 enrolled with a friend; the remaining six were offered the option but chose to enroll alone. Their costs to attend Washington College are fully covered, and a condition of their enrollment limits annual borrowing, should they need it, to $2,500.

The school also promises extra support throughout their time on campus in the form of seminars and mentoring. Donors, including San Francisco-based Bank of the West, a unit of BNP Paribas SA, are covering slightly less than half the cost while the school and federal grants cover the rest.

Bair's buddy system could help students who might otherwise feel alienated at the overwhelmingly white, rural campus. "Being in school with friends will affirm your own sense that you belong in college," said Strayhorn. Carter said that some George's Brigade students may be aided by simply having someone on campus like them who could tell them, "Yes, I understand your experience and I support you."

That will be especially important at Washington College. "One of our concerns is not just to help them feel comfortable at college but also in this part of the state," said Knight, who is serving as a mentor to one of the George's Brigade students. "When examining the challenges, you have to look at the context of where the college is located."

Strayhorn, Carter, and other diversity scholars agreed that the program showed promise, but was only a start. "When we talk about diversity, we talk about the whole institution," said Carter. "The fabric of the institution needs to be reexamined ... extending to the coursework, activities, the curriculum."Still, "the payoff [of the George's Brigade program] could be pretty significant over the long haul," Strayhorn said.

Bair is already seeing results. This year's freshman class at Washington College is the most diverse in the school's 234-year history. Close to 19 percent of freshmen are black or Hispanic, compared with 7 percent of the previous year's entire student body, according to the school and Education Department data.

"She's working on an issue that so many institutions of higher education struggle with," Bial said of Bair. "It's so important."

Print Citations

CMS: Nasiripour, Shahien. "Sheila Bair's One Weird Trick to Make Her College Less White." In *The Reference Shelf: Education Reform*, edited by Betsy Maury, 136–139. Ipswich, MA: H.W. Wilson, 2017.

MLA: Nasiripour, Shahien. "Sheila Bair's One Weird Trick to Make Her College Less White." *The Reference Shelf: Education Reform*. Ed. Betsy Maury. Ipswich: H.W. Wilson, 2017. 136–139. Print.

APA: Nasiripour, S. (2017). Sheila Bair's one weird trick to make her college less white. In Betsy Maury (Ed.), *The reference shelf: Education reform* (pp. 136–139). Ipswich, MA: H.W. Wilson. (Original work published 2016)

Bernie Sanders Just Introduced His Free College Tuition Plan

By George Zornick
The Nation, April 3, 2017

President Donald Trump doesn't appear willing nor interested in addressing astronomical student-debt levels, which long since crested above $1 trillion. In fact, his administration has made it easier for for-profit colleges to rip off students, and recently scrapped Obama-era regulations that limited rates loan-guarantee agencies can charge people who defaulted on student loans. His budget also proposed cutting $5 billion in higher-education funding for low-income Americans. Perhaps that's not surprising from a president who just finalized a $25 million settlement stemming from his scam for-profit university.

That's a financial tragedy for the millions who hold student-loan debt and the students who will matriculate while Trump is president. But Trump's unwillingness to even motion toward a student-debt plan creates a massive political opening for Democrats.

Senator Bernie Sanders stepped into that breach Monday afternoon, introducing a bill with Senator Elizabeth Warren, Representative Keith Ellison, and several other members of Congress. The College for All Act aims to eliminate tuition and fees at public four-year colleges and universities for students from families that make up to $125,000 per year. The bill would make community college tuition-free for all income levels.

Clearly the bill will go nowhere in a Republican Congress, and with Trump in the White House. But Sanders and several of the co-sponsors clearly see the bill as a valuable organizing tool. "Our job is to bring forward a progressive agenda," said Sanders. "Our job now is to go out in every state in this country.... We can win this fight when millions of Americans stand up and demand this legislation."

"We need organized events at every college campus across the country," said Representative Pramila Jayapal, a Sanders-backed candidate who ran last year on a pledge to introduce this bill in the House.

One year ago today, tuition-free college was a catalyst of Sanders's presidential campaign, where he captured close to three-quarters of the under-35 vote during the primary. The College for All Act is substantially the same as his campaign plan, though the income cut-off is new. Hillary Clinton frequently assailed the Sanders plan's lack of an income limit, often offering some variation of the line "I don't think taxpayers should be paying to send Donald Trump's kids to college," as she said during one debate.

"Our job is to bring forward a progressive agenda," said Sanders. "Our job now is to go out in every state in this country. . . . We can win this fight when millions of Americans stand up and demand this legislation."

When Clinton released an updated tuition plan after the primary was over, it borrowed many of Sanders's subsidized-tuition elements, but also had a $125,000 income threshold. This is essentially what Sanders is now proposing, though Clinton's proposal made the initial cutoff $85,000 per year and raised it incrementally to $125,000. The College for All Act starts at $125,000 outright. (This is similar to a plan New York Governor Andrew Cuomo introduced this year, which Sanders also backed.)

The act would have the government pay 67 percent of tuition subsidies at public colleges and universities, while asking state and tribal governments to pay the other third. Sanders's office pegs the cost of the legislation at $600 billion, and it would be financed by a tax on Wall Street speculation.

The legislation also weaves in several other progressive higher-education proposals. It ends the federal government's ability to profit from student loans—any excess revenue would be plowed back into Pell Grants under the legislation. "It is obscene that the United States government is making a profit off the backs of people who are trying to get an education," said Warren, who has railed against the revenue excesses for years.

It would also allow students to refinance existing loans at low rates, and would cut the government lending rate for new undergraduate borrowers to 1.88 percent.

The United States Students Association, the American Federation of Teachers, the National Education Association, and other groups have endorsed the legislation, and might be helpful in organizing support going forward.

There are five Senate co-sponsors for the bill (Warren, Kamala Harris, Richard Blumenthal, Chris Murphy, and Kirsten Gillibrand) and fourteen in the House, including Ellison, co-chair of the Progressive Caucus and deputy DNC chair.

That count alone shows the political momentum behind this issue. When Sanders introduced a similar bill in 2015, it had zero co-sponsors.

Print Citations

CMS: Zornick, George. "Bernie Sanders Just Introduced His Free College Tuition Plan." In *The Reference Shelf: Education Reform*, edited by Betsy Maury, 140–142. Ipswich, MA: H.W. Wilson, 2017.

MLA: Zornick, George. "Bernie Sanders Just Introduced His Free College Tuition Plan." The Reference Shelf: Education Reform. Ed. Betsy Maury. Ipswich: H.W. Wilson, 2017. 140–142. Print.

APA: Zornick, G. (2017). Bernie Sanders just introduced his free college tuition plan. In Betsy Maury (Ed.), The reference shelf: Education reform (pp. 140–142). Ipswich, MA: H.W. Wilson. (Original work published 2017)

10 Public High School Teachers Explain Why They're Worried about Trump's Pick for Education Secretary

By De Elizabeth
Teen Vogue, January 31, 2017

President Donald Trump has nominated Betsy DeVos for the position of education secretary, and she seems to be one of the most controversial of all his picks.

DeVos has been outspoken about "school choice," and she is a supporter of school vouchers, which give students the opportunity to use public funds for private schools. She is also a supporter of charter schools, and has publicly criticized Common Core—the set of standards that demonstrate what students are supposed to know at each level.

Because of her stances and lack of experience in education, DeVos has been criticized by public school advocates. With regard to her "school choice" agenda, the American Civil Liberties Union of Michigan has referred to her position as "misguided," explaining that the focus on for-profit schools can have detrimental effects on public schools.

After DeVos's confirmation hearing earlier this month, criticism only intensified. At her hearing, it became clear that DeVos was not familiar with some key federal laws that aim to protect students with disabilities. Additionally, she hedged on the topic of enforcing sexual assault laws on college campuses. When asked if she would uphold Title IX as it relates to sexual assault, DeVos wouldn't give a clear answer, saying, "Senator, I know that there's a lot of conflicting ideas and opinions around that guidance." Lastly, many citizens were concerned when DeVos implied that schools should be equipped with guns for protection from "potential grizzlies."

In the weeks since her hearing, disability advocates, Title IX advocates, and even teachers and administrators have voiced their concerns regarding DeVos's nomination. In fact, Senator Bob Casey of Pennsylvania has reportedly received over 50,000 letters and emails objecting to DeVos as education secretary. It's easy to see that the reaction to her nomination has been swift and visceral.

Teen Vogue talked to 10 public high school teachers from all over the country to find out what they think of DeVos's nomination. Read on to learn what they had to say.

Betsy DeVos has a vision that threatens the fundamental stability of our public school systems in America. Since she has spent the last 20 years using her considerable wealth and political influence to advocate for privatization and vouchers, she has missed the fact that the federal government plays an important role in overseeing our public schools and making sure that all students have access to quality education. She also has no knowledge or experience with student loan programs, when the federal government is the largest provider of said loans. Lastly, her confirmation hearing revealed that she was also unaware of federal reporting requirements for harassment, discipline, and bullying for public schools. While she says her motivation is to improve educational opportunities for students through "school choice," her vision is about turning public schools into private entities which would exist to earn profits for corporations. —***Nancy, a public high school English teacher in New York***

I think the most troublesome indicator that she is not qualified is that she has no experience with public education. Not only has she never worked in public education, she does not have the experience of being the parent of a child in public education. This tells me that she does not know what educators, parents, or students need from public education—which would be the very first requirement for someone who is the head of the department of education. DeVos is a champion of charters, vouchers, and private schools. As a teacher of at-risk students in an alternative school, I can tell you the answer is not taking funding away from public programs. My students and my fellow teachers deserve to be represented by someone who is interested in championing the diverse needs of a diverse body of public school students. When I see Betsy DeVos, I do not see someone who represents my students, and that's a problem. —***Courtney, a high school English teacher in New York***

I believe Betsy DeVos will do anything she can to dismantle our current education system. Her support of private, for-profit schools is troubling on many levels. Based on her answers in her hearing, she is unfamiliar with the very concepts that we have professional development meetings about. Overall, I do not feel confident in her abilities to serve as Secretary of Education. She has never taught in a public school and her children did not attend public schools. Her proficiency is lacking in the world of public education, and I seriously doubt her growth would prove satisfactory within the testing window. As a fine arts teacher, I am also deeply concerned that the arts would be the first to go. The recent Every Student Succeeds Act includes the arts as part of the definition of a 'well-rounded education,' and I worry that DeVos would ignore or change that definition to exclude or eliminate the fine arts all together. —***Mallory, a high school theater teacher in Georgia***

DeVos is so far removed from the world of public education. She threatens to create an entirely new set of challenges in addition to the ones we face every day as public school teachers. She doesn't understand the importance of educating every student, regardless of need or ability, which is the exact reason public schools exist. Without being able to even answer questions about this concept, I can't imagine her making any appropriate decisions for our benefit. —*Laura, a high school music teacher in Massachusetts*

Watching the confirmation hearing for Ms. DeVos, I had a strong visceral response at the injustice of such an unqualified person being chosen to oversee our public schools seemingly because she has donated so many millions to the Republicans. In Michigan, she spent millions, not in support of public schools, but to dismantle them. Ms. DeVos helped fund the loopholes that allow charter schools in MI to discriminate against students with disabilities; no wonder she didn't know that the Individuals With Disabilities Education Act (IDEA) was federal law. Any classroom teacher or parent of a learner with disabilities can quote from it. It isn't just law, it's the right thing to do. —*Rachel, a high school English teacher in Massachusetts*

I am not just concerned about Betsy DeVos's nomination, but I am baffled. She is in no way qualified for the position. Not only does she not have any education experience, but she never even attended public schools and therefore has no idea of their importance, the issues that school systems face, or how to fix them. In addition to this, records prove that she has severely damaged school systems she has been involved in. There are serious issues with our schools. Teachers don't always feel valued. Education too often is spoken of in terms of fads pushed by multi-million education companies, rather than what best serves students. There are some students who live in poverty, or face outside issues that affect their ability to learn. We need to work on these issues. And we simply cannot do that if we have someone who is against the rights of our most vulnerable students, and has no experience in education. —*Karra, a high school English teacher in New Mexico*

DeVos's lack of experience as an educator is deeply concerning, and was shown during her nomination hearing. Her unfamiliarity with ideas that are central to assessing the growth of students and educators seems peculiar for someone who will be in charge of ensuring the success of our schools. Furthermore, her background as a political donor seems antithetical to the president's promise to "drain the swamp" of corruption. Lastly, the aggressive push toward school choice, intentions aside, seems to ignore the deeper issues that lead to drastic inequalities in our education system. There seems to be this alarmist notion that our public education system is floundering without taking into account the massive amount of diversity in our educational landscape. There are deeper issues such as racial segregation, racial inequality, and income inequality, which I believe school choice doesn't fully address. Her deep devotion to the school choice principle seems simply grounded in ideological reasons, as opposed to evidence-based research. —*Nick, a high school science teacher in Missouri*

"Betsy DeVos has a vision that threatens the fundamental stability of our public school systems in America."

There are so many fears about DeVos. For me, what is striking is her ... lack of knowledge about students with disabilities. This is a woman who would not qualify to be a teacher, principal, or administrator, but is being considered for Education Secretary. Like everything in this Trump world we now live in, it seems that knowledge, truth, fact, and qualifications are unnecessary. ***—Debra, a high school English teacher in Virginia***

As a high school Latin teacher, I work with two concepts that Betsy DeVos seems to know nothing about: languages and students with disabilities. I know that languages will find a way to continue, but her lack of knowledge regarding students with disabilities scares me. She basically admitted that she knows nothing of the federal laws that we, as teachers, have to follow every day. I would be fired if I acted the way she did, and I honestly would not even have a job as a teacher with the qualifications that she brings to the table. Many teachers have master's degrees and even PhDs. We know what we are doing. We studied long and hard to get the jobs we have. Teaching is not easy. We need to support public education and bolster it so that all children receive a fair and appropriate education. ***—Taylor, a high school Latin teacher in Virginia***

I believe that Betsy DeVos, if confirmed, would be one of the worst things to happen to public education in the 21st century. ... As a public school teacher, I believe that education is a civil right. I teach some of our community's most vulnerable students and I feel that DeVos does not have their best interest at heart. I am truly fearful about what her appointment would mean. We are already over-testing our students and trying to draw correlations between test scores and teacher abilities. We are already unable to address all of the needs of our students in terms of meals, shelter, stability at home, access to technology outside of school, and social needs. If we continue to ignore the correlations between economic status and education, we will have a harder time advancing as a society. I am deeply opposed to DeVos's appointment and am consistently working against the possibility of her being confirmed as our next secretary of education. I am hopeful that the delay of the committee vote is a signal that everyone can agree that she is absolutely not qualified. ***—Emily, a high school business & tech teacher in Illinois***

Some names have been changed.

Print Citations

CMS: Elizabeth, De. "10 Public High School Teachers Explain Why They're Worried about Trump's Pick for Education Secretary." In *The Reference Shelf: Education Reform*, edited by Betsy Maury, 143–147 Ipswich, MA: H.W. Wilson, 2017.

MLA: Elizabeth, De. "10 Public High School Teachers Explain Why They're Worried about Trump's Pick for Education Secretary." *The Reference Shelf: Education Reform*. Ed. Betsy Maury. Ipswich: H.W. Wilson, 2017. 143–147. Print.

APA: Elizabeth, D. (2017). 10 public high scholl teachers explain why they're worried about Trump's pick for education secretary. In Betsy Maury (Ed.), *The reference shelf: Education reform* (pp. 143–147). Ipswich, MA: H.W. Wilson. (Original work published 2017)

The Outsized Role of Parent Contributions in Elementary School Finance

By Emily Workman
New America, May 2, 2017

Our nation's neediest students—those facing the greatest risk for academic failure and with the greatest need for supports—are disproportionately attending schools that serve large numbers of students from low-income families. Their schools are often inadequately funded, which means the students often lack access to many of the academic and enrichment supports that their peers in more affluent schools or districts receive. A contributing factor to this inequity is complicated school funding formulas and local property tax provisions that inadvertently direct less money to the schools serving lower-income students.

Of course, those contributors to inequity are well-known. A new report from the Center for American Progress (CAP), however, highlights an oft-overlooked additional source of revenue for some of the most affluent schools and districts in the nation—private donations from parents of students through parent-teacher associations (PTAs). These donations further exacerbate inequity.

The report shows that the "50 richest PTAs raised nearly $43 million, an average of $867 for each student enrolled in those schools." This is significant when you consider that researchers from the National Bureau of Economic Research have found that for every additional $1000 in per-student spending, there is a significant increase in test scores—greater than the effects of many other initiatives aimed at increasing student achievement. In fact, NBER claims that no other large scale reforms have had such a significant impact. In short, money in fact does matter.

The CAP report holds up Horace Mann Elementary School in Northwest Washington, DC—one of the most affluent schools in the city—as an example of the impact parent donations can have. Horace Mann spent an additional $1600 per student in the 2013-14 school year, which paid for additional staffing including new art, music, and physical education teachers and classroom aides. Other common investments made by PTAs include after-school programs, clubs, drama programs, field trips, supplies and materials for teachers, equipment, and other enrichment programs.

Interestingly, 35 of the 50 richest PTAs are elementary schools. Since we know that the knowledge and learning experiences gained in the early grades sets the foundation upon which future learning is built, all students in elementary schools in particular—especially the most disadvantaged—need every opportunity to access supports that will help them succeed. Yet, many of these supports are beyond the financial means of a low-income school's budget.

The authors argue that district leaders have a responsibility to "promote greater transparency of private contributions and create systems to allocate all resources equitably." They make a number of recommendations for how district leaders should address this issue, including conducting an annual needs assessment for every school and supporting partnerships between schools. They also present a number of approaches to directly tackle inequities in parent donations, including redistributing donations, restricting the use of funds, incorporating predicted donations into school budgets, and encouraging donations to districts.

The report offers Montgomery County in Maryland as an example of a district that restricts the usage of funds by prohibiting the use of parent donations for school staffing. This policy can help maintain equity because teacher quality is shown to be the greatest in-school factor on student achievement.

Also included in the report are two districts that require PTAs turn over a portion of funds raised for redistribution across all schools in the district. Portland Public Schools in Oregon, for example, collects one-third of the PTA's donations. Similarly, the Santa Monica-Malibu School District in California requires that funds raised for "specific schools intended to replace personnel, programs or services cut by the Board in the process of budget reduction, unless sufficient funds are received to restore" be placed in an equity fund and distributed across all the district schools.

Tackling this issue, however, requires great care as district leaders must balance the desire to create greater equity across schools without deterring parents from making contributions to public schools.

States can also take action. In an interview, Mike Griffith from the Education Commission of the States explained that New Mexico accounts for PTA contributions in the state's funding formula so that schools receiving large amounts of private donations receive less state funding. With the passage of the Every Student Succeeds Act (ESSA) in 2015, states are now required to report expenses at the school level, in addition to the district level, which will go a long way in increasing the transparency of private donations and their use.

Tackling this issue, however, requires great care as district leaders must balance the desire to create greater equity across schools without deterring parents from making contributions to public schools. A parent's incentive to contribute additional monies to schools is often directly related to a desire to provide their child with additional educational opportunities and redistributing their funds to other students can serve as a disincentive to donate. In fact, largely as a result of the 2011 policy put in place in the Santa Monica-Malibu School District, some parents are pushing for a separation of the district whereby the more affluent Malibu schools will create their own district, as reported by Dana Goldstein with the *New York Times*. A question of whether redistribution policies will serve as an impetus for re-segregation can't be ignored.

On the other hand, based on CAP's analyses comparing districts with equitable distribution policies in place to demographically similar districts without, the authors found that having those policies in place did not significantly influence contributions in the districts analyzed. The study was limited, however, since they were unable to compare contributions before and after the policies were put in place.

CAP's report highlights an important factor in school funding that is often overlooked, but perhaps even more significant is that the report joins an abundance of evidence that proves there are flagrant funding inequities across public schools that continue to perpetuate the large achievement gap that exists.

Print Citations

CMS: Workman, Emily. "The Outsized Role of Parent Contributions in Elementary School Finance." In *The Reference Shelf: Education Reform*, edited by Betsy Maury, 148–150. Ipswich, MA: H.W. Wilson, 2017.

MLA: Workman, Emily. "The Outsized Role of Parent Contributions in Elementary School Finance." *The Reference Shelf: Education Reform*. Ed. Betsy Maury. Ipswich: H.W. Wilson, 2017. 148–150. Print.

APA: Workman, E. (2017). The outsized role of parent contribution in elementary school finance. In Betsy Maury (Ed.), *The reference shelf: Education reform* (pp. 148–150). Ipswich, MA: H.W. Wilson. (Original work published 2017)

5
Education Technology

Credit: Jim Lo Scalzo-Pool/Getty Images

U.S. President Barack Obama tours a seventh grade classroom that uses technology to enhance students' learning experience, prior to delivering remarks on the ConnectED Initiative at Buck Lodge Middle School February 4, 2014 in Adelphi, Maryland. As part of the president's ConnectED program, Obama has tasked the Federal Communications Commission to help to build high-speed digital connections to America's schools and libraries, with the goal of getting 99-percent of American students to next-generation broadband and wireless technology within five years.

Hi-Teach: Education in the Digital Age

The Information Age or Digital Age is the current era in human history, named for a global revolution in access and control of information. From the dawn of personal computing to the explosion of Internet technology, the Digital Age is all about data and, since the beginning, educators, researchers, and legislators have been trying to figure out how this technological revolution can be harnessed to improve the education system. As of 2017, it is arguable that educators have not yet found the perfect formula to revolutionize education in the same way that information technology has revolutionized global commerce and communication. However, despite slow gains, the effort continues, driven by visionaries who see the potential for a more inclusive, open educational environment driven by mass data and computing.

Access to the Web

One of the most important issues affecting the future of education in the Digital Age is the debate over net neutrality, the idea that the Internet should be a public resource, regulated and managed by public servants, like the telephone and federal mail system, rather than run by corporations for profit. In 2003, legal scholar and Internet pioneer Tim Wu wrote an article suggesting that the Internet was becoming so important to humanity that the technology needed to be protected to prevent discrimination, an idea that he called "network neutrality."[1]

From the beginning, the Web was an open system, meaning that any person could visit any website or use any Web service with equal levels of access. The Web has thus been a fundamentally "democratic" system, where consumer interest and choice determines which sites or services thrive. Wu realized, however, that this system could change in ways that threatened the democratic nature of the Web. To provide an example of how this might work, consider the popular streaming service Netflix, which is an independent company that competes with traditional cable television providers and was able to become a dominant force in entertainment because of the open Web. Internet Service Providers (ISPs) like Comcast, AT&T, and TimeWarner, create the digital networks that provide Internet access and profit by charging consumers a fee to access their networks. These same companies also offer television and streaming services and compete with companies like Netflix for consumers. Without regulation, ISPs can slow down or restrict access to competing companies, like Netflix, in order to encourage users to switch to their streaming services.[2] In a deregulated system, therefore, ISPs essentially own the Web and their potential for profit, rather than consumer choice, will determine what services remain available.

Internet service providers invest in infrastructure, laying the cables that form the backbone of the Internet, and so argue they should be free to manage traffic to maximize profit. Deregulation advocates argue that government regulation discourages companies from investing in infrastructure and that corporate competition will lead to growth and innovation.[3] Opponents argue that the open Internet already provides sufficient profit for ISPs and that the open Internet is already a proven forum for innovation, with companies like Google, Facebook, Twitter, and Amazon, made possible by the open system that enabled these initially small-scale developments to compete.[4] Neutrality encourages independent and non-profit web development, which is why the Web has become an important forum for free speech and expression and an essential educational tool for the public.

A majority of Americans do not believe that corporations will act in the public interest if left to their own devices and, regardless of political ideology, the vast majority support neutrality. In a University of Delaware survey in 2014, for instance, nearly 81 percent opposed allowing ISPs to charge websites higher rates for faster speeds.[5] The Federal Communications Commission (FCC), the branch of the federal government responsible for regulating communications, officially adopted net neutrality rules that prohibited corporations from slowing down or speeding up traffic on a tiered service model.

Corporations have mounted a massive multibillion-dollar campaign against neutrality. A review by the National Institute on Money in State Politics found that 265 Republican members of Congress had personally taken donations from antineutrality corporations like Comcast, NBCUniversal, AT&T, and Time Warner, ranging from less than $1,000 to more than $150,000.[6] This campaign essentially bought the support of the Republican party and President Trump. Trump appointed Ajit Pai, a former lawyer for Verizon Communications, to lead the FCC and Pai has announced his intention to favor corporations over public interest and to essentially dismantle existing neutrality protections.[7]

The net neutrality debate is important to education at every level. In the twenty-first century, students in K-12 and in higher education increasingly rely on the Internet to complete schoolwork and this is also an essential way for teachers to blend lessons with real-world skills. Training students to locate, evaluate, and utilize Web sources for research and other purposes translates into basic computer literacy skills that are increasingly essential for work and many aspects of daily life.

However, the fact that Internet access is already a privatized system in which users pay ISPs for access, coupled with the fact that ISPs do not invest in high speed Internet systems in some rural or economically disadvantaged areas, means that Internet access is not evenly distributed. This creates what some have called the "broadband gap" or, in reference to education specifically, the "homework gap," defined as the divide between those with access to high speed Internet and those without. According to Pew Research center information from 2015, 31.4 percent of households with income less than $50,000 lack access to high speed Internet. For households with less than $25,000, nearly 40 percent lack access. This essentially means that more than 5 million homes with school-aged children lack access to high speed Internet, thus putting parents and students at an increasingly severe disadvantage to other students.[8]

Antineutrality proponents, like FCC head Ajit Pai, believe the free market will handle this problem. Freed from government regulations that limit profit, ISPs will allegedly be more likely to expand and perhaps even to lower costs. This claim is illogical because the free-market system encourages corporations to pursue profit and not to act in the public interest. The broadband debate is essentially the same as the debate that resulted in the formation of the FCC in 1934, in an effort to ensure that telephone, wire, and radio communications were made available to as many Americans as possible, without discrimination, and at a reasonable price. Citizens must decide if they agree with the Trump administration, and therefore trust that corporations will act in the public interest or that competition will force corporations make changes that will benefit the public, or if they believe that the government must step in to prevent monopolization and to ensure that the Internet develops as a public, rather than corporate, resource.

The Unrealized Online Education Revolution

Economists have coined the term "disruption" for a development in a field that is so transformative that it fundamentally alters the standard business model. Companies like Amazon and Ebay became disruptors in their respective markets, leading many traditional competitors to become more or less obsolete. The first online classes debuted in the 1980s, and have since become a staple of higher education. Advocates hoped that online education would disrupt the education field, helping to provide more egalitarian options for a wider variety of potential students. Advocates envisioned that the lower level of investment required from educational institutions would mean that online classes would be more affordable and would be designed for students unable to attend traditional classes.

Unfortunately, online education has failed to become the positive disruptive force envisioned by early innovators, in part because many educational institutions did not embrace the potential of the medium. Many institutions offered online education at the same rate as traditional classes and failed to design online curricula to appeal to nontraditional students. Students who succeed in online classes must be able to effectively manage their own time and to thrive without much direct teacher/student interaction. By contrast, many of the students who opt for online classes are working students and nontraditional students who have less experience with traditional education and are therefore often ill-prepared for the higher level of personal initiative needed to succeed in online education. A five-year study in 2011 tracked 51,000 community college students in Washington state and found that those who took online classes were less likely to earn degrees or transfer to four-year colleges and were more likely to withdraw or fail their classes.[9]

One of the biggest trends in online education of the 2010s were the massive open online courses (MOOCs), which are online classes that are made available to large numbers of students. There are many different types of MOOCs, from free, open enrollment lectures made available to a potentially unlimited number of learners, to more narrowly tailored programs that operate on a fee-based system (though generally much less than a traditional class) and can be used to obtain credit towards a degree or certificate. Early proponents described MOOCs as a potentially revolutionizing innovation that could open up educational opportunities for thousands or millions of nontraditional students, but this potential has been largely unrealized by 2017.

The University of California invested in a three-year pilot program to create an entirely "digital" branch of the university that would utilize online classes and MOOCs to broaden the university's market. Despite a huge investment and high hopes, data from the program collected in 2015 showed that, between 2012 and 2015, only 250 students finished classes through the online arm of the institution. Other big investments in the MOOC model have failed in similar ways. For instance, edX, a joint $60 million project by Harvard University and Massachusetts Institute of Technology (MIT), has been able to offer thousands of online courses to students, but statistics from the program found that more than half of edX registrants quit after only a week in one of the company's classes. Research from Harvard and MIT in 2015 further suggested that only about a quarter of those who took MOOCs for college credit earned credit from the class.[10]

Online education is not only a higher education issue, but increasingly applies to the K-12 education system as well. At this level, many K-12 public, private, and charter schools offer online classes and, in five states, students are required to take at least one class online, as a way to prepare them for later online schooling and work. Another trend has been the idea of creating entirely online schools that allow students, sometimes in different states, to perform most or all of their work online. As of 2015, 30 states and Washington, DC, had fully online K-12 schools and supporters argue that these programs have tremendous potential for nontraditional and special-needs students. For instance, virtual schooling provides children in military families to remain in the same program even as their families move. Unfortunately, researchers have found that online students do not perform as well as traditional students and are more likely to fail or drop out of classes or school.[11]

For instance, in a number of states, private companies offer online education to students through "virtual charter" schools, thus providing a charter school option to students who do not have an equivalent traditional institution in their area.[12] In 2015, the Center for Research on Education Outcomes (CREDO), released the results of a long-term study of online charter schools revealing that students in virtual charters fell behind traditional students by 72 days of reading instruction and 180 days of mathematics. The study thus showed that a year enrolled in a virtual charter school was essentially equivalent to a year with no schooling of any kind.[13] Researchers conducting the study found, unsurprisingly, that the average teenager lacks the discipline and self-motivation needed to succeed in an entirely virtual educational environment and that insufficient supervision and poor-quality guidance essentially meant that the entire virtual high school program had failed from end to end.[14] As the primary problem seems to be that students fare better with direct, face-to-face guidance to keep them on track, it is possible that future programs might experiment with streaming video communication to simulate the effect of more personal interaction and guidance. In any case, the current model works only for a select group of students and provides another example of how the online revolution in education has not yet come to fruition.

Is the Information Age Bad for Education?

It is possible that educators and innovators simply have not found the right model to unlock the potential of digital education. New innovations like game learning and personalized curriculum programs, might point the way towards a more harmonious partnership between education and technology in the future. As of 2017, however, it is uncertain whether the Information Age will further the goal of creating a more informed public or whether digital tools simply create more distractions and new problems for teachers and students. Some research indicates that the Web can be a positive influence, such as a 2008 study showing that using the Internet can, in moderation, increase brain function.[15] By contrast, research has also found that the increasing tendency of individuals to "multitask" by shifting quickly between websites or mixing work with social media, discourages concentration and has negative effects on an individual's ability to recall specific data.[16]

One growing problem is that the Web has made it possible for students to more easily plagiarize by either copying and pasting data from the Web or through anonymous online markets where unscrupulous students can purchase papers and outsource their classwork. Beyond the increased potential for cheating, some have become concerned that information overload and the ease of accessing information in the digital environment discourages critical thinking. The "fake news" controversy surrounding the 2016 election demonstrated the seemingly widespread inability to differentiate between legitimate and illegitimate sources of information. Millions of Americans, including President Donald Trump, embraced, shared, and promoted false information presented through websites masquerading as news outlets and it is unclear whether Trump and allies legitimately believed this information or used it to intentionally mislead the public. What is clear, is that millions of Americans are willing to trust often outrageous and completely unsubstantiated claims made by public figures or published on the Web without suspicion or skepticism. It is unclear whether this means that Americans lack sufficient training in critical thinking or is it simply a reflection of the fact that individuals are less critical of claims that confirm preexisting beliefs.

Micah L. Issitt

Works Used

Champeau, Rachel. "First-Time Internet Users Find Boost in Brain Function after Just One Week." *UCLA Newsroom*. University of California Los Angeles. Oct 19 2009. Web. 30 Apr 2017.

Coughlan, Sean. "Online Schools 'Worse Than Traditional Teachers'." *BBC News*. BBC. Nov 4 2015. Web. 30 Apr 2017.

Derousseau, Ryan. "California's Multimillion-Dollar Online Education Flop Is Another Blow for MOOCs." *The Hechingter Report*. Teachers College at Columbia University. Apr 14 2015. Web. 30 Apr 2017.

Ehrenfreund, Max. "New Poll: Republicans and Democrats Both Overwhelmingly Support Net Neutrality." *The Washington Post*. Nash Holdings. Nov 12 2014. Web. 30 Apr 2017.

Fung, Brian. "The Future of Net Neutrality in Trump's America." *Forbes*. Forbes Inc. Apr 5 2017. Web. 30 Apr 2017.

Horrigan, John B. "The Numbers Behind the Broadband 'Homework Gap'." *Pew Research Center*. Apr 20 2015. Web. 11 May 2017.

Kaufman, Micha. "We Can't Be Neutral on Net Neutrality." *Forbes*. Forbes Inc. Nov 14 2014. Web. 30 Apr 2017.

Levitin, Daniel J. "Why the Modern World Is Bad for Your Brain." *The Guardian*. Guardian News and Media. Jan 18 2015. Web. 4 May 2017.

Madrigal, Alexis C. and Adrienne Lafrance. "Net Neutrality: A Guide to (and History of) a Contested Idea." *The Atlantic*. The Atlantic Monthly Group. Apr 25 2014. Web. 30 Apr 2017.

"Net Neutrality Won: Here's the Essay That Started It All." *Recode*. Vox Media. Jun 14 2016. Web. 30 Apr 2017.

Reardon, Marguerite. "Net Neutrality: How We Got from There to Here." *CNet*. CBS Interactive. Feb 24 2015. Web. 30 Apr 2017.

Rosenfeld, Steven. "A Leading Charter School Advocate's Stunning Admission: Online Public Schools Are a Colossal Disaster." *Salon*. Salon Inc. Feb 15 2016. Web. 30 Apr 2017.

Samuelsohn, Darren. "Virtual Schools Are Booming: Who's Paying Attention?" *Politico*. Politico. Sep 23 2015. Web. 11 May 2017.

Sottek, T.C. "The 265 Members of Congress Who Sold You Out to ISPs, and How Much It Cost to Buy Them." *The Verge*. Vox Media. Mar 29 2017. Web. 30 Apr 2017.

Strauss, Valerie. "Study on Online Charter Schools: 'It Is Literally as if the Kid Did Not Go to School for an Entire Year'." *The Washington Post*. Nash Holdings. Oct 31 2015. Web. 30 Apr 2017.

"The Trouble with Online College." *The New York Times*. The New York Times Co. Feb 18 2013. Web. 30 Apr 2017.

Notes

1. "Net Neutrality Won: Here's the Essay That Started It All," *Recode*.
2. Madrigal and Lafrance, "Net Netrality: A Guide to (and History of) a Contested Idea."
3. Reardon, "Net Neutrality: How We Got from There to Here."
4. Kaufman, "We Can't Be Neutral on Net Neutrality."
5. Ehrenfreund, "New Poll: Republicans and Democrats Both Overwhelmingly Support Net Neutrality."

6. Sottek, "The 265 Members of Congress Who Sold You Out to ISPs, and How Much It Cost to Buy Them."
7. Fung, "The Future of Net Neutrality in Trump's America."
8. Horrigan, "The Numbers Behind the Broadband 'Homework Gap'."
9. "The Trouble with Online College," The New York Times.
10. Derousseau, "California's Multimillion-Dollar Online Education Flop is Another Blow for MOOCs."
11. Samuelsohn, "Virtual Schools Are Booming: Who's Paying Attention?"
12. Coughlan, "Online Schools 'Worse Than Traditional Teachers'."
13. Strauss, "Study on Online Charter Schools: 'It Is Literally as if the Kid Did Not Go to School for an Entire Year'."
14. Rosenfeld, "A Leading Charter School Advocate's Stunning Admission: Online Public Schools Are a Colossal Disaster."
15. Champeau, "First-Time Internet Users Find Boost in Brain Function after Just One Week."
16. Levitin, "Why the Modern World Is Bad for Your Brain."

Computing in the Classroom: From the "Teaching Machine" to the Promise of Twenty-First-Century Learning Technology

By Sophia Nguyen
Harvard Magazine, March-April, 2015

On November 11, 1953, psychology professor B.F. Skinner sat in a fourth-grade math class, perturbed. It was Parents Day at his daughter Deborah's school. The lesson seemed grossly inefficient: students proceeded through the material in lockstep, at the same pace; their graded assignments were returned to them sluggishly.

A leading proponent of what he called "radical behaviorism," Skinner had devoted his career to studying feedback. He denied the existence of free will and dismissed inner mental states as explanations for outward action. Instead, he focused on the environment and the organism's response. He had trained rats to push levers and pigeons to play Ping-Pong. A signed photo of Ivan Pavlov presided over his study in Cambridge. Turning his attention to a particular subset of the human animal—the schoolchild—Skinner invented his Teaching Machine.

Roughly the size and shape of a typewriter, the machine allowed a student to progress independently through a curriculum, answering test items and getting instant feedback with a few pulls of a lever. "The student quickly learns to be right. His work is pleasurable. He does not have to force himself to study," Skinner claimed. "A classroom in which machines are being used is usually the scene of intense concentration." With hardly any hindrance from peers or teachers, thousands of students could receive knowledge directly from a single textbook writer. He told the *Harvard Crimson*, "There is no reason why the school room should be any less mechanized than the kitchen."

Sixty years later, Skinner's reductionist ideas about teaching and learning continue to haunt public education—especially as it's once again being called upon to embrace technology. In December 2014, as part of a nationwide event promoting computer-science education called Hour of Code, Barack Obama hunched over a laptop alongside a group of New Jersey middle-schoolers, becoming the first president to write a line of code. The public-policy world frames computer science in K-12 education as a matter of economic urgency. Digital fluency is often called a twenty-first-century skill, equally necessary for personal workplace success and for the maintenance of America's competitive edge.

Teaching machines with capabilities beyond Skinner's imagining have proliferated in this century. The barest twitch of curiosity can be satisfied with swift thumbs and a pocket-sized interface. The possibilities seem endless: virtual realities that immerse students in remote habitats or historical eras; learners mastering skills and content through digital games; kids everywhere achieving basic fluency in code, as their forebears once had to learn cursive. Even as researchers invent new ways to use machines for learning, they realize that the culture of the classroom may itself need to advance, in tandem with technology—a difficult proposition, when bandwidth is already taken up by battles over high-stakes testing, budgets, and teacher tenure.

Rich Halverson, education professor and associate director of the University of Wisconsin's Games Learning Society, diagnoses the problem this way: "When you manage an education system that's as rich in potential as ours with a sense of crisis, all crisis does is shut down possibility. We try to reach for the proven, for the stuff that works. Practices on the edge get ignored."

Our needs have changed, and our capabilities have grown—but we still speak like latter-day Skinners. The education writer Audrey Watters, guest lecturing last semester for the Harvard Graduate School of Education (HGSE) class "The Future of Learning at Scale," traced the behaviorist echoes in the current chatter surrounding tech-culture innovations like "gamification." As Skinner once used food pellets to induce pigeons to roll a ball back and forth with their beaks, corporate and education leaders alike have embraced the idea of dispensing nuggets of fun to shape desired behavior in humans. For businesses, gamification-based training promises to maximize profits and employee productivity; for schools, it seems like a way to motivate students to perform rote memorization—and to do so cost-effectively. The education system continues to pursue Skinner's goal of efficiency and automation.

"The current system is outmoded," declares Paul Reville, Keppel professor of practice of educational policy and administration, who spoke at a September HGSE event. "We have a batch-processing, mass-production model of education that served us very well if we wanted to achieve a society in which we were sending a lot of people into low-skill, low-knowledge jobs," he says. "But for high-skill, high-knowledge jobs in a postindustrial information age, we need a very different system."

The digital society and economy, saturated by screens, require rethinking what school can and should do for today's schoolchildren.

Beyond Playing at Games

Meaningful choices—and the open-ended, experimental spirit of play—are essential to a deep game experience, says Jessica Hammer '99, a Carnegie Mellon professor who teaches game design. "Or else you're making what I like to call 'kick the puppy' games," she says. "Would you like to kick this puppy, yes or no? That's not much of a game." Games have more richness than is dreamt of in gamification's philosophy.

In the foundational studies of computer games conducted in the 1980s, education researchers asked what made the repetitive tasks of feeding quarters into a machine and controlling a joystick more appealing than the repetitive tasks of schoolwork. They wanted to apply the mechanics of games' reward systems to make educational software just as engrossing. Some titles became classics, many of them simulations like Sid Meier's Civilization, or Oregon Trail, created by three student teachers at Carleton College. Many others flopped. Their use of a drill-and-practice mechanic to teach content made them look an awful lot like multiple-choice tests, except that they used a cartoon monster to gobble up the right answer. This brittle sort of fun became known as "chocolate-covered broccoli"—the Teaching Machine, with shinier levers.

"Learning by doing has more conditions for success than teaching by telling," says Wirth professor in learning technologies Christopher Dede. This tenet has guided his decades of work in developing virtual and augmented realities for science students. His recent collaborator, associate professor of education Tina Grotzer, took more time to warm to simulations. With her background in cognitive science, Grotzer eventually came to appreciate the pedagogical value of virtual worlds, due to her particular interest in how learners reason about complex causality.

Environmental science poses a particular challenge for science teachers, she explains. Demonstrating a chemical reaction or physics principle right before students' eyes is eminently doable: a beaker fizzes; a catapult flings a tennis ball. Cause and effect occur within a graspable timeframe. Students can complete a hands-on lab activity from start to finish within a single class period.

Not so in environmental science, in which developments unfold on a much longer scale, exacerbating the mind's natural tendency to focus on events rather than processes. It's hard for students to track complex causality when it's "bottom-up, and distributed," says Grotzer. Nonobvious variables further frustrate the efforts of children (and many adults) to understand systems such as food webs and global weather patterns.

"A lot of students have been taught to see science as facts rather than a process of making meaning," explains Dede. He and Grotzer designed EcoMUVE (Multi-User Virtual Environment) as a simulation with a mystery at its heart. Students explore the environment around a pond at many different time points. They use a virtual net to trawl for organisms in the water, and other tools to record data about oxygen levels and temperature. They can plot changes over time on a graph, and use their avatar to speak with the characters strolling in the area. One day in late summer, pixelated carcasses turn up on the shore: a fish kill. The students must investigate what went wrong, proposing hypotheses and gathering evidence.

Called upon to put their knowledge to use, learners enter a different mindset than is usual in the classroom. Unlike in an exam, says Grotzer, "They don't know what information to bring to bear to the experience. They're not cued."

"For me, it's about getting them to wear the shoes of a scientist to see how they fit," says Dede. "The primary barrier is that they don't think they can do it."

He doesn't characterize his virtual environments as games, though they bear a family resemblance. They often have objectives (find out why the whale has washed up on the beach; trace an epidemic through a nineteenth-century town), but because that objective is discovery, the activities have a noncompetitive, exploratory bent. Calling it a "simulation" rather than a "game" also lowers schools' resistance to trying out the new activity. After three decades of experience, Dede firmly believes that "psychological and cultural barriers seem to slow education down more than every other field."

Even so, "We've loosened up about games," says Eric Klopfer, director of MIT's Education Arcade, who has also worked with Dede on augmented realities. Klopfer recalls a time when teachers would tell him, "'Just don't use the word game in my school, because the principal will kick it right out.' And now, in fact, there are people who are saying just the opposite: 'Ooh, is that a game? I'd love to try that out in my school.'"

With the founding of hubs like Wisconsin's Games Learning Society (GLS) and MIT's Games to Teach Initiative (the forerunner to the Education Arcade) in the early 2000s, the ventures of the more risk-tolerant academic world have fed the larger industry new pedagogical models, game projects, and the occasional young talent. In turn, without investing in the educational market themselves, the biggest companies support the diversity of the larger habitat. Zynga (behind FarmVille and Words with Friends) operates co.lab, offering office space, tools, and mentoring to young ed-tech companies, including some that germinated as university projects. Electronic Arts (SimCity, Madden NFL) funds the nonprofit GlassLab, which develops its own games and aspires to be a resource for commercial developers who need assessment metrics and data to make their projects more educationally sound.

"Have you been on iTunes lately?" says Rich Halverson. "Good God, the world of games and games for learning is at an unprecedented glut!" But, he notes, demand has lagged. Education games remain marginal in schools: a special treat for kids who finish their work, or a remedial intervention for those who can't. Halverson believes that this underuse of a powerful resource further widens the digital divide already disadvantaging poor and minority students. Families who know of and can afford these enrichment channels will seek them out.

Halverson cites the linguist James Paul Gee, whose 2003 book *What Video Games Have to Teach Us About Learning and Literacy* claimed that Pokemon could be considered "perhaps the best literacy curriculum ever conceived." Its trading cards enabled millions of kids to master a complex taxonomy of imaginary creatures, all with specialized traits. Compare the average middle-school classroom to what Halverson calls the "learning space" within games themselves, and in the culture surrounding games—for example, the online game Minecraft and its array of blueprints, discussion boards, and how-to videos. Which provides a more authentic model for how to pursue work and personal interests in the twenty-first century?

"Think about how you do your work," Halverson instructs. "You're probably sitting in front of a computer right now. You've got a big project you're trying to come up with. You're on the phone talking to some dude from Wisconsin, taking notes.

You probably have something on your wall with all the sources you're going to put together for the article. There are online resources and how-to guides for how to write. You're putting all of this stuff together. You've created your own learning environment."

From Playing to Programming

"Games are perhaps the first designed interactive systems our species invented," writes Eric Zimmerman, a games designer and professor at New York University. "Games like Chess, Go, and Parcheesi are much like digital computers, machines for creating and storing numerical states. In this sense, computers didn't create games; games created computers." In his essay "Manifesto for the Ludic Century," Zimmerman argues that the rise of computers parallels the resurgent cultural interest in games. Future generations will understand their world in terms of games and systems, and will respond to it as players and designers—navigating, manipulating, and improving upon them.

Yasmin Kafai, Ed.D. '93, an education professor at University of Pennsylvania, first explored how game creation and computer programming could be brought together in the classroom while a Harvard graduate student working in the MIT lab of Seymour Papert. As early as the 1960s, when salesmen still hawked versions of the Teaching Machine from door to door, Papert pioneered the idea of computers in the classroom, paired with a radically different philosophy: "constructionism." This theory proposed that learners do not passively receive knowledge but actively build it—and that they do this best when they get to manipulate materials in a way that feels meaningful.

Digital fluency is often called a twenty-first-century skill, equally necessary for personal workplace success and for the maintenance of America's competitive edge.

For "Project Headlight," a program beginning in 1985 that brought hundreds of computers into a public elementary school in Boston, Papert's team developed activities that immersed students in the programming language he had invented, LOGO. Following his pedagogical ideals, the researchers didn't want the computer lab to seem like a locked room at the end of a long hallway, essentially removed from daily life and learning. They wanted to know what students were naturally interested in. "These were the days of Sonic the Hedgehog, Super-Mario," recalls Kafai. "Kids told me that they really wanted to program their own games."

For a brief period in the early 1980s, it was relatively commonplace for avid gamers to dabble in programming; a range of books taught users how to make or modify games using languages like BASIC and Pascal. Kafai designed a curriculum in which older students would design software for children in the lower grades, in subjects ranging from fractions to marine habitats. The kids quickly realized that creating Nintendo-style games was beyond their skill set, but in art class Kafai had them think like professionals, designing boxes and creating advertisements of the kind that they might find in stores.

Ironically, the advent of multimedia CD-ROMS and software packages—and soon after, Internet browsers—made the personal computer feel so friendly that programming seemed irrelevant to its operation. Now that computers came preloaded and densely written with default systems and applications, they did everything the average user required. This technological wizardry deterred people from peeking behind the curtain. Creation and design were once again thought of as the province of experts; schools restricted themselves to teaching PowerPoint and touch-typing.

As programming was exiled from the classroom, researchers like MIT's Mitchel Resnick and Natalie Rusk, Ed.M. '89, gave it safe haven in the extracurricular context, through a program called the Computer Clubhouse. In true constructionist style, Resnick and Rusk envisioned members learning through design activities: controlling robots, digitally composing music, editing an animation. With the support of adult mentors and teachers, Clubhouse youth would build computational confidence. Within 15 years, the network of Clubhouses had spread to more than 100 sites, with a focus on low-income communities.

Starting in 2003, Resnick collaborated with Kafai and others to develop the programming tool Scratch, imagining that it would be used in Clubhouse-style settings. In some ways, Scratch was the inheritor of LOGO's legacy, but with a few key differences. Where LOGO had been designed with mathematics in mind, Scratch was intended to be media-centric, a tool for self-expression: kids loved the idea of making their own interactive stories, animations, and games, hardly realizing that the projects made use of algebra and algorithms. Additionally, the Scratch "grammar" would be composed of command "blocks" that could snap together, like Lego bricks, to achieve different effects. This liberated learners from the frustration of typos, or the flummoxing syntax of traditional programming languages. For a finishing touch, the interface would have a prominent "Share" icon—and along with it, an online community where users could display, comment on, and peer into the backend of projects. The research team built social values like collaboration, tinkering, and remixing into the culture of coding itself.

A public with staggeringly uneven rates of digital illiteracy creates ravines between the creators and the users; those who design the system and those at its mercy.

Since Scratch launched in 2007, it has been translated into more than 40 languages and used by millions worldwide—including people well outside the target age group (eight to 16), like the hundreds enrolled in Harvard's most popular class, CS 50: "Introduction to Computer Science." It's even used in primary school classrooms. In 2009, the online community hosted by MIT spun off the forum

ScratchEd under the leadership of Karen Brennan (now an assistant professor of education at HGSE). There, educators can show off sample lessons and offer troubleshooting and other advice. Though their local administrations may not be able to mandate computation in the classroom, in this virtual space they can show one another what's possible.

Teaching the Teachers

As others work toward systemic change on the policy level, urging states to create certification pathways for computer-science teachers and establish standards in the subject, Karen Brennan and the ScratchEd research team exert their efforts from the opposite end. They want to empower educators to integrate coding into the classroom independently, absent official guidance and mandates. Last fall, Brennan published a free Creative Computing Curriculum Guide that she created with former student Christan Balch, Ed.M. '14, and ScratchEd research program manager Michelle Chung, Ed.M. '10. Its 150 colorfully designed pages are divided into manageable units and sessions, under cheerful section headings that suggest "Possible Paths" and "Things to Try," and offer space for "Notes to Self" and "Feeling stuck? That's ok!" Chung says that they wanted to actively promote a "choose your own adventure" ethos, so teachers will feel emboldened to adapt the lesson plans freely. If Skinner once compared teachers to line cooks, Brennan and her team imagine them as chefs.

A growing component of their work is to convene educators in person as well as online. After the first few tutorials they ran, Brennan remembers, "We had this puzzle." Participants kept returning to introductory workshops long after they'd stopped needing what she calls "our song-and-dance 'Introduction to Scratch' piece." The program leaders soon realized that the attendees were attracted less to the workshop's content than to the opportunity to interact with colleagues. So ScratchEd began to host monthly meetups at the MIT Media Lab, welcoming participants at all levels to gather, collectively set an agenda, and share their frustrations, success stories, and expertise.

Soon the sessions attracted teachers from as far away as New York and Philadelphia—and once, a woman who'd taken a red-eye flight from San Diego to make the Saturday morning meeting. The team realized that they had hit upon an unexpected vein of potential energy. "What is that ephemeral quality? Can we package that, can we communicate it? Because it's very different from many types of professional learning that teachers are encountering," says Brennan.

In the fall of 2014, a trio of local educators took the reins of the original meetup group. They now host the gatherings at Kennedy Longfellow School in Cambridge, in a computer lab recently remodeled to accommodate round tables surrounded by carts of robotics kits, laptops, and tablets. For the November meeting, held on the cusp of the nationwide Computer Science Education Week and the Hour of Code, participants included teachers, parents, and library and technology specialists, from public and private schools. Some wanted to learn strategies for running an afterschool club; others wondered how to convince other teachers to allocate already scarce time to the uncertain prospect of grappling with computers. Empathy, and experience within the system, cooled their natural evangelism; none wanted to pile onto the pressures most teachers already feel. Talk of individual projects—using Scratch to build a hurricane simulator, or to animate verbs as a study aid for Spanish and French classes—led to deeper discussions of classroom dynamics: colleagues' general reluctance to take risks, or how a coding activity often goes more smoothly when the kids take charge.

Heather French, Ed.M. '13, who has worked as an instructional technology specialist in the Cambridge public-school district since her graduation, attests that teaching "digital confidence is often the most challenging part of my job." When frustrated by the technology they use—whether a misformatted Google Application or a tangled snarl of code—children and adults reflexively ask her to intervene. A self-taught programmer herself, French believes that part of her job is to teach them how to find the answers themselves: "They just need the courage to try."

Students are accustomed to feeling this uncertainty; teachers, less so. Implicitly, many regard expertise as their source of legitimacy: a store of knowledge, in the form of facts, to be transmitted to the children. They want all the solutions to all possible problems before they feel comfortable leading a lesson—and because computers are only beginning to return in the classroom in these new ways, few have that expertise.

In a talk called "Getting Unstuck" for an HGSE-wide event last September, Brennan addressed teachers' fears of encountering an intractable technical issue that causes the day's lesson to break down. During her research, she reported, young independent Scratch learners had suggested some strategies for when a project malfunctions: reread the code with a critical eye, to check for mistakes; enlist the help of a collaborator, to see the project with fresh eyes; find successful examples to analyze and emulate. These were helpful, Brennan said, but also suggestive of a broader lesson—that teachers could model problem-solving for their students even if they didn't have all the solutions. Indeed, a small degree of uncertainty might be preferable: making room for more spontaneous discovery, and more authentic and rewarding classroom interactions.

With its collaborative spirit, the meetup is a mode of professional development that matches this pedagogy. Recently, Brennan and Michelle Chung released a Meetup Kit in the style of their curriculum guide, so that the model can be replicated and remixed elsewhere.

Rebooting School

At the Cambridge gathering last fall, there was a general sense that the rising profile of events like Hour of Code could make real inroads into schools' uncertainty about investing more energy in tech. Still, a persistent worry encroached on the excitement: that the enthusiasm would come up against calcified classroom culture and dissipate. How could they prevent digital media from becoming a faddish one-off, forgotten amid competing demands on educators? "My fear," confessed Ingrid

Gustafson, one of the meetup's core leaders and one of French's technology colleagues in the Cambridge schools, "is that we're building a path to nowhere."

When she's not bothered by such doubts, Gustafson speaks glowingly about projects that, to her, seem like signs of a way forward. Last year, she helped develop an activity for sixth-graders who had recently played with Grotzer and Dede's EcoMUVE forest simulation and were then assigned to present what they hypothesized about the virtual world they'd explored. After a visiting artist taught them about scientific illustration and painting techniques, the students drew food webs as accurately and aesthetically as possible. Then they used MakeyMakeys—circuitry toolkits that make ordinary objects into touchpads—to hook the paper models up to Scratch simulations that they coded themselves, practicing the new computational concepts they had learned, like loops, conditionals, and sequencing. When a student touched a deer on the food web, it would appear in the virtual ecosystem and interact with other organisms. Beyond the lessons in art, biology, and computer science, the sixth-graders learned something deeper and possibly more enduring: that the digital realm is not just a received environment, with expertly designed features beyond their control; it's a world in which they can communicate and create. Gustafson recently received a $15,000 state grant to bring the EcoMUVE activity to all sixth-graders in the district. She and her colleagues hope that this new introduction to Scratch programming will work in tandem with the existing robotics unit for the seventh-graders. The faculty will build upon their collective knowledge, institutionalizing computational creativity one year at a time.

As the digital realm has permeated almost every aspect of modern life, institutions like schools remain vital levelers. They promote more democratic and equitable participation in society's virtual marketplaces and town halls. A public with staggeringly uneven rates of digital illiteracy creates ravines between the creators and the users; those who design the system and those at its mercy. As media theorist Douglas Rushkoff warns, "Program or be programmed."

B.F. Skinner's machine was rudimentary, its interface only the narrowest of windows through which students squinted at curricula printed on cylinders of paper. The windows are so much larger now, offering portals to seemingly infinite information. The advanced features of the new Teaching Machines could be used to realize Skinner's ideal school: every learner an island, in front of a glowing screen; all students proceeding at different paces through the same exact motions; teachers reduced to technicians.

Indeed, when computers first entered classrooms on a mass scale, it was as banks of monitors installed to speed up rote learning, under a "one size fits all" philosophy. Seymour Papert criticized this transformation as "the shift from a radically subversive instrument in the classroom to a blunted conservative instrument in the computer lab." He proposed an alternative to the concept of the computer programming the child: "In my vision, the child programs the computer." He imagined another way for machines to revolutionize classrooms.

The call to reexamine what teachers teach can bring renewed discussions of how. With tools like augmented reality, games, and coding, it's possible to imagine a model of schooling that departs from its behaviorist past—creating a Ludic Education for a Ludic Age, promoting inquiry, collaboration, experimentation, and play. In this vision, teachers and students are partners in a joint venture. They open up the Teaching Machine to peer into its guts and gears—tinkering, failing, and trying again, to see what they can make of it together. The machines can return education to what it's always been: a project that's intrinsically human.

Print Citations

CMS: Nguyen, Sophia. "Computing in the Classroom from the 'Teaching Machine' to the Promise of Twenty-First-Century Learning Technology." In *The Reference Shelf: Education Reform*, edited by Betsy Maury, 161–170. Ipswich, MA: H.W. Wilson, 2017.

MLA: Nguyen, Sophia. "Computing in the Classroom from the 'Teaching Machine' to the Promise of Twenty-First-Century Learning Technology." *The Reference Shelf: Education Reform*. Ed. Betsy Maury. Ipswich: H.W. Wilson, 2017. 161–170. Print.

APA: Nguyen, S. (2017). Computing in the classroom from the "Teaching Machine" to the promise of twenty-first-century learning technology. In Betsy Maury (Ed.), *The reference shelf: Education reform* (pp. 161–170). Ipswich, MA: H.W. Wilson. (Original work published 2015)

Ex-FCC Chair Blasts Efforts to Change Lifeline, Net Neutrality, Privacy Rules

By Benjamin Herold
Education Week, April 5, 2017

From net neutrality to online privacy to universal-service programs, the administration of President Donald Trump has taken direct aim at a number of the signature policy changes enacted by the Federal Communications Commission under the leadership of former chairman Tom Wheeler.

Wheeler isn't happy.

"They seem to be looking backwards and saying, 'How do we undo everything we voted against when we were in the minority?' Wheeler told *Education Week* in an interview here at the annual conference of the Consortium for School Networking, where he was being honored for his work to expand access to affordable high-speed internet service.

"Every school ought to be worried," he said.

During Wheeler's tenure, the Democrat-controlled FCC passed a number of major reforms via party-line votes. The commission expanded and overhauled the E-rate program, which helps schools and libraries pay for telecommunications services. It changed the federal Lifeline program to allow low-income families to use federal subsidies to pay for home broadband service. With its landmark Open Internet Order, the commission claimed the authority to regulate broadband service providers and declared that they must treat all online content the same.

And shortly before he stepped down in January, Wheeler pushed through new regulations that would have prevented broadband carriers from tracking and selling their customers' data.

But nearly as soon as President Trump tapped Republican Ajit Pai as the commission's new chair, the FCC set about the process of unwinding those efforts:

- On February 3, Pai reversed an earlier FCC decision to approve nine companies as eligible broadband providers under the federal Lifeline program, which provides low-income consumers with a monthly subsidy of $9.25 to help offset the cost of phone or internet service;
- Less than a week later, the Pai-led FCC quashed an internal report documenting the success of the multibillion dollar E-rate program;
- In late March, Pai announced that the FCC would relinquish responsibility

for designating eligible Lifeline providers to states, reversing a Wheeler-led order that claimed that power for the commission; and

- On April 3, Trump signed a law overturning internet privacy protections enacted by the FCC under Wheeler that would have prevented broadband service providers from tracking and selling their customers' data.

Up next could be net neutrality, which might prove the most contentious of all. When the FCC weighted related rules in 2014, the agency was flooded with comments from the public, many of them urging the commission to fight to protect the flow of free and open content over the internet.

To date, Chairman Pai has declined *Education Week's* requests for an interview. His written dissents to the Wheeler-era orders, as well as his recent statements and blog posts, suggest that he supports the general principles of expanding broadband access and preserving an open internet, but takes issue with what he sees as regulatory overreach by the FCC in seeking to enact those principles.

The answer is not to cut things back, or do it on a state-grant basis, a block-grant basis, or a per-pupil basis. We need to reach all students, and give every student the opportunity.

Wheeler told *Education Week* he doesn't buy it, questioning his successor's commitment to expanding broadband access for schools and families. "It's what we always hear: 'Oh, yeah, I'm all for it,' even as they're eviscerating it," he said. Following is a transcript of Wheeler's conversation with *Education Week,* edited for length and clarity.

Let's start with net neutrality. What are the stakes for K-12 schools?

If you don't have a fast, fair and open Internet, how can you provide the kind of access to information that students need?

An example that I dealt with at the end of my term was "zero rating." Carriers set up a system where they say, "This will be the blessed content. It will have a [lower] charge when you subscribe. And by the way, this happens to be the content I own." Innovative new services and ideas then have to compete against that which the network provider has already said it's going to favor. And you can't have fair competition.

The most important part of the Open Internet Rule was that we put a referee on the field. Because who knows how the internet is going to evolve? You need to have somebody there to throw a flag and say, "No, that's not just and reasonable."

Is there a feasible scenario where the types of online content that schools are using are relegated to a slow lane? Or is that fear overwrought?

The issue isn't who can come up with the worst imaginable scenario. The reality is that absent the Open Internet rules, there's nobody on the case if and when something like that happens. Internet service providers are left to make the rules. And that's not good for anybody but the ISPs. We're talking about four companies: Comcast, AT&T, Verizon, and Charter. They're the ones who benefit from [rolling back net neutrality.] Everybody who uses the internet doesn't benefit.

One issue where there has already been action is Lifeline. Chairman Pai moved to send decision-making around designating eligible broadband providers to the states. Do you agree with him that this will make the program stronger and expand broadband access for low-income families?

No. It's just more double speak. It's what we always hear: "Oh, yeah, I'm all for it," even as they're eviscerating it. Let's remember that the people who are now running the commission voted against Lifeline [reform] in the first iteration.

So you think that this specific action will "eviscerate" Lifeline broadband access?

When you make it hard for [companies] to get an eligible telecommunications carrier designation by forcing them to go to fifty-plus jurisdictions, then you make it hard for them to provide Lifeline service. It's that simple. You can say "Oh, I'm all for [expanded broadband access]" all you want, but you are making it harder and more expensive for people to get.

Chairman Pai argues that one of the benefits of sending the decision-making back to the states would be "more cops on the beat" to ferret out waste, fraud and abuse.

I think the people who don't support Lifeline in the first place, or don't support E-rate in the first place, always go and hide behind the "waste, fraud and abuse" smokescreen.

You don't think Chairman Pai supports E-rate and Lifeline?

He didn't vote for them either time.

You don't think he's committed to the policy goal of expanding broadband access for schools and low-income families?

He can speak for himself. I'm not going to speak for him.

Do school and libraries have reason to be afraid about what's going to happen with E-rate?

Again, the people who are running the commission right now are the people who voted against the expansion and modernization of the E-rate program. And, the minute they got in office what did they do? They repudiated a report that we put out talking about the [E-rate's] successes and how the program could be further improved. They immediately pulled that back and said, "This is not what the commission stands for. This is no longer commission policy."

The facts speak for themselves. We'll wait and see what happens, but it is of great concern.

What do you think schools and libraries should be paying attention to with E-rate moving forward?

If it goes to a per-pupil [payment system], I think that's a real problem. That is particularly hard on rural schools, where the greatest challenges are. It means that rural schools end up paying, as a percentage, more for the broadband.

This is an issue where we have a national challenge. The answer is not to cut things back, or do it on a state-grant basis, a block-grant basis, or a per-pupil basis. We need to reach all students, and give every student the opportunity.

What about the bill President Trump signed Tuesday rolling back online privacy protections?

Every student ought to be worried about that. And every school ought to be worried about that. Because suddenly, all of the information that goes across the network is available to be sold.

Let's go back. So the first thing [the new administration did] was come in and pull back on the E-rate report. The second thing was make it harder [for companies to get designated as a Lifeline provider.] The third thing was gut the privacy protections. The fourth thing is the Trump administration proposes a budget that cuts back heavily on education. And we're supposed to sit here and think that this is a benign environment? I think the facts speak for themselves. We need to see this as a precursor.

On privacy, why should ISPs be regulated differently than internet companies such as Facebook and Google, who are allowed to mine customer data and use it for advertising?

Simple: With Facebook, I am voluntarily saying, "You know what? Yeah. I'll trade you my information for a service." And if I don't like Google, I can go to Bing. If I don't like Bing's privacy policy, I can go to Mozilla.

But two-thirds of the American people have one choice or less in who they get to subscribe to for their internet service. The networks are monopoly providers.

When I go on my wireless device, and I make a telephone call, Verizon or AT&T cannot turn around and sell that information from the telephone call. When I use the same device and the same network to go on the web, they can turn around and sell that information.

Why is that right? If my information as to who I'm calling should be protected, why isn't my information as to who I'm visiting on the web protected likewise?

How do you see all these recent policy changes fitting together?

I wish they had an agenda in which they were looking forward and saying, "Here's some of the new opportunities and new challenges of the new connected society."

Instead, they seem to be looking backwards and saying, "How do we undo everything we voted against when were in the minority?"

Isn't that the way politics works? The Republicans won.

Hey, I used to always say elections have consequences, and the Republicans used to always complain about me saying that.

Last question: Do you have any regrets that you didn't do things in a more bipartisan manner, so that maybe some of your efforts might have withstood the transition?

I was able many times to work together with [Republican commissioner] Michael O'Rielly. He was great to work with. It's very difficult to find a compromise unless people will really engage on addressing issue rather than throwing up smokescreens. And that was what I found in other circumstances.

Print Citations

CMS: Herold, Benjamin. "Ex-FCC Chair Blasts Efforts to Change Lifeline, Net Neutrality, Privacy Rules." In *The Reference Shelf: Education Reform*, edited by Betsy Maury, 171–175. Ipswich, MA: H.W. Wilson, 2017.

MLA: Herold, Benjamin. "Ex-FCC Chair Blasts Efforts to Change Lifeline, Net Neutrality, Privacy Rules." *The Reference Shelf: Education Reform*. Ed. Betsy Maury. Ipswich: H.W. Wilson, 2017. 171–175. Print.

APA: Herold, B. (2017). Ex-FCC chair blasts efforts to change lifeline, net neutrality, privacy rules. In Betsy Maury (Ed.), *The reference shelf: Education reform* (pp. 171–175). Ipswich, MA: H.W. Wilson. (Original work published 2017)

Transforming The EdTech Ecosystem: A Checklist for Investing

By Barbara Kurhsan
Forbes, November 7, 2016
With contributing authors Leslie Broudo Mitts, Ph.D., and John Wendel, Ph.D.

In 2016, the news from the world of edtech investment is that the number of deals is down, capital is drying up, and a higher percentage of both volume and capital is moving into later stage investments. However, these quantitative metrics do not tell us how these investments are qualitatively altering students' educational experiences. Instead of being concerned primarily about the valuation of edtech investments, we should be concerned about the value of edtech investments to communities, school systems, and teachers—and especially to the students themselves.

We offer a checklist for edtech investing that puts this qualitative value goal as a central consideration to ensure that investments address problems and opportunities that are essential to the core "business" of education rather than simply those that are of interest to investors and entrepreneurs.

Our perspective is informed by our experience as practitioners, educators, and researchers, not only in the education space, but also in areas such as healthcare and consumer packaged goods innovation where technology has often been applied with mixed results. Similar to edtech offerings, the fundamental issues in these areas are often left unaddressed. What we see instead and in large number are edtech entrepreneurs who develop apps that address periphery problems rather than problems that are at the core of teaching and learning.

For example, consider apps that aim to help teachers and administrators measure student attendance or discipline, assist parents with tracking homework assignments, facilitate new networks for tutoring, mentoring, and admissions or gamify reading and time management. We do not mean to suggest that these types of apps are not useful. However, they do not truly challenge the broken social and cultural framework of education that has existed for decades, and instead assume a structured, disciplined and hierarchical framework rather than innovate the pedagogy.

Such solutions work forward from the existing technology rather than backwards from the desired outcomes. Where are the innovations that will move us beyond an education system that was developed to serve an agricultural society?

Failure in edtech is not simply wasted capital; failure produces clutter, noise and confusion and, most importantly, lost time for students who only have one opportunity to receive an education.

These issues are important for several reasons. Existing solutions involves resources, including time and capital that crowd the edtech market and give the false sense that the edtech community is "working on the problem." In an informal experiment we conducted, we found that edtech entrepreneurs described the intended end results of their ventured using metrics related to school adoption and student/teacher usage. Using these metrics, ultimately such would-be solutions would be self-referential, justified by achieving their own end result. In no cases did entrepreneurs' metrics include implications for the lived experiences of students and teachers or address how the solution would change students' lives or impact their communities now or in the future.

These were not the questions that the entrepreneurs with whom we interacted could speak to, and in some cases, had even considered.

- **Address the whole child:** Entrepreneurs will miss opportunities by pretending that challenges related to education do not exist. Edtech offerings need to account for how related challenges in health care, housing, and family care could impact their solution to ensure that their solutions can be successfully implemented. How would the offering help a student who has moved between homeless shelters for the past six months?
- **Do your homework:** Not being aware of the existing literature is not an excuse for developing a solution that fails to address the realities of education. Entrepreneurs need to understand the theoretical models underlying their proposed solutions and "stress test" it through the lens of other theoretical models. Explore or seek out experts in the areas of user experience, linguistics, or anthropology to ensure that no innovative "stone" is left unturned in developing, testing and strengthening the proposed offering. What is the research basis for the solution, and is the interpretation of that research consistent with the proposed solution?
- **Innovate to transform the ecosystem:** Avoid focusing on technology "widgets" that bureaucratize what is already being counted and instead reconceptualize and re-imagine what is possible but has yet to be created. Be mindful of proposing an innovation that merely uses technology to do what is already being done without technology, such as counting attendance using an electronic system rather than using paper. Would the solution be easily understood by a teacher or student in a one-room schoolhouse in 1835? If so, it isn't transformational.

The components of this checklist are essential to consider given the high price of failure in the edtech space. Failure in edtech is not simply wasted capital; failure produces clutter, noise and confusion and, most importantly, lost time for students who only have one opportunity to receive an education.

The field of edtech has not seen a great deal of creativity and ingenuity in developing solutions that will "move the needle" for students. We believe that this is a result of many factors. First, edtech entrepreneurship attracts teachers who have rich classroom experience but who lack business experience. In addition, there is a huge amount of capital in the edtech investment market, which potentially results in a lack of discipline in who enters the edtech space and what kinds of solutions they bring. We also understand that education lends itself to be understood—and addressed—in black and white terms, totalized either as a "union problem" or posited as multiple opportunities for control that simple apps can satisfy.

Too many U.S. high school graduates are functionally illiterate or innumerate. Unlike the legerdemain of product innovation, we can't address issues in education simply by re-branding, re-messaging, changing the formulation, or pitching to a new market. It is therefore important for edtech solutions to follow the value chain backwards by using technology that works backwards in a transformative way from shared end goals. Taking another look at the checklist, we offer this comparison.

Emphasizing the change metrics above will help drive edtech ventures that are "gamechangers" and that are integrated solutions to education problems. We do not mean to suggest that such "gamechangers" do not currently exist, but we believe that they are not widespread. We must take steps to shift the emphasis of edtech investments away from the reification of the entrepreneur and towards the merit of the problem that the solution seeks to address. Our checklist is a first step in a needed reset in edtech investing not only because it maintains a focus on outcomes that are qualitative rather than quantitative, but also because the metrics emphasize the imperative that the proposed solutions effect real transformation in students' lives.

Print Citations

CMS: Kurhsan, Barbara. "Transforming the EdTech Ecosystem: A Checklist for Investing." In *The Reference Shelf: Education Reform*, edited by Betsy Maury, 176–178. Ipswich, MA: H.W. Wilson, 2017.

MLA: Kurhsan, Barbara. "Transforming the EdTech Ecosystem: A Checklist for Investing." *The Reference Shelf: Education Reform*. Ed. Betsy Maury. Ipswich: H.W. Wilson, 2017. 176–178. Print.

APA: Kurhsan, B. (2017). Transforming the edtech ecosystem: A checklist for investing. In Betsy Maury (Ed.), *The reference shelf: Education reform* (pp. 176–178). Ipswich, MA: H.W. Wilson. (Original work published 2016)

Online Education Pioneer Boots Up a Jobs Program for the Tech Industry

By Tom Simonite
MIT Technology Review, December 14, 2016

Sebastian Thrun smiles a little awkwardly as he explains why he no longer believes in the educational revolution he sold to the world just a few years ago.

The lean, balding robotics pioneer has been instrumental in convincing investors, governments, and colleges to splurge millions on the online college education platforms dubbed MOOCs, or massive online open courses, billed as opening up quality education to anyone on Earth. Thrun, a Stanford professor, helped birth the frenzy when he put his introductory artificial intelligence course online in 2011, accidentally attracting 160,000 students.

Amazed by the response, he took time out from Stanford and also from a side job working on autonomous cars and other research at Google to found Udacity, a company offering MOOCs in computing, math, and physics.

It attracted $160 million in venture capital investment and teamed up with San Jose State University to offer courses valid for college credit. But within two years of Udacity's launch, Thrun began to question whether MOOCs could make much of a mark on the world in their current form.

Udacity's completion rates were as low as 2 percent, and the people who made it through were mostly the kind of well-motivated students already served well by conventional institutions. Meanwhile, it was clear that many people sought out MOOCs to improve their employment prospects, but providers seemed more focused on emulating colleges than serving that need.

Thrun, now Udacity's president, didn't waste much time turning the company away from its founding ideas to market itself as a gateway to a new job in the tech industry. The company partners with employers such as Amazon and Facebook to offer "nanodegrees" that are tightly vocational. "We are happy we moved out of the MOOC space," he says. "We are able to outpace universities with curricula that you wouldn't find in any university, that empower students to find jobs."

Udacity works with its corporate partners to create courses intended to produce job candidates with skills those same companies find in short supply, such as machine learning and mobile app development. More than 30 companies, such as Intel and Samsung, have signed up with Udacity as "hiring partners" that gain access to graduating students before they hit the wider job market.

Thrun says this model allows Udacity to fill an important—and lucrative—education gap that college-style MOOCs don't. He argues that technology has created new jobs and changed existing ones faster than colleges can keep up, and that many people can't afford the time and expense of conventional education anyway.

Sebastian Thrun helped stoke the hype around massive online open college courses—but has pivoted his own startup to focus on vocational training instead.

"There's growing mismatch between people's educational needs and this idea of once-in-a-lifetime education at college," he says. "That made sense when people had one job for life. Now technology moves fast and people are forced into new jobs quickly."

Udacity currently offers 12 nanodegrees, ranging from front-end Web developer (created with help from companies including AT&T and Google) to self-driving car engineer (shaped by partners including Mercedes-Benz and Uber's trucking division, Otto). Some 3,000 people have graduated from nanodegree programs in the past two years, and 13,000 more are currently enrolled. Around 900 people have gotten jobs related to the program they studied.

Students pay $199 a month for most nanodegrees, and work through courses at their own pace. Taking six months to finish is typical, and to give students additional motivation, for most courses the company refunds half your tuition if you finish within a year. For some courses, paying $299 a month gives you the right to a full refund if you don't get a job within six months of graduation. (So far only one person has taken up that deal.) Student fees provide most of Udacity's revenue, although some partner companies contribute financially as well. By contrast, many coding and other technology boot camps require students to enroll full-time, and fees can be much higher.

Haddigan signed up for Udacity's front-end Web developer nanodegree late in 2014 in the hope of finding better prospects than he had working as an art seller, a job he landed after graduating with a fine arts degree. He praises the personal feedback provided on coding exercises and project work, and career counseling offered once a course is done.

Haddigan completed his course in about five months, working on it before and after work most days. Worries that his atypical education might hold him back evaporated when he got the first position he applied for after completing the Udacity class. He is now a Web developer with IntuitSolutions, a Philadelphia company specializing in creating e-commerce sites.

Haddigan thinks that a growing need for technology skills has made companies more open-minded to alternative backgrounds like his own. "They are willing to overlook things like whether you have a formal degree as long as you have the know-how," he says.

That kind of thinking led IBM's Watson group to work with Udacity to co-create the Artificial Intelligence Engineer Nanodegree (Amazon and Chinese ride-sharing company DiDi also contributed). Rob High, chief technology officer for the Watson group, says researchers inventing new artificial intelligence techniques will continue to come from conventional, elite educational backgrounds. But large numbers of less elite programmers and managers also need to understand the technology if IBM and others are to deploy it broadly, he says.

The way Udacity's new model neatly matches the motivations of students and tech companies suggests it could become well established even outside technology, says David Passmore, a professor of education at Penn State University.

The company's reasonable tuition and sharp focus on jobs has value in an era when tuition is more expensive than ever, he says. The way Udacity works with companies to create courses provides them a relatively easy and direct way to shape the skills in the job market, says Passmore, who could see it easily adapted to industries like manufacturing.

Thrun doesn't have plans to expand beyond technology, where Udacity's brand and his network are strongest, but Erik Brynjolfsson, director of the MIT Initiative on the Digital Economy, says that still leaves a large market, since technology skills are now needed in every industry.

Print Citations

CMS: Simonite, Tom. "Online Education Pioneer Boots Up a Jobs Program for the Tech Industry." In *The Reference Shelf: Education Reform*, edited by Betsy Maury, 179–181. Ipswich, MA: H.W. Wilson, 2017.

MLA: Simonite, Tom. "Online Education Pioneer Boots Up a Jobs Program for the Tech Industry." *The Reference Shelf: Education Reform*. Ed. Betsy Maury. Ipswich: H.W. Wilson, 2017. 179–181. Print.

APA: Simonite, T. (2017). Online education pioneer boots up a jobs program for the tech industry. In Betsy Maury (Ed.), *The reference shelf: Education reform* (pp. 179–181). Ipswich, MA: H.W. Wilson. (Original work published 2016)

The New Cheating Economy

By Brad Wolverton

The Chroncicle of Higher Education, August 28, 2016

Fifteen credits were all he needed. That's what the school district in California where Adam Sambrano works as a career-guidance specialist required for a bump in pay. But when he saw the syllabus for a graduate course he'd enrolled in last year at Arizona State University, he knew he was in trouble. Among the assignments was a 19-page paper, longer than anything he'd ever written. The idea of that much research worried Mr. Sambrano, who also spends time serving in the Army National Guard.

Before the class started, he went on Craigslist and enlisted the service of a professional cheater. For $1,000—less than the monthly housing allowance he was receiving through the GI Bill, he says—Mr. Sambrano hired a stranger to take his entire course.

He transferred $500 upfront, "From Adam for ASU," according to a receipt obtained by the *Chronicle*. Then he just waited for the cheater to do his work.

On any given day, thousands of students go online seeking academic relief. They are first-years and transfers overwhelmed by the curriculum, international students with poor English skills, lazy undergrads with easy access to a credit card. They are nurses, teachers, and government workers too busy to pursue the advanced degrees they've decided they need. The *Chronicle* spoke with people who run cheating companies and those who do the cheating. The demand has been around for decades. But the industry is in rapid transition.

Just as higher education is changing, embracing a revolution in online learning, the cheating business is transforming as well, finding new and more insidious ways to undermine academic integrity. A decade ago, cheating consisted largely of students' buying papers off the internet. That's still where much of the money is. But in recent years, a new underground economy has emerged, offering any academic service a student could want. Now it's not just a paper or one-off assignment. It's the quiz next week, the assignment after that, the answers served up on the final. Increasingly, it's the whole class. And if students are paying someone to take one course, what's stopping them from buying their entire degree?

The whole-class market is maturing fast. More than a dozen websites now specialize in taking entire online courses, including BoostMyGrade.com, OnlineClassHelp.com, and TakeYourClass.com. One of them, NoNeedtoStudy.com, advertises that it has completed courses for more than 11,000 students at such colleges as Duke, Michigan State, even Harvard.

As cheating companies expand their reach, colleges have little incentive to slow their growth. There's no money in catching the cheaters. But there's a lot of money in upping enrollment.

Two professors at Western Carolina University were so concerned about the encroachment of cheating that they set up a fake online class to learn more about the industry's tactics, and see what they could detect. About a dozen students agreed to enroll in the introductory psychology course, including John Baley, then a graduate student in clinical psychology. They were provided with fake names, email addresses, and ID numbers, plus a pot of money for cheating services. Half were asked to cheat, and they did so in a variety of ways, collaborating inappropriately with classmates, buying papers, and paying others to take tests.

Mr. Baley went looking for a company to take the whole class for him. He typed a few words into his browser—"cheat for me in my online class"—and turned up dozens of results. Many sites seemed untrustworthy: Their content was misspelled or grammatically incorrect, or their customer-service reps had trouble with basic English. Some requested confidential banking information or asked him to enter it into a website with no security protection. But one company impressed him. Its representatives responded promptly, explained how their colleagues would complete the course, and guaranteed a B or better—or his money back. He agreed to pay the company $900, half upfront, and handed over his course username and password.

Over the next 10 weeks, the company, which Mr. Baley declined to name, to protect any further research, passed him from the customer-service staff to the management team to the person who took his course. At each stage, he says, he dealt with people who were efficient, responsive, and reliable. In fact, the cheaters performed better than he thought they would. They completed every assignment without prompting, at one point providing a written script for a video presentation with less than 36 hours' notice.

The instructors, Alvin Malesky, an associate professor of psychology, and Robert Crow, an assistant professor of educational research, used Turnitin and Google to check students' work for plagiarism and monitored them to see if groups were taking exams at the same time. The professors caught several students plagiarizing material. But they didn't spot the paid test takers, purchased papers, or coordinated assignments. And they had no clue that a person in New York to whom Mr. Baley had mailed his books was behind the As they were giving. Even when professors knew that students were cheating, and were trying to catch them, they came up short. Mr. Baley's only frustration was with the barrage of marketing he got. His Facebook and Instagram feeds were saturated with ads for cheating companies, he says. That didn't let up for months. Two years after the company took his class, its representatives are still trying to enlist him to refer other students as clients.

Like any underground industry, academic cheating has its share of sloppy opportunists and savvy operators. Most work in the shadows. Click on a website that offers academic work for hire, and you'll probably find little information about the people or company behind it. The owners often use aliases and mislead prospective customers with fake addresses and exaggerated claims.

No Need to Study LLC lists its corporate address as 19 East 52nd Street, in New York, but complaints filed with the Better Business Bureau say that address does not exist. A representative for the company said in an email that it is a virtual business offering services exclusively online and does not have an office open to the public. A dissertation-writing service that claims to be based in Chicago seems to operate out of Pakistan. "In order to create a best academic assignment that rank #1 among other assignments," it website says, "then you will seek for a dedicated and experienced writer's help."

Even more-established companies can be difficult to track down. The headquarters of one, Student Network Resources, appears to be in the middle of a New Jersey cornfield.

A half-mile away, in a generic strip mall, it maintains a post-office box in a packing-and-shipping store. The owner of the store says he forwards the mail to Florida. It goes to the company's founder and president, Mark DeGaeta.

Mr. DeGaeta got the idea for Student Network Resources in the late 1990s, when he was still in high school, he says in an email to the *Chronicle*. Over the years, he has registered more than a dozen domains, including PaperDue.com and HelpMyEssay.com, which funnel work to his company, whose name is relatively unknown. When students place a request through one of the sites, they enter their name, email address, and as much information about the assignment as possible, including due date and level (undergraduate, master's, or doctoral). That information goes into Student Network's system, where a price is set based on the difficulty of the assignment. The job is posted to a private board for writers, stripped of any personal details about the student. From there, a willing writer picks up the order and corresponds with the client through a private channel in which students often disclose personal information about themselves and their courses. Then the writer delivers the completed assignment.

Mr. DeGaeta is mum about the revenue he has brought in, but the business appears to be lucrative. Two longtime writers say they've earned as much as $10,000 a month. At peak times, the company says on its website, most of its 150 writers earn more than $1,800 a week. Writers typically pocket half the price of an order; the company gets the rest. If those numbers are accurate, annual revenue for Student Network Resources would be in the millions. The company has only two employees. The founder has made a good living, according to public records. He owns an apartment in a tony neighborhood of New York, near the United Nations building, and seems to reside near Miami Beach. But his business has fallen off in recent years, he says, as the industry has expanded overseas.

The company emphatically denies that it is a cheating service. It says it tells customers that they may not use its material for academic credit—and requires them to acknowledge as much before purchasing papers, during the research process, and before receiving the work. "We vehemently protect our copyright," Mr. DeGaeta said in a written statement. "If the customer decides to use our material as a reference they must cite Student Network Resources Inc." Several current and former writers told the *Chronicle* that they had believed that. Amelia Albanese, a former community-college tutor who worked for the company in 2010, says she thought she was writing sample papers for tutors and teachers. When she realized she was doing students' work, she quit.

As cheating companies expand their reach, colleges have little incentive to slow their growth. There's no money in catching the cheaters. But there's a lot of money in upping enrollment.

"I worked at a college," she says, "and if the students I worked with had cheated, I would have been furious."

The company's business depends on covering its tracks. A memo it sent to writers last year gives step-by-step instructions for wiping the metadata from documents they produce. "Every document that you submit must have 100% blank 'Summary' properties," the memo says. "You can make the Author' field (and other fields) blank by default for all new documents by going to 'Preferences' -- > 'User Information' and replacing the content of the 'First:' and 'Last:' fields with a blank space." According to Mr. DeGaeta, the memo was aimed at preventing writers from poaching clients. But if there's no trace of a cheater on a document, a college has no way of knowing—or if an instructor suspects something, no proof—that the student didn't do the work.

Cheating has become second nature to many students. In studies, more than two-thirds of college students say they've cheated on an assignment. As many as half say they'd be willing to purchase one. To them, higher education is just another transaction, less about learning than about obtaining a credential. The market, which includes hundreds of websites and apps, offers a slippery slope of options. Students looking for class notes and sample tests can find years' worth on Koofers.com, which archives exams from dozens of colleges. And a growing number of companies, including Course Hero and Chegg, offer online tutoring that attempts to stay above the fray (one expert calls such services a "gateway drug").

Many students turn to websites like Yahoo Answers or Reddit to find solutions to homework problems. And every month, hundreds of students put assignments up for bid on Freelancer.com and Upwork, where they might get a paper written for the cost of a few lattes.

It's not uncommon for students to disclose personal details in their orders, which anyone online can see. This spring a student from the University of North Carolina at Charlotte included an attachment to his Upwork order that identified his institution and the introductory philosophy class he was looking for help in. A few days later, a Ph.D. candidate in Britain went on the same site to solicit help with his dissertation. A document he attached to his order included his name and his adviser's. Some of the most explicit exchanges happen on Craigslist, which has become a hub of cheating activity. Over two days in April, the *Chronicle* analyzed Craigslist posts in seven cities in which a cheater or cheating service offered to complete whole courses for students. The search turned up more than 200 ads. In many cases, the same ads ran in multiple cities, suggesting a coordinated marketing effort.

Craigslist posters appealed to students by acknowledging how little time they had for busywork. "Online classes are a pain in the ass," said one Chicago-area ad. Others outright asked students to hand over their online credentials. "You can trust us with your login and password information," said a Phoenix post. "We will do every section of your online class including discussion boards, tests, assignments, and quizzes."

The *Chronicle* exchanged messages with several Craigslist posters to inquire about the cost of their service and how it worked. One person who has posted regularly in the Los Angeles area said he had been in business for 10 years and had a staff of "over 20 experts." His prices, he said, depended on the number of hours it would take to complete a class, not how well a student wanted to do.

"We always get As and B's," he said in a text message. "Calculation based classes are $750. All others are $600. Anyone quoting different is not a pro and doesn't know what they are doing. Cheap quotes = F grades."

"Oh," he added, "and you can split up the payments."

Another poster said his prices depended on the institution. "A course from Penn State World Campus requires more effort than a course from Post University," he said in an email. "Previously, I completed a remedial English course for a client at Kaplan University. This person requested a 'B' for $90/week for eight weeks. Another client at a Cal State University required an 'A' in a four week upper division Asian Studies course for $300/week."

The most common way students cheat is through a simple web search—typing, for example, "essay," "essay help," or "write my essay." As many as half of the visits to some sites used for cheating come through search engines, the *Chronicle* found.

The companies that have made the biggest strides in the business have mastered the search game. Search-engine optimization efforts have helped Ultius, founded in 2011, grow fast. The Delaware-based company, with a call center in Las Vegas, has hired more than 40 employees, including engineers and customer-service representatives, according to job ads. It has contracted with more than 1,400 writers.

That growth has coincided with a surge in traffic. Over a recent three-month stretch, the site drew about 520,000 visits, according to a *Chronicle* analysis of data compiled by SimilarWeb. Thirty to 40 percent of Ultius's traffic comes from students' web searches, according to estimates on Alexa, which measures internet usage. Ultius is the No. 1 or No. 2 search result that pops up when someone Googles "buy a term paper," "buy a research paper," or about a dozen other phrases that indicate an intent to purchase a completed assignment, according to a *Chronicle* analysis of search data compiled by Spyfu, a search-engine optimization tool.

Boban Dedovic, 27, the company's chairman, helped start it after three semesters as a student at the University of Maryland at College Park, during which he worked as a tutor. To him, Ultius is a technology company that connects customers to writers, he says via email. He denies that Ultius is part of the cheating industry, referring to it as a "doc prep service." In a written statement, the company says it works hard to ensure that its customers don't misuse its services, informing them of its fair-use policy (that its work is meant for reference only and must be properly cited) at least three times and requiring them to accept it. When the company suspects a problem, it conducts an investigation, drafts an internal report, and, if it finds a violation, disables the customer's account. However, the company says, it cannot individually monitor every one of its orders.

Ultius protects its business by keeping those orders private. When a student posts an assignment on Craigslist or other sites, looking for someone to pick it up, Google indexes that text, making it visible in searches. But the customer experience at Ultius occurs behind a wall, in the same way a bank keeps its clients' information private. Because Google can't create a record of those pages, professors wouldn't be able to find them.

The company's dealings with one Ph.D. candidate illustrate the increasingly complex work that students are outsourcing, while faculty members remain in the dark. Last year, Ultius contracted with a student who described herself as a "single active duty parent" to help write a concept paper for her doctoral program, records show. The job included revisions requested by the chair of her dissertation committee.

The Ph.D. student requested that Ultius complete a literature review and produce a theoretical framework for her dissertation. The order required the company to find data on migration patterns and economic growth in Jamaica, and to apply advanced economic theory. The company did the work, but the customer was so displeased with it that she filed a complaint with the Better Business Bureau. That complaint details the case.

Ultius considers customer service a top priority, and despite 19 complaints in the past three years, mainly minor beefs over papers and assignments, it maintains an A+ rating from the BBB.

The Ph.D. student threatened to go public with her story, but more often it's the paid cheaters who make threats. After Mr. Sambrano, the high-school guidance specialist, transferred $500 to have the whole course at Arizona State done for him, he stopped hearing from his Craigslist cheater and filed a PayPal claim against him. The cheater advised him to drop the claim or he'd hand over evidence of the arrangement to the university. Mr. Sambrano, afraid he'd be expelled, dropped the charge. He says he ended up doing the class himself.

In another case, if not for a cheater turning a student in, a college may never have known that the student was paying someone else to log in to the course and complete the work.

In May an undergraduate at Colorado State University-Global Campus, dissatisfied with the quality of the work done for him, filed a PayPal claim. Angered, the cheater gave the student's name to the instructor, along with text messages, screen shots of the student's portal, and payment records detailing how the student had arranged to have the entire course done for him, says Jon M. Bellum, the provost. CSU-Global, an online institution with about 15,000 students, had its

Colleges have tried technology to combat cheating. Several thousand institutions around the world use the anti-plagiarism software Turnitin, which says it has a database of some 600 million papers. But a recent study found that custom work is "virtually undetectable."

information-technology department look at the IP addresses used for the student's coursework and found more than one. Mr. Bellum would not disclose the penalty the student faced, citing privacy law, but says such abuses can result in expulsion. Often, though, the university is not aware of the violation.

Colleges have tried technology to combat cheating. Several thousand institutions around the world use the anti-plagiarism software Turnitin, which says it has a database of some 600 million papers. But a recent study found that custom work is "virtually undetectable."

Coursera, an online education platform employed by dozens of prominent colleges, uses webcams and "keyboard dynamics," which attempt to verify students' identities on the basis of their typing patterns. But that doesn't do much good if the cheater is always typing. CSU-Global says it spends about $60,000 a year administering random identity checks on its students. The tests require them to provide answers to personal questions like what banks service their loans or what streets they've lived on. If they don't answer accurately, they can't log in to their classes. About 2 percent of identity checks result in students' getting locked out of the CSU system.

Other institutions have blocked access to sites that help students cheat. Victor Valley College, in California, has prevented anyone on a campus computer from accessing the website of Student Network Resources. But students can turn to their own laptops or other devices. The biggest key to fighting the problem is faculty engagement, says Tricia Bertram Gallant, a former president of the International Center for Academic Integrity. She often speaks with professors about the business, she says, and finds them surprised that someone else could be doing students' work. "When I tell them about contract cheating, they're shocked," she says. "They basically say, 'What? That goes on?'"

Others are in denial that it could happen in their classes. And even those who know about it and want to stop it say they're too busy, or feel that the fight is futile, with new cheating companies popping up all the time.

But some professors are catching on. Last fall, Megan Elwood Madden, an associate professor in the School of Geology and Geophysics at the University of Oklahoma, spotted a suspicious passage in a student's paper. She ran it through Turnitin, finding several plagiarized sources but no match for the bulk of the text. So she Googled the student's research topic and found the assignment posted on Course Hero with the student's request for help. A web search did not turn up the text the student had handed in, because it was hidden in Course Hero's system. But once Ms. Elwood Madden had logged in to the site, she could see communication between the student and a contractor suggesting that the student had had the work completed for him, the professor said in an email. She discovered that the student had used Course Hero to arrange work in at least four other classes as well. The revelations led the university to expel the student.

Such stories are rare, academic-integrity officers say, because there are so few would-be enforcers in pursuit. After the *Chronicle* published an article about the Western Carolina experiment, two federal law-enforcement officials contacted the professors, eager to hear more about the business.

William Josephson, a former assistant attorney general in New York who has investigated fraud, says companies that assume false identities violate federal laws governing interstate commerce. Laws in at least 17 states prohibit students from using cheating services to complete their assignments. But prosecutors aren't enforcing them.

Faculty members on the front lines are no more active. That's also true in other countries where the cheating industry has developed. This spring, Marcus J. Ball, a higher-education reformer in Britain, came across an advertisement for academic cheating services on the wall of a London subway station.

The ad offended Mr. Ball, who began emailing college administrators and professors, trying to persuade them to sign a petition for the British government to debate the issue of contract cheating. His goal was to create a "unified block" of people willing to stand up to the cheating companies, with hopes of taking the fight to Canada, the United States, and elsewhere. In May, Mr. Ball contacted more than 250 college officials including academic-integrity leaders in several countries. Only five responded.

"Academics are constantly complaining about the essay-mill problem," he said in the email. But when presented with a "practical way forward to potentially solve the problem, they don't engage."

Last year, Ms. Bertram Gallant, who is director of the academic-integrity office at the University of California at San Diego, organized a dozen international experts to study the growth of contract cheating and how to stop it. The group laid out a series of big goals. Chief among them: Mobilize faculty members and students to demand laws making it more difficult for cheating companies to operate. It is creating a tool kit to help professors detect and prevent cheating. And it is organizing an international awareness day to bring more attention to the problem. But the group can only muster so much fight. "There's just not enough of us who care," says Ms. Bertram Gallant. "It's a very small cadre internationally who really dedicate our lives to working on this issue, and that's just not enough people." College leaders haven't helped, she says. Many have failed to make the issue a priority. Few colleges have academic-integrity offices, she says, or devote dollars to the problem. "There is a lot of money to support these companies, but not a lot of money to support our research," she says. "All the money is going to the illegal part of the industry, and none of it is going to combat the industry."

Colleges also might need to rethink their approach, says Ms. Bertram Gallant. As online education continues to grow, and cheating companies have more opportunities to infiltrate classes, institutions would do well to enlist people with the skills to ferret out violations, she says. While educators may be equipped to catch plagiarism, they don't have the tools to track a paid cheater who is assuming someone else's identity.

Instead, colleges continue to rely on proud traditions to fight the scourge of cheating. This fall, as students return to campus, some colleges will require them to sign an honor code. Others will spell out for them the potential consequences of academic dishonesty.

In October, academic-integrity officials at the University of Oklahoma plan to hold a session to warn new students about paper mills. The tool they're using to combat cheating? Tea bags. To remind the students of the importance of ethics, the university is encouraging them have a cup of "integri-tea."

Dan Bauman and Ben Myers contributed reporting to this article.

Print Citations

CMS: Wolverton, Brad. "The New Cheating Economy." In *The Reference Shelf: Education Reform*, edited by Betsy Maury, 182–190. Ipswich, MA: H.W. Wilson, 2017.

MLA: Wolverton, Brad. "The New Cheating Economy."*The Reference Shelf: Education Reform*. Ed. Betsy Maury. Ipswich: H.W. Wilson, 2017. 182–190. Print.

APA: Wolverton, B. (2017). The new cheating economy. In Betsy Maury (Ed.), *The reference shelf: Education reform* (pp. 182–190). Ipswich, MA: H.W. Wilson. (Original work published 2016)

Bibliography

Anderson, Melinda. "How the Stress of Racism Affects Learning." *The Atlantic*. The Atlantic Monthly Group. Oct 11 2016. Web. 30 Apr 2017.

Ansell, Susan. "Achievement Gap." *Education Week*. Aug 3 2004. Web. 30 Apr 2017.

Barnwell, Paul. "Are Teachers Becoming Obsolete?" *The Atlantic*. The Atlantic Monthly Group. Feb 15 2017. Web. 28 Apr 2017.

Bendix, Aria. "Trump's Education Budget Revealed." *The Atlantic*. The Atlantic Monthly Group. Mar 16 2017. Web. 30 Apr 2017.

Braun, Henry, Jenkins, Frank, and Wendy Grigg. "A Closer Look at Charter Schools Using Hierarchical Linear Modeling." *IES*. National Center for Education Statistics. Aug 2006. Web. 25 Apr 2017.

Braun, Henry, Jenkins, Frank, and Wendy Grigg. "Comparing Private Schools and Public Schools Using Hierarchical Linear Modeling." *IES*. National Center for Education Statistics. Jul 2006. Web. 28 Apr 2017.

Broussard, Meredith. "Why Poor Schools Can't Win at Standardized Testing." *The Atlantic*. The Atlantic Monthly Group. Jul 15 2014. Web. 5 May 2017.

Bukhari, Jeff. "If Trump Repeals the Estate Tax, the Federal Government Will Hardly Notice." *Fortune*. Fortune Inc. Apr 27 2017. Web. 10 May 2017.

Camera, Lauren. "Achievement Gap between White and Black Students Still Gaping." *U.S. News*. U.S. News and World Report. Jan 13 2016. Web. 30 Apr 2017.

Carey, Kevin. "Dismal Voucher Results Surprise Researchers as DeVos Era Begins." *The New York Times*. The New York Times Co. Feb 23 2017. Web. 30 Apr 2017.

Carnoy, Martin. "School Vouchers Are Not a Proven Strategy for Improving Student Achievement." *EPI*. Economic Policy Institute. Feb 28 2017. Web 28 Apr 2017.

Champeau, Rachel. "First-Time Internet Users Find Boost in Brain Function after Just One Week." *UCLA Newsroom*. University of California Los Angeles. Oct 19 2009. Web. 30 Apr 2017.

"Charter School Financial Impact Model." *MGT of America*. MGT of America, Inc. Sep 11 2014. Web. 25 Apr 2017.

Coughlan, Sean. "Online Schools 'Worse Than Traditional Teachers'." *BBC News*. BBC. Nov 4 2015. Web. 30 Apr 2017.

Danner, Christi and Melissa Stanger. "The 50 Most Expensive High Schools in America." *Business Insider*. Web. 30 Apr 2017.

Davis, Julie Hirschfeld, Rappeport, Alan, Kelly, Kate, and Abrams, Rachel. "Trump's Tax Plan: Low Rate for Corporations, and for Companies Like His." *The New York Times*. The New York Times Co. Apr 25 2017. Web. 30 Apr 2017.

Derousseau, Ryan. "California's Multimillion-Dollar Online Education Flop Is

Another Blow for MOOCs." *The Hechingter Report*. Teachers College at Columbia University. Apr 14 2015. Web. 30 Apr 2017.

Desilver, Drew. "U.S. Students' Academic Achievement Still Lags That of Their Peers in Many Other Countries." *Pew Research*. Pew Research Center. Feb 15 2017. Web. 25 Apr. 2017.

Doyle, William. "Why Finland Has the Best Schools." *LA Times*. Tronc Media. Mar 18 2016. Web. 10 May 2017.

Ehrenfreund, Max. "New Poll: Republicans and Democrats Both Overwhelmingly Support Net Neutrality." *The Washington Post*. Nash Holdings. Nov 12 2014. Web. 30 Apr 2017.

"Epilogue: Securing the Republic." The Founders' Constitution. Chapter 18, Doc. 16. *University of Chicago*. 1987. Web. 30 Apr 2017.

"Evaluation of the Public Charter Schools Program." *PPSS*. Policy and Program Studies Service. US Department of Education. 2004. Web. 25 Apr 2017.

Figlio, David and Krzysztof Karbownik. "Evaluation of Ohio's EdChoice Scholarship Program: Selection, Competition, and Performance Effects." *Thomas B. Fordham Institute*. July 2016. Web. 28 Apr 2017.

Fung, Brian. "The Future of Net Neutrality in Trump's America." *Forbes*. Forbes Inc. Apr 5 2017. Web. 30 Apr 2017.

Godsey, Michael. "The Deconstruction of the K-12 Teacher." *The Atlantic*. The Atlantic Monthly Group. Mar 25 2015. Web. 28 Apr 2017.

Hanford, Emily. "The Troubled History of Vocational Education." *American Radio Works*. American Public Media. Sep 9 2014. Web. 28 Apr 2016.

Harding, Luke. "Leak Reveals Rex Tillerson Was Director of Bahamas-Based US-Russian Oil Firm." *The Guardian*. Guardian News and Media. Dec 18 2016. Web. 30 Apr 2017.

Heim, Joe. "On the World Stage, U.S. Students Fall Behind." *The Washington Post*. Nash Holdings. Dec 6 2016. Web. 25 Apr 2017.

Henderson, A. Scott and Paul Lee Thomas. *James Baldwin: Challenging Authors*. Boston: Sense Press, 2014.

Hiaasen, Scott and Kathleen McGrory. "Florida Charter Schools: Big Money, Little Oversight." *Miami Herald*. Miami Herald Media Company. Sep 19 2011. Web. 28 Apr 2017.

Horrigan, John B. "The Numbers Behind the Broadband 'Homework Gap'." *Pew Research Center*. Apr 20 2015. Web. 11 May 2017.

Jennings, Jack. "Proportion of U.S. Students in Private Schools Is 10 Percent and Declining." *Huffpost*. Huffington Post. Mar 28 2013. Web. 25 Apr 2017.

Kamenetz, Anya. "Americans Like Their Schools Just Fine—But Not Yours." *NPR*. National Public Radio. Aug 23 2016. Web. 30 Apr 2017.

Kamenetz, Anya. *The Test: Why Our Schools are Obsessed with Standardized Testing—But You Don't Have to Be*. New York: PublicAffairs, 2015.

Kaufman, Micha. "We Can't be Neutral on Net Neutrality." *Forbes*. Forbes Inc. Nov 14 2014. Web. 30 Apr 2017.

Keller, Jared. "Did Massachusetts Just End the Country's Charter School Debate?" *PSMAG*. Pacific Standard. Nov 8 2016. Web. 25 Apr 2017.

Kertscher, Tom. "Were the Founding Fathers 'Ordinary People'?" *Politifact*. Politifact. Jul 2 2015. Web. 5 May 2017.

Kohli, Sonali. "Modern-Day Segregation in Public Schools." *The Atlantic*. The Atlantic Monthly Group. Nov 18, 2014. Web. 28 Apr 2017.

Le Miere, Jason. "It's Not Just Trump: Poll Says His Cabinet and Other Republican Leaders Are Unpopular Too." *Newsweek*. Mar 20 2017. Web. 25 Apr 2017.

Lehmann, Evan. "Conservatives Lose Faith in Science over Last 40 Years." *Scientific American*. Nature America, Inc. Mar 30 2012. Web. 30 Apr 2017.

Levitin, Daniel J. "Why the Modern World Is Bad for Your Brain." *The Guardian*. Guardian News and Media. Jan 18 2015. Web. 4 May 2017.

Long, Heather. "U.S. Inequality Keeps Getting Uglier." *CNN Money*. Cable News Network. Dec 22 2016. Web. 30 Apr 2017.

Lorin, Janet. "Who's Profiting from $1.2 Trillion of Federal Student Loans?" *Bloomberg*. Bloomberg. Dec 11, 2015. Web. 30 Apr 2017.

Lynch, Matthew. "Poverty and School Funding: Why Low-Income Students Often Suffer." *Huffington Post*. Huffington Post. Oct 15 2014. Web. 10 May 2017.

Madrigal, Alexis C. and Adrienne Lafrance. "Net Neutrality: A Guide to (and History of) a Contested Idea." *The Atlantic*. The Atlantic Monthly Group. Apr 25 2014. Web. 30 Apr 2017.

Masci, David. "About One-Fifth of Adults Globally Have No Formal Schooling." *Pew Research*. Pew Research Center. Jan 11 2017. Web. 25 Apr 2017.

McEachin, Andrew, Stecher, Brian, and Grace Evans. "Not Everyone Has a Choice." *U.S. News*. U.S. News and World Report. Aug 31, 2015. Web. 30 Apr 2017.

McElwee, Sean. "These 5 Chards Prove That the Economy Does Better under Democratic Presidents." *Salon*. Salon Media Group, Inc. Dec 28 2015. Web. 30 Apr 2017.

Miller, Alison Derbenwick. "Why We Must Have Computer Science in More Schools and Classrooms." *Forbes*. Forbes Inc. Nov 14 2014. Web. 28 Apr 2017.

Mitchell, Josh. "More Than 40% of Student Borrowers Aren't Making Payments." *The Wall Street Journal*. Dow Jones & Co. Apr 7 2016. Web. 30 Apr 2017.

"Moving Beyond Computer Literacy: Why Schools Should Teach Computer Science." *NCWIT*. National Center for Women & Information Technology. 2016. Web. 28 Apr 2017.

"Net Neutrality Won: Here's the Essay That Started It All." *Recode*. Vox Media. Jun 14 2016. Web. 30 Apr 2017.

Nicks, Denver. "CEOs Make 335 Times What Workers Earn." *Money*. Time, Inc. May 17 2016. Web. 30 Apr 2017.

Oakes, Jeannie. *Keeping Track: How Schools Structure Inequality*. New Haven, CT: Yale University Press, 2005.

Paperny, Tanya. "How Lobsters Are Keeping Students in School." *The Atlantic*. Atlantic Monthly Group. Oct 11 2016. Web. 28 Apr 2017.

Patten, Eileen. "Racial, Gender Wage Gaps Persist in U.S. Despite Some Progress." *Pew Research*. Pew Research Center. Jul 1 2016. Web. 3 May 2017.

"Race and Ethnicity in a New Era of Public Funding for Private Schools." *Southern Education*. Southern Education Foundation. Mar 2016. Web. 28 Apr. 2017.

Radu, Lucian. "John Dewey and Progressivism in American Education." *Bulletin of the Transilvania University of Brasov*. Vol. 4, No. 53 (2011), 85–90.

Reardon, Marguerite. "Net Neutrality: How We Got from There to Here." *CNet*. CBS Interactive. Feb 24 2015. Web. 30 Apr 2017.

Reeves, Richard V. "The Other American Dream: Social Mobility, Race and Opportunity." *Brookings*. Brookings Institution. Aug 28 2013. Web. 5 May 2017.

Resmovits, Joy. "Betsy DeVos Says It's 'Possible' Her Family Has Contributed $200 Million to the Republican Party." *Los Angeles Times*. Los Angeles Times. Jan 17 2017. Web. 25 Apr 2017.

"Results from the 2016 Education Next Poll." *Education Next*. Program on Education Policy and Governance. Harvard Kennedy School. 2016. Web. 25 Apr 2017.

Rosenfeld, Steven. "A Leading Charter School Advocate's Stunning Admission: Online Public Schools Are a Colossal Disaster." *Salon*. Salon Inc. Feb 15 2016. Web. 30 Apr 2017.

Ryan, Julia. "American Schools vs. the World: Expensive, Unequal, Bad at Math." *The Atlantic*. The Atlantic Monthly Group. Dec 3 2013. Web. 25 Apr 2017.

Saad, Lydia. "U.S. Education Ratings Show Record Political Polarization." *Gallup*. Gallup Org. Aug 17, 2016. Web. 24 Apr 2017.

Samuelsohn, Darren. "Virtual Schools Are Booming. Who's Paying Attention?" *Politico*. Politico. Sep 23 2015. Web. 11 May 2017.

Savitz, Eric. "5 School Technologies to Watch: Pesonalized Learning Is Here." *Forbes*. Forbes Inc. Oct 22 2012. Web. 28 Apr 2017.

Schoen, John W. "Why Does a College Degree Cost So Much?" *CNBC*. NBC. 2017. Web. 30 Apr 2017.

Singer, Alan. "Results Are In: Common Core Fails Tests and Kids." *Huffington Post*. Huffington Post. May 2 2016. Web. 28 Apr 2017.

Sottek, T.C. "The 265 Members of Congress Who Sold You Out to ISPs, and How Much It Cost to Buy Them." *The Verge*. Vox Media. Mar 29 2017. Web. 30 Apr 2017.

Stern, Sheldon M. and Jeremy A. Stern. "The State of State U.S. History Standards 2011." EdExcellence. *Thomas B. Fordham Institute*. Feb 2011. Web. 30 Apr 2017.

Stiglitz, Joseph. "Equal Opportunity, Our National Myth." *The New York Times*. The New York Times Co. Feb 16, 2013. Web. 28 Apr 2017.

Stratford, Michael. "A Look at Betsy DeVos' Charitable Giving." *Politico*. Politico LLC. Dec 5 2016. Web. 30 Apr 2017.

Strauss, Valerie. "How Public Opinion about New PISA Test Scores Is Being Manipulated." *The Washington Post*. Nash Holdings. Dec 1 2013. Web. 25 Apr 2017.

Strauss, Valerie. "Study on Online Charter Schools: 'It Is Literally as if the Kid Did Not Go to School for an Entire Year'." *The Washington Post*. Nash Holdings. Oct 31 2015. Web. 30 Apr 2017.

Strauss, Valerie. "Welfare for the Rich? Private School Tax Credit Programs." *The Washington Post*. Nash Holdings. Feb 28 2013. Web. 30 Apr 2017.

Strauss, Valerie. "Why the Movement to Privatize Public Education Is a Very Bad Idea." *The Washington Post*. Nash Holdings. Jul 14 2016. Web. 30 Apr 2017.

"The Trouble with Online College." *The New York Times*. The New York Times Co. Feb 18 2013. Web. 30 Apr 2017.

"Trump: Secretary DeVos Right Choice to Address Education 'Crisis'." *VOA News*. Voice of America. Feb 14 2017. Web. 30 Apr 2017.

"Tuition and Fees and Room and Board over Time." *CollegeBoard*. Trends in Higher Education. 2017. Web. 30 Apr 2017.

Websites

National Education Association

www.nea.org

A professional organization that provides support for teachers, administrators, and staff of educational institutions. Established in 1857, the NEA is the largest professional organization in the United States and plays an important role in creating and promoting education reform policies.

Federal Communication Commission (FCC)

www.fcc.gov

The Federal Communications Commission (FCC), initiated in 1934, is a federal agency responsible for regulating communication by television, telephone, satellite, and cable. The FCC's primary purpose is to ensure that essential communications technologies are protected in the public interest and are made available to the greatest number of citizens at a reasonable cost.

US Department of Education

www.ed.gov

The United States Department of Education is the branch of the federal government charged with determining executive policy on education. The organization was founded in 1980 and is currently under the direction of conservative reform advocate Betsy DeVos.

American Federation of Teachers

www.aft.org

The American Federation of Teachers (AFT) is a labor union founded in 1916 that serves American teachers and other school professionals. The AFT primarily serves the public education industry and the organization has supported political candidates whose policies are seen as beneficial to public education.

Thomas B. Fordham Institute

www.edexcellence.net

The Thomas B. Fordham Institute is an influential conservative think tank that conducts research on education and contributes to policy recommendations for legislators and administrators. Specifically, the institute primarily studies the effectiveness of educational policies produced at the federal and state levels.

Brookings Institution

www.brooking.edu

The Brookings Institution is one of the nation's oldest political think tanks, created in 1916, studying research on education, governance, foreign policy, and economic development. Brookings studies and provides policy recommendations on education policy and reform legislation.

Pew Research Center

www.pewresearch.org

The Pew Research Center is one of the nation's most respected research organizations, conducting and analyzing research on a variety of social and governmental policy issues. Pew Research conducts studies on educational achievement and policy and conducts surveys measuring public opinion on public figures and reform proposals.

American Council on Education (ACE)

www.acenet.edu

The American Council on Education is a research organization that studies the higher education system. The ACE funds and analyzes studies on higher education development, reform, and legislative proposals that affect the nation's higher education system.

National Center for Education Statistics (NCES)

www.nces.ed.gov

The National Center for Education Statistics is a branch of the US Department of Education that collects and analyzes statistical information on US education, public school financing, and other related issues. The NCES analyses can be used to guide legislators in developing new educational policies and helps to determine changes in education financing.

Index